AGRICULTURAL DEVELOPMENT AND TRADE LIBERALISATION: IMPLICATIONS FOR A SMALL ISLAND STATE

AGRICULTURAL DEVELOPMENT AND TRADE LIBERALISATION: IMPLICATIONS FOR A SMALL ISLAND STATE

RENUKA MAHADEVAN AND
JOHN ASAFU-ADJAYE

Nova Science Publishers, Inc.
New York

For permission to use material from this book please contact us:
Telephone 631-231-7269; Fax 631-231-8175
Web Site: http://www.novapublishers.com

LIBRARY OF CONGRESS CATALOGING-IN-PUBLICATION DATA

Mahadevan, Renuka.
Agricultural development and trade liberalisation : implications for a small island state / Renuka Mahadevan and John Asafu-Adjaye.
p. cm.
Includes bibliographical references and index.
ISBN 978-1-60456-916-2 (hardcover)
1. Sugar trade--Fiji. 2. Free trade--Fiji. I. Asafu-Adjaye, John. II. Title.
HD9118.F53M34 2008
382'.41361099611--dc22 2008025303

Published by Nova Science Publishers, Inc. ✣ New York

CONTENTS

PREFACE

This book reports the findings of the joint research work carried out by the authors to empirically assess the economic and environmental impacts of agricultural trade liberalisation on Fiji's economy, as well as the environmental effects of increased agricultural production and trade. The main aim of the research is to propose supportive policies to enhance sustainable economic development in Fiji. The research was funded by the Australian Centre for International Agricultural Research (ACIAR). Other institutions that assisted with the research include the Fiji Ministry of Agriculture, The Fiji Ministry of Finance and Economic Planning, the University of the South Pacific (USP), and the Australian Bureau of Agricultural and Resource Economics (ABARE).

Fiji, like most African, Caribbean and Pacific (ACP) countries, faces immense challenges in the coming years from various developments in its trading regime. Examples include the loss of the European Union's preferential access to sugar, the impending Economic Partnership Agreement with the EU, and various types of regional and global trade arrangements. In this book, we use Fiji as a case study to analyse the impacts of these policies and to propose policies to mitigate any adverse impacts.

The book fills a current gap in knowledge and makes a contribution to the policy debate on the impacts of agricultural trade liberalisation in a number of areas. First, Fiji makes a good case study of sugar preference erosion as it is the recipient of the second largest EU sugar quota allocation and given the high level of heterogeneity within the ACP region, a single country analysis has more to offer by unmasking impacts on a wide range of macroeconomic variables as well as the effect on key sectors of the economy. Second, previous studies have used the popular Global Trade Analysis Project (GTAP) model which is a computable general equilibrium (CGE) model for trade analysis with two possible shortcomings. The GTAP model only allows for comparative static analysis and is thus unable to trace what happens through time or provide an insight to short and medium term impacts unlike the dynamic CGE model used in this study. This intertemporal dimension facilitates an understanding of the adjustment costs borne by the economy undergoing reform, thereby making better informed policy decisions. Also, the multi-regional nature of the GTAP model does not account for the high level of heterogeneity within the ACP region.

This book is aimed at a wide cross-section of readers including policymakers, policy analysts, researchers and postgraduate students in various fields such as agriculture and natural resources, international trade, and economic modeling. The material is presented in such a way that a non-technical audience would also greatly benefit from the analysis as the focus of the book is on policy making. We believe the lessons drawn from the Fiji experience are valuable for other developing agricultural economies facing the need for agricultural reform and development and the inevitable wave of trade liberalisation.

We gratefully acknowledge the financial support provided by ACIAR to facilitate the research project. We are also grateful for the invaluable in-kind support provided by the Australian and Fijian participating institutions which contributed immensely to the successful completion of the project. Special mention goes to Dr Theo Levantis, formerly of ABARE, who provided technical support for the modification of the Fiji CGE model. We are grateful to Mr Sunil Kumar, lecturer, School of Economics at USP, who assisted with data collection for the update of the Fiji input-output table. We also acknowledge the contributions made to the project by the staff of the Ministry of Agriculture, in particular those based at Nadi, for organising the logistics and execution of the field surveys. Special mention goes to Mr Osea Bolawaqatubu and Mr Atish Prasad.

Renuka Mahadevan and John Asafu-Adjaye
School of Economics, The University of Queensland
St Lucia Campus, Brisbane, Australia

ABBREVIATIONS AND ACRONYMS

ABARE	Australia Bureau of Agricultural and Resource Economics
ACIAR	Australian Centre for International Agricultural Research
ACP	African, Caribbean and Pacific
ADB	Asian Development Bank
ALTA	Agricultural Landlords and Tenants Act
APO	Asian Productivity Organisation
AusAID	Australian Agency for International Aid
CGE	Computable General Equilibrium
HDI	Human Development Index
NLTA	Native Land Trust Act
NLTB	Native Land Trust Board
CSR	Colonial Sugar Refinery
DEA	Data Envelopment Analysis
EBA	Everything But Arms
EC	European Community
EPA	Economic Partnership Agreement
EU	European Union
FDI	Foreign direct investment
FSC	Fiji Sugar Corporation
FTA	Free trade agreement
GATT	General Agreement on Trade and Tariffs
GDP	Gross Domestic Product
GSP	Generalised System of Preferences
ICT	Information and Communication Technology
IMF	International Monetary Fund
I-O	Input-output
LDCs	Less developed countries
LMC	Landell Mills Commodities
LP	Linear programming
MNCs	Multinational companies
PACER	Pacific Agreement for Closer Economic Relations
PICs	Pacific Island countries
PICTA	Pacific Island Countries Trade Agreement

POCS	Pure Obtainable Cane Sugar
RTA	Regional trade agreement
SPARTECA	South Pacific Regional Trade and Economic Cooperation Agreement
TCTS	Tons of cane required to produce one ton of sugar
TE	Technical efficiency
UNDP	United Nations Development Program
USP	University of the South Pacific
VAT	Value added tax
WTO	World Trade Organisation

Chapter 1

INTRODUCTION

BACKGROUND

Although Fiji is one of the largest and most developed Pacific island countries with a total land area of 18,376 km^2, it is a small nation with a population of 846,085 in 2005. Of Fiji's 320 islands, Viti Velu (where the capital Suva is located), Vanua Levu and Taveuni are the three main islands (Figure 1.1). With a per capita income of US$3,514 in 2005 (ADB 2006), Fiji is classified as a lower middle-income country. However, Fiji is a development enigma. While there has certainly been some growth in the economy, the economy has been riddled with problems. The four military coups so far have critically destabilized the economy on many fronts – but politics does not stop there and runs deep into Fiji's economic mainstay, the sugar industry. The sugar industry has been uncompetitive for a while now and its viability is seriously questioned with the withdrawal of the European Union's sugar subsidies at the end of 2007.

Fiji is chosen as a case study to highlight the problems of sugar reform in the ACP countries due to the withdrawal of the European Union (EU) sugar subsidy for two reasons. First, the value of EU transfers to Fiji amounts to about 3% of Fiji's Gross Domestic Product (GDP). This is quite substantial and, relative to the other ACP countries, Fiji is the second largest recipient of EU income transfers. Second, and more importantly, the problems in Fiji's sugar industry present a classic case to discuss agricultural reform in general. Often, agricultural reform is patchy, concentrated in some areas and neglected others. Thus, reform policy may not succeed because of the failure to consider policy making in a holistic framework. In that regard, this case study of Fiji highlights the importance of an integrated and well-coordinated approach to policy implementation, especially when an industry is tightly and vertically integrated. This calls for a similar reassessment of reform measures in other types of agriculture as well.

In addition, the withdrawal of EU subsidies places an emphasis on trade liberalisation for Fiji. Thus, there is a need to understand the various types of trade arrangements available and the possible impacts on the economy. Therefore, this book is a timely effort to study in detail some of the prospects, challenges, efforts and actions taken by Fiji to sustain agricultural growth, particularly sugarcane, and to cope with trade liberalisation as part of its economic development strategy. The key challenge for any economy is to remain competitive and undertake reform. Thus, various policy options are identified (not because other options are less important) for the reason that they hold important lessons for all developing agricultural economies that face trade reform. By critically raising a number of policy issues, we shed light on new questions for research and policy discussion.

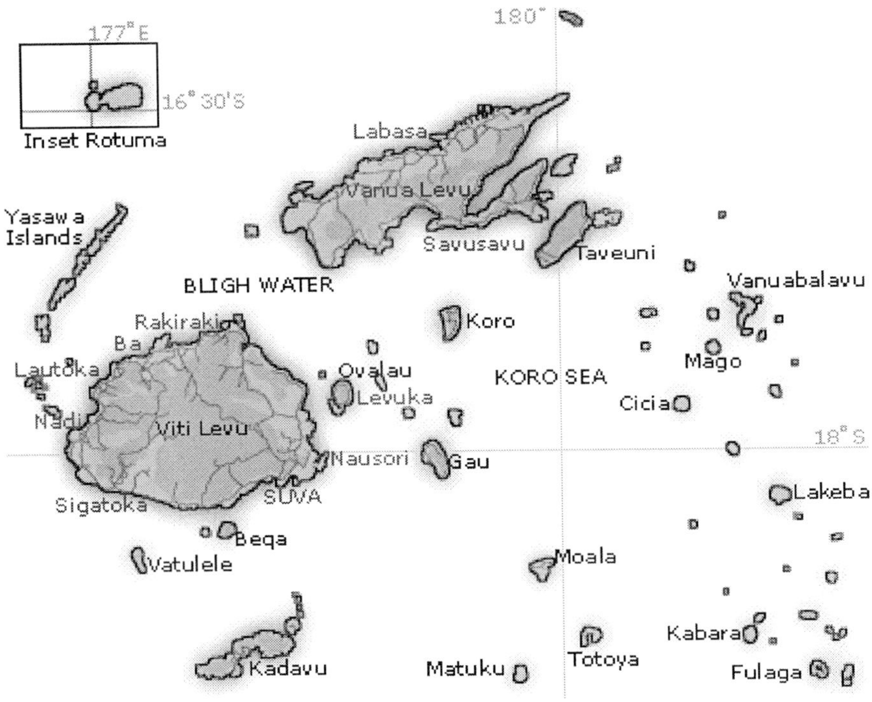

Source: http://www.fiji.gov.fj/publish/fiji_map.shtml

Figure 1.1. Map of Fiji.

This volume is divided into two main parts. The first part studies selected key areas such as structural transformation, export-led growth, productivity growth of sugar cane farmers, the neglect and impact of soil erosion on sugar cane farms, and the political economy of the sugar cane industry. The resulting implications for soil conservation policy and sugar cane reform to take on a holistic and integrated approach has important lessons in the way agricultural policy in general should be viewed in developing countries.

The second part of this volume focuses on trade liberalisation and examines the impacts of a number of scenarios on a wide range of macroeconomic indicators. The scenarios include: the European Union's removal of sugar price subsidies; unilateral trade liberalisation versus multilateral trade liberalisation; various forms of regional trade agreements (such as the Pacific Island Countries Trade Agreement, the Pacific Agreement for Closer Economic Relations and the Economic Partnership Agreements) as compared to global trade liberalisation. Various policy measures to assist developing countries to meet the challenges of trade liberalisation are discussed.

A brief outline of the objectives of the subsequent chapters is as follows:

Chapter 2. The Fijian Economy

This chapter begins with a brief overview of Fiji's history, macroeconomic performance and reforms undertaken by the government. Then a discussion on the importance of various sectors and the investigation of inter-industry causality links between the sectors in terms of their GDP contribution and their relation to economy-wide GDP growth is presented using the Toda Yamamoto procedure. A similar analysis on causality is also applied to study the importance of the export-led growth strategy. Policy implications from the two analyses shed light on the need for diversification on sectoral output and trade-related matters.

Chapter 3. The Sugar Industry

This chapter begins with a discussion on the global sugar market and producers: in particular, the EU sugar regime and preferences given to ACP countries. The historical perspective of Fiji's sugar industry helps to understand the issues in the political economy of the industry (such as the problems of the land tenure system and ethnic issues in sugar production). Problems related to the various institutions involved in sugar production highlights the difficulty in undertaking sugar reform appropriately and speedily. Lastly, the performance and structure of the sugar industry is reviewed and a broad summary of the areas in which efficiency improvements are needed is provided to set the stage for discussion in the next few chapters.

Chapter 4. Productivity of Cane Farmers

Here, a farm-level survey is used to study the productivity performance of sugarcane farmers using the parametric approach of the random coefficient stochastic production frontier and the non-parametric approach given by Data Envelope Analysis. Measures of overall technical and scale efficiency, as well as input-specific technical efficiency, are computed. Various socio-economic factors affecting technical efficiency are also investigated and analysed. These, together with data on farmers' perceptions of problems and attitudes towards cane farming and the operation of sugar institutions shed light on where Fiji's sugar industry is heading and the extent of its viability in the global market.

Chapter 5. The Lack of Soil Conservation on Cane Farms

Recent evidence in Fiji suggests that the problem of land degradation in particular is worsening and this has adversely affected cane and sugar yield. Thus, this chapter is devoted to examining the impacts of soil erosion within the framework of technical efficiency in cane production. The following questions are addressed: What is the effect of soil erosion on cane output and what is the cost to cane farmers and the sugar industry? If soil conservation were undertaken, would the extent or type of conservation significantly affect cane output? In addition, factors affecting the perception of the soil erosion problem and the extent of soil conservation effort on cane farms are also empirically investigated for soil conservation policy.

Chapter 6. Reforming the Cane and Sugar Industry

This chapter is devoted to issues related to both the cane and sugar industries. A review and critique of past key reform proposals of the industries sets the stage for discussion. This is followed by a consideration of a wide range of problems that have plagued the industries such as, poor weather conditions, farming practices, the cane payment system, milling operations and the support services for harvesting and transportation. The need for an integrated set of measures is necessary for a more holistic approach to policymaking and the effective implementation of reform.

Chapter 7. The Dynamic Computable General Equilibrium Model

This chapter describes the dynamic computable general equilibrium model, which is used in the analyses in chapters 8 and 9. It begins with a discussion of the different economic models and goes on to explain the general equilibrium approach, contrasting it to other modeling approaches. This is followed by a brief overview of previous economy-wide models of the Fiji economy. The remainder of the chapter is devoted to describing the theoretical structure of the model. This includes a description of the sectors in the model, the input/output structure and the key equations of the model. Finally, information is given on the model solution and closure.

Chapter 8. Impacts of Trade Liberalisation Policies

In this chapter, the computable general equilibrium model is used to understand and compare the effects of five different sets of trade liberalisation policies. The first scenario investigates the effects of unilateral trade liberalisation by Fiji. This is followed by an analysis of two types of regional trade agreements: namely, the Pacific Island Countries Trade Agreement, and a combination of this trade agreement and the Pacific Agreement for Closer Economic Relations. The last two scenarios investigated are partial trade liberalisation involving only tariff removal and full-trade liberalisation involving removal of both tariff and non-tariff barriers.

Chapter 9. The Loss of EU Sugar Preferences, Impact of the EU Development Aid, EPA, and Fiji's Structural Reform

The EU-ACP sugar reform began in 2007 and, in January 2008, the EPA was meant to take effect. The impacts of these events on Fiji are analysed in conjunction with EU development aid to better understand the growth path of Fiji's future for policy. The results from the various scenarios (e.g., partial/gradual sugar price cuts, one-off full price cut for sugar exports, and so on) are compared and contrasted for policy making. In addition, impacts from internal structural reforms to cope with the loss of the EU sugar subsidy are also studied. These include industrial policies to boost the performance of the agricultural, tourism, fisheries and garment sectors.

Chapter 10. Fiji at its Crossroads: Where to Now?

By providing a summary of the findings of the previous chapters, this chapter discusses the challenges and opportunities for Fiji in its agricultural development and trade liberalisation strategies. The policy options for the government in its pursuit are critically examined in the context of the changing environment faced by its agricultural and export sectors.

Chapter 2

THE FIJIAN ECONOMY

INTRODUCTION

Fiji gained independence in 1970 but its record of economic development in the last three decades has been disappointing and is now a matter of serious concern. While the government has attempted various reforms since the 1980s to better manage the economy, they have been far from effective (Reddy *et al.* 2004b). In addition, the economy is riddled with many other problems: the political and economic turmoil generated by the coups affect investor confidence and economic growth; poverty and unemployment are high; the agricultural sector is susceptible to natural disasters; a complex land tenure pattern restricts access of individuals and groups to land with secure tenure; the sugar industry, which is the mainstay of the economy, is uncompetitive and its viability is threatened by the loss of EU sugar preferences at the end of 2007; the mounting pressure to liberalise trade and the possibility of various trade arrangements present many challenges for a small island state like Fiji.

The purpose of this chapter is to highlight some of these issues to set the tone for the remaining chapters. The next two sections provide a brief overview of Fiji's history and macroeconomic performance as well as the policies undertaken. This is followed by an outline of the trends over time in output, employment, and labour productivity of the agriculture, manufacturing and other sectors. The fifth section presents the empirical evidence on the causality links between these sectors. Section six examines the importance of an export-led growth strategy for selected growth sectors and the final section concludes.

HISTORY OF FIJI

The small island nation of Fiji was first sighted in 1643, but reports of cannibalism and the ritual killing of the elderly frightened the visiting sailors. Racism and fear drove one explorer, D'Urville, to burn Fijian villages to the ground in 1838. In light of the history of violent confrontation with outsiders, the British arrived and following the collapse of the attempt at organised government under King Cakobau, Fiji was voluntarily ceded to Great Britain on 10th October 1874. But in 1970, Fiji gained independence to become a self-governing nation under the Commonwealth. This situation changed following the 1987 military coups when Fiji was declared a republic and ceased to be a member of the Commonwealth. Fiji re-entered the Commonwealth in October 1997 but, following the civilian coup in 2000, was expelled again from the Commonwealth and re-admitted after democracy was restored after the 2001 elections.

Fiji is a multi-cultural and multi-racial country. While all Fiji citizens are known as Fiji Islanders, native Fijians comprise about 51.1% of the total population, followed by Indians who make up 44% – the rest are either Rotumans, Chinese, Europeans or other Pacific islanders. While indigenous Fijians are usually classed as Melanesians, they are actually a mix of both Polynesian and Melanesian elements. Indians are descendents of Indian labourers brought by the British to work in the sugar plantations during Fiji's indenture period. The indenture system ended in 1916, but many Indians chose to stay on in Fiji and since then have become a vital part of Fiji's economy.

MACROECONOMIC PERFORMANCE

The performance of Fiji's economy can be described as sluggish and unstable and, in general, exhibits a declining trend as seen in table 2.1. The economy's real GDP grew annually by 4.12% in the period 1971–1986, but declined in 1987 due to the coups in May and September of that year. After the coups the currency was devalued by a total of 35% in 1987 and 1988 to stabilise the economy, to stop capital flight, to dampen import demand, to encourage exports and create employment. There was, however, a recovery in the 1991–99 period and inward private investment continued to be attracted primarily to the garment and tourism industries – but the economy was still hindered by weak private investment and increased emigration. The May 2000 putsch once again adversely affected the economy with a -1.7% growth, but the economy recovered more quickly to register an annual growth rate of 2.45% over 2001–05 (as seen in table 2.1) – but the December 2006 coup was clearly a disruption that Fiji could have done without. The Reserve Bank of Fiji (RBF) predicted economic growth to decline by 3.1% in 2007.[1]

Inflation in Fiji was high during the 1970s, but has generally declined over time and is not a serious issue except for the occasional rise due to the 1987 coups when it rose to 11.7%. Fiji has also been on a managed exchange rate with the Fijian dollar tied to a basket of other foreign currencies, thus enabling control over inflation, especially imported inflation. It can be seen that unemployment rates have not declined and hovered higher – around the 8% mark – after the 2000 coup. The ranking for Fiji on the UNDP Human Development Index (HDI) had fallen from 44th position in 1995 to 92nd in 2005 – unemployment could be an underlying factor among others.

Overall, the focus of macroeconomic management has not enabled an adequate level of savings and investment, or fiscal prudence. Gross domestic investment as a ratio of GDP has been declining since the mid 1980s. From an average of 20.6% during 1981–90, the ratio has steadily declined to an average of 13% from 1991–2005. The low rate of private investment, not exceeding 5% since 1990, reflects concerns regarding political stability and the expiry of

[1] Speech by the RBF Governor on the opening of a Westpac Bank Branch on Denerau Island, Fiji, 3rd September 2007.http://www.fijilive.com/archive/showpdf.php?pdf=2007/09/rbf_govn_speech_sept.pdf

land leases since 1997. Foreign direct investment (FDI), too, has been persistently low between 1985 and 2004, averaging about 5%. Gross domestic savings have often been less than 10% of GDP since 1990, so monetary resources are not available to expand investment capacity when needed. The low savings can be attributed to low wage levels, high poverty and high urban employment at around 14%.

Table 2.1. Some Macroeconomic Indicators on Fiji (%)

Indicator	1971–86	1987–90	1991–99	2000	2001–05	2000–05
Real GDP Growth	4.12	-0.94	2.76	-1.66	2.45	1.77
Inflation Rate	3.53	6.56	3.7	3.0	2.82	2.95
Unemployment Rate	8.9*	7.5	6.4	7.6	8.2	8.1

Notes:

1. Above values are averaged over the years using 1990 as a base year.
2. * This is averaged over 1976–1986.

Source: Reserve Bank of Fiji, Quarterly Review.

As in the case of many governments in the position of governing a country after independence, Fiji embarked on a public sector-led growth strategy. However, with low economic growth, government revenue grew slowly and the government resorted to deficit financing. Consequently, the national debt level has spiraled to reach 52% of GDP in 2005, although only about 9% of it is foreign debt. While foreign aid to Fiji as a proportion of GDP has been reduced from 3.7% of GDP in 1990 to 2.5% in 2005, it is nevertheless quite substantial at US$ 51.1 million (UNDP 2006). However, much of it is often not properly managed to provide long run benefits.

Also, Fiji's balance of payments position has not been particularly healthy in the last few decades. The change in foreign reserves has been positive except for some events such as the 1987 coup, the 33% devaluation in 1988, the 1993 and 1994 hurricane Kina and the 20% devaluation in 1998. Fiji's balance of trade is traditionally negative, though the balance on the current account has moved into the black on six occasions since independence in 1970. The overall balance of payments has been positive more often than negative since 1970.

In general, the Fijian economic story is far from being good news. It is undeniable that the coups and ineffective reform and structural adjustments have slowed down the development of the economy. However, Fiji faces no less a challenge than other developing economies, which is the need to be competitive.

Macroeconomic Policies and Reform

Like most developing countries, Fiji adopted an economic strategy largely based on protection of domestic industries and a large public enterprise sector. Due to the widespread failure of this approach to generate sufficient economic growth and because of the changing world economic order, economic policy makers have adopted open market-oriented reform policies since the mid 1980s. Some of these reform measures are reviewed briefly to show that Fiji still has a long way to go in getting reform to work effectively. Perhaps there is some truth in Tisdell's (1996) view that Pacific island countries need to be cautious about adopting the market-based approach to policy making as the social, economic, political, and institutional structures may not be suited for a full-scale market-based economy.

With the labour market, statutory wage guidelines were removed to promote enterprise bargaining, but there is still inflexibility due to disagreement between the key stakeholders on appropriate changes to protect the interests of workers, employers and the government. The employers seek minimum intervention to enable them to make changes to maintain a competitive edge. However, the unions in Fiji are very powerful and have resisted some changes, such as the setting of wage increments. Such disagreements finally led to changes in various laws in 1991, including the Industrial Associations Act, the Trade Union Recognition Act, the Trade Union Act, and the Trade Dispute Act – see Chand (1998) for details.

Like the labour market, reform in the financial sector has been inconsistent as some changes indicate a move towards flexibility and less intervention, while others suggest more state intervention – see Reddy *et al.* (2004b) for examples. In general, the partial and selective reform has been at a slow pace, possibly reflecting the cautious attitude of the government. There is also no equity market in Fiji. While it might be argued that this does not to allow entrepreneurs the opportunity to test if investors are willing to take a risk for a greater return, this is hardly a concern in Fiji given the ample domestic funds due to low investment rates in the economy. Thus, there is limited means of channeling household and institutional savings outside the commercial banking lending system into productive investment. The capital market, on the other hand, has remained distorted for a very long time as the allocation of capital is highly influenced by political factors. Access to credit from the Fiji Development Bank and other lending institutions is based on ethnicity and sometimes on provincialism.

As far as investment and trade liberalisation is concerned, there has been resistance from the local branches of MNCs that are already established in Fiji. They are not keen to see competition from imports or from new firms being set up in the country. In general, lobbying activities related to this resistance are quite strong. But bureaucracy at the government level for approving foreign permits for investment[2] has greatly hampered FDI. Furthermore, liberalising the product market without sufficiently liberalising the labour market (as land and labour are still heavily protected), does not improve the investment environment as overseas firms making low-cost products will have an edge over the local producers.

Political instability is another major disruption to the reform process as it affects policy certainty and results in a loss of human and financial capital. Reddy *et al.* (2004a) revealed that human capital loss increased from just over 2000 persons/year in the pre-coup period 1987 to over 5000 persons/year after 1987. Along with this, there was a substantial financial loss of approximately F$40 million per year. Ghani (2005), on the other hand, estimates that emigrant transfers equaled 2.3% of GDP annually on average since 1987. It was reported by McKenzie (2006) that 13.5% of Fiji's population is living abroad. Such large emigration almost always involves only the skilled workers – and they are mostly Indian Fijians, as there has been a drastic reduction in the proportion of Indians in the population from 49% in 1986

[2] This can take more than one year and there is no one-stop centre where all other required processing can be done. For instance, after approval is given, there are other related approvals an investor needs from places such as the Ministry of Land, Fisheries or Tourism.

to 37% in 2005 (Government of Fiji 2006a). This has implications for the sustainability of growth in the economy because of a reduction in financial resources available for investment as well as erosion of the tax base. Nevertheless, as a result of migration since 2003, remittance has become the third largest foreign exchange earner. The Reserve Bank of Fiji revealed that by 2004 estimates, remittance earned F$300 million of foreign exchange. In the short term, the brain drain can be resolved by improving law and order and the political environment – in the long term, by reducing the wage gap between Fiji and the destination countries.

By and large, perhaps the most urgent reform required is, ironically, in the public sector itself, which is administratively large and represents two-thirds of national paid employment. It is said to over employ (partly due to positive discrimination in appointing and promoting indigenous Fijians in the civil service after the military coup in 1987), and is hence inefficient and a waste of resources. The large government has also created room for bad governance, misuse and abuse of public funds as highlighted by the Auditor General on an annual basis (Readdy and Prasad 2002). In addition, since independence, Fiji has witnessed political competition that has led to increased government expenditure (Reddy *et al.* 2004b). Response to natural disasters and affirmative action policies have been used to transfer large amounts of state resources into mobilising support for political re-election, and this reduces the funds available for development-related expenditure. Between 1985 and 2003 alone, Fiji had four elections and 10 different governments, which were elected under different platforms and promises. Thus, there is very little opportunity for continued foresight in the provision of long-term benefits for the economy. This has impacted negatively on land policy and infrastructure development; it has affected utility supply as seen in the electricity and water crisis since 2002 due to huge shortages and low production capacity.

THE GROWTH SECTORS

As seen in the government's 5-year development plans following independence, Fiji focused on the development of the agricultural sector, public infrastructure and the promotion of the urban industrial sector through protection of domestic industries. After the 1987 coups, a more outward-oriented strategy was pursued and, today, Fiji is dependent on a number of key industries, notably sugar, tourism, garments and fisheries. While Fiji is still an agricultural economy, industrialisation has changed the structure of the economy over time.

Table 2.2 shows the declining share of agriculture, forestry and fishing since 1990. However, within this sector, agriculture has been falling (from about 20% in 1985 to 10% in 2005) while forestry and fishing have expanded quite rapidly. The manufacturing sector, on the other hand, comprises textile, clothing and footwear production, sugar production, beverage and tobacco production, food processing and wood and metal-based industries. Although its share over time has not changed much within this sector, sugar production, which is the mainstay of the economy, saw its share decline from 13.1% in 2000 to 9.7% in 2005 while the clothing and footwear saw its 2005 production halved from 2004. The beverage and tobacco production share has risen particularly due to mineral water production given Fiji's success in marketing this product whose exports increased significantly from F$5.9 million in 1999 to $45.7 million in 2003.

Table 2.2. Sectoral Composition of Real GDP (%)

Sector	1975	1985	1990	1995	2000	2005
Agriculture, Forestry, Source: http://www.fiji.gov.fj/publish/fiji_map.shtml Figure 1.1. Map of Fiji. Fishing	19.9	16.26	16.66	18.34	17.03	14.31
Mining and Quarrying	1.0	0.83	1.06	2.36	0.95	0.82
Manufacturing	10.1	11.97	12.66	13.53	13.95	13.15
Electricity, Gas & Water	1.6	1.96	2.01	3.61	2.93	2.63
Construction	4.4	7.26	7.30	4.12	4.44	5.30
Trade, Hotels & Restaurants	21.6	18.45	18.49	15.08	15.77	19.96
Transport & Communications	8.3	9.24	9.03	11.26	15.98	17.28
Finance, Insurance & Bus. Services	16.3	7.59	8.17	12.99	13.19	12.07
Community & Other Services	18.0	26.43	24.62	18.71	19.02	18.79

Source: Prasad and Tisdell (2006) and Fiji Islands Bureau of Statistics (2006).

Within services, tourism, as the lead industry, has impacts on the retail trade and hotels, as well as transport and communications and hence an increase in the shares of these sub-sectors. Tourism contributes about 20% to GDP and about 40,000 people are directly employed in this industry (Reserve Bank of Fiji 2006). As seen in table 2.3, tourism is the biggest foreign exchange earner, surpassing sugar; sugar exports have been on a declining trend since the mid 1990s.

It can be further seen that the fisheries sector looks quite promising, although its performance has been described as erratic since 1999 with fresh fish rather than canned fish comprising the bulk of fish exports. Some of the decline in fishing has been attributed to lower catch rates as a result of over fishing within Fiji's exclusive economic zone and adverse climatic conditions.

Table 2.3. Exports of Fiji's Key Industries (F$million)

	1985	1995	2001	2005
Tourism	161.4	405	496	733.2
Sugar	111.8	276.1	221.6	217.9
Fish	11.7	113	91.2	82.9
Garments	2.1	185	305.2	120.4

Source: Fiji Bureau of Statistics and the Reserve Bank of Fiji, various issues.

The Challenges Faced by Key Industries

Their small size exposes many Pacific island economies to problems, including the inability to influence export and import prices, the inability to enjoy economies of scale, and the small domestic market. The narrow resource base also allows specialisation in a limited number of export goods. This section highlights the challenges faced by industries such as sugar, agriculture in general, fisheries, garments and tourism.

The Sugar Industry

With the sugar industry, the impending problem is the loss of EU sugar preferences at the end of 2007. Since a few chapters in this book are already devoted to this issue, here, we discuss the implications of the consequent loss of income to a large population dependent on the sugar industry due to a fall in sugarcane production. Compounded with the existing danger in the non renewal of land leases since 1997 (see Chapter Three), ADB (2005) estimates the displacement of jobs for 12,000 workers who will exit the industry due to low productivity and inability to sustain profits in the wake of the fall in sugar prices. To help these farmers, the ADB started the Alternative Livelihood Project in 2006 with the aim of enabling farmers to diversify their income base while still being involved in agricultural production.

The Agricultural Sector

The agricultural sector is still a key sphere of the Fijian economy and there are reports that domestic production is insufficient to cater for local demand driven by tourism (Government of Fiji 2006b). In fact, the import food bill has doubled in a decade to reach F$377.2 million in 2005 and more effort should be taken to strengthen backward linkages between the agricultural sector and tourism.

However, there are many obstacles to revitalising the agricultural sector. First, although there are many crops like dalo, yagona, ginger, pulses, rice, fresh fruits (such as pineapple, papaya and mango) and vegetables that are grown in Fiji, the incentive to grow these crops is hampered by the lack of a support structure in marketing,[3] stable prices, a steady market to supply, and transportation of produce to crop centres for sale.[4] Livestock, on the other hand, is seen to require a good amount of start-up cash that may not be readily available as banks are often reluctant to provide loans without collateral – micro finance schemes are not well established in Fiji to provide loans to farmers. The Ministry of Agriculture simply does not have the resources to provide incentives to improve the situation or offer sufficient advice to increase farm productivity.

In addition, there are limitations to the total area of land suitable for productive use, although the overall population density of 31.3 person/km^2 is not high. This is mainly due to the fact that almost 70% of the land area of the two main islands, Viti Levu and Vanua Levu (which cover 87% of the total land area), is steep mountains terrain, deeply incised by river valleys and generally unsuitable for agriculture. To make matters worse, the weather conditions are not always conducive for agricultural production either. The World Bank

[3] It is still early days to tell how effective the newly established Agricultural Marketing Authority will be.

[4] Anecdotal evidence, as well as farmers surveyed in 2004, reveals that the export of a lot of agricultural produce is monopolised by a few who exploit the rural community involved in the direct production of these crops due to the lack of a well-developed market. In addition, products (such as yaqona, root crops and ginger) which start off as government initiatives are often handed over to important politicians and hard lobbyists who are not necessarily efficient and have their own interests at heart.

(2006b) estimates Fiji's disaster index at 40/50 related to natural disasters[5] (cyclones, floods, droughts, earthquakes, volcanic eruptions) and this is the second highest among nine of the largest PICs.

Table 2.4. Share of the Subsistence Economy in Sectoral GDP (%)

Sector	2000	2005
Agriculture	34.7	37.7
Fisheries	32.2	34.2
Forestry	47.6	41.4

Source: Fiji Bureau of Statistics and the Reserve Bank of Fiji, various issues.

The other problem with the agricultural sector and other primary industries is that it is not sufficiently commercialised. Most of the rural communities involved in crop production have small plots of land and, therefore, the subsistence sector within this industry is large. Although the total subsistence share in the primary sector has declined from 47.4% in 1985 to 38.6% in 2005, table 2.4 shows a breakdown that indicates the shares are still high for a lower middle-income country such as Fiji.

The existence of the subsistence economy – and hence the low levels of commercialisation – are features of a primitive sector (Kaldor 1967 and Seavoy 2000). Kaldor clearly recognized that food production is a necessary precondition for economic development when he said: "It is no accident that in England, as elsewhere in Europe, the so-called agricultural revolution historically preceded the industrial revolution. In countries where this agricultural revolution failed to occur … [and] even if … it did get started, it could not be long sustained." While Seavoy (2000) goes further to say that commercialising policies must be enforced with political power for economic development, Malaysia is a success story in that regard.

Lastly, improvements in agricultural productivity are, however, necessary as this leads to increased incomes for agricultural workers and provides a broad domestic market for manufactured goods in an indirect manner. But relative to manufacturing, the agricultural labour productivity is low and this makes it difficult to boost production. First, agricultural production in Fiji is very labour intensive and given the significant out migration from the rural to urban sector, there is a lack of skilled labour in agriculture and this affects productivity. Second, the large subsistence sector is often reflective of the less efficient use of labour (Seavoy 2000). Third, the uncertainty surrounding the non-renewal of land leases deters investment in inputs. The lack of modernization and commercialization in the agricultural sector does not allow for the establishment of agro industries that are necessary for value-added production.

There was, however, one failed attempt by the government in its set up of the 'Commodity Development Framework', a four-year master plan endorsed in 1997. This plan emphasised the need for diversification as a basis of agricultural development in Fiji. It particularly considered commercializing agricultural commodities for export and increased

[5] Whereas in a large country, like Australia, such natural disasters are likely to leave a large part of it untouched, while in small countries most of it may be devastated and, consequently, few internal resources may remain available to respond to the disaster.

private sector development, as well as the establishment of major commodity councils. But this program was a F$69 million fiasco and criticism levied against it included: the reversal to government investment; support provided to commodities with no apparent competitive advantage; the absence of systematic and transparent criteria for allocation of funds; and failure to address real issues such as the chronic financing and working capital problems facing the sector (see http://www.fijilive.com/news/ 6 Feb 2002 and *The Times* 28 Jan 2002).

The Fisheries Sector

One sector that has huge potential but not fully exploited (and is the fourth largest export earner after tourism, sugar and garment exports), is the fisheries sector, which accounted for about 5% of Fiji's GDP in 2005. The problem lies in the lack of domestic fishing fleets as local producers do not have the capacity to acquire long liners and therefore do not fish in the extended economic zones. Instead, the majority of the catching is done by foreign boats, and access fees paid by foreign vessels amount to about one-twentieth of the value of fish caught in Pacific waters (Oxfam 2006a).

Other constraints include the lack of related infrastructure (such as fishing wharves) and electricity for refrigeration and processing in rural areas. Although there has been expansion in this sector, especially due to tuna exports to the US and the high-value 'sashimi' market, private investment still remains sluggish despite the numerous incentives[6] provided (Government of Fiji 2006b). The high transportation costs due to long distances make it difficult for Fiji to compete in the traditional processed fish market and thus 80% of the fish exported is fresh fish. It is, nevertheless, possible for Fiji to consider product differentiation as an alternative strategy by targeting niche markets for processed fish products (smoked, flavoured, prepared fillets) that produce more value added. Currently, fish processing is dominated by distant water fishing nations such as China, Indonesia, Japan, the Philippines, South Korea, and the US. Other problems that need to be curbed include illegal fishing, and fishing in areas where there are no fisheries conservation and management measures, thus depleting the fish stock.

Fiji cannot afford to ignore this sector for two reasons. First, as the EU is the world's largest tuna market and thus has vested interest in the ongoing negotiations of a regional fisheries agreement with the ACP economies to promote more sustainable fisheries in the Pacific region.[7] This is an important issue given the recent stalled World Trade Organization round talks where fisheries subsidies were to be discussed. Another obstacle is the application of increasingly stringent food safety standards, which act as a trade barrier and encourage the Pacific to export only raw or semi-processed fish products to avoid compliance costs. The second reason the fisheries sector is important to Fiji is that it is dominated by indigenous Fijians, who the Fiji government has pledged to support to maintain equity as a rule.

The Natural Resource Sector

The forestry sector on average contributes 1.3% of GDP and 3.4% of export earnings. There is huge potential in this sector as the country has more than 50% forest cover with 850,000 ha (47% native forest), 42,000 ha pine plantation and 51,000 ha of hardwood

---

[6] These include fiscal duty concessions for fishing boats, specialised fishing gear, equipment and bait.

[7] The EU currently has three bilateral fisheries agreement with Kiribati, Federal States of Micronesia and the Solomon Islands (Oxfam 2006a).

plantation (Government of Fiji 2006b). The hardwood plantations, including mahogany, have enormous value-adding potential of up to US$200 million annually. But Fiji has been slow to cash in on its natural resource sector. This is due to a lack of infrastructure support, inadequate skilled personnel, poor timber utilization, and the ability to sustain quality and quantity for domestic export markets. There is, however, increased activity in the pine industry and the commercial exploitation of the maturing mahogany crop begun in 2004 is expected to boost the forestry industry. The recent construction of a Timber Industry Training Institute and a Forestry Training Centre is also expected to yield benefits in the long run, while the 2007 budget has set aside F$20 million for the further development of the fisheries and forestry sector.

If properly developed and managed to sustain growth, the agriculture, fisheries and forestry sector has immense potential to provide employment and growth for the economy. Furthermore, most of these activities are concentrated in the rural or outer islands where much poverty remains, although the rural sector contributed around 40% of domestic exports in 2004. Without specific strategies in place for this sector, Fiji is at a big risk if it was to increasingly rely more heavily on the manufacturing sector. This is a lesson to be learnt from Malaysia which is an economic success story. Malaysia started as an agricultural economy and reached a phase of industrial expansion. However, it has now renewed emphasis on the role of agriculture as an engine of growth. This is because heavy reliance on the manufacturing sector and services sectors can increase the vulnerability to external shocks given the pace of globalisation. Thus, diversification is required not just within the primary sector, but also a balanced growth approach towards manufacturing and services to help cushion adverse impacts on any one sector.

The Garments Sector

Prior to the mid 1980s, the garment industry was non existent and it originated as a product of the post-1987 coup strategy of export-led development. It evolved on the back of the preferential trading agreement with the South Pacific Regional Trade and Economic Cooperation Agreement (SPARTECA) in 1980, the import credit scheme in 1991, the tax-free zone and factory scheme in 1987, and the multi-fibre agreement.[8] In fact, from 1997 to 2001, garments replaced sugar as the country's leading export sector. Before the coup on 2000, the garment industry played a major role in employment creation as it employed some 18,000 to 20,000 workers – mainly unskilled female workers who made up about 75% of those employed. Today, it employs about 12,000 to 15,000 workers (Hannan 2005).

However, recently, there were fears that the garment industry was hollowing out because of factors such as: the increasing competition from China and Southeast Asia; the end of the tax-free factor and import credit schemes in 2000; the erosion of the preferential trading agreements with SPARTECA; and the expiry of the multi-fibre agreement at the end of 2004 (Storey 2005). Fortunately, due to strong lobbying from Fiji's then Prime Minister, Laisenia Qarase, the Australian government passed the Textile, Clothing and Footwear Investment

[8] The SPARTECA allowed garment manufacturers in Fiji preferential but non-reciprocal access to the markets of Australia and New Zealand in the form of duty-free and unrestricted or concessional access. The import credit scheme allowed Australian fabric to be shipped to Fiji at a competitive price and used in re-imported goods to the Australian market. The tax-free factory scheme included incentives of tax holiday, duty exemptions on capital goods and raw materials and freedom to repatriate capital profits for 13 years. The multi-fibre agreement is a global agreement where Fiji garment exports enter the US under export quotas.

Program Amendment Bill in late 2004 to guarantee Fiji's export agreement under SPARTECA for an additional seven years.[9] But there is concern among Fijian garment manufacturers that if Australia signs a bilateral free trade agreement with China, they would be further disadvantaged (Hannan 2005).

The main problem with this sector is its over reliance on trade preferences – it mirrors the sugar industry's failure to restructure and improve competitiveness by moving up the value chain while being protected. Today, this sector remains low-skill, low-wage, low-technology with a cut, make and trim focus. It has very limited backward and forward supply linkages, which can be seen in the lack of fabric making and dyeing capacity (Oxfam 2004b).

Tourism

Given the problems in the sugar and the garment sectors, tourism was hailed as the cornerstone of growth and development. This has been reflected in the vigour with which the government has been pushing state resources in favour of tourism in the numerous incentives and aid packages to boost the performance of this sector.[10] Since 1998, tourism has been the biggest foreign exchange earner generating on average about 30% of total exports and tourist arrivals have increased from 190,000 in 1987 to 500,000 in 2005.

But tourism has its own set of problems as it has been adversely affected by the domestic political uncertainty (and hence delayed investment) seen in the 1987 and 2000 coups. As well, it has been affected by external events such as the US terrorist attacks of 2001, the Bali bombing in 2002, the 2003 severe acute respiratory syndrome, the 2002 revolt by the mobile force in Vanuatu and the army in Papua New Guinea. Thus, tourism demand in Fiji is volatile and subject to external shocks.

Another drawback for tourism is that a large part of the income leaks out of the country because of the high degree of foreign ownership in tourism-related activities, particularly accommodation. Most of the food, where the bulk of the expenditure is concentrated, is also imported. In addition, secondary tourism activities such as eco-tourism and entertainment facilities are still poorly developed relative to other major competing destinations such as Bali and the Australian Gold Coast, thus leading to fewer days spent in Fiji (Government of Fiji 2006b). The problem of labour migration has also left this industry with a short supply of skilled workers. To support human resource development, construction of a Tourism and Hospitality Training School commenced in 2005. Lastly, the land-lease system serves as a disincentive to investment. Prasad and Tisdell (2006) explain that, in addition to the normal lease payment, 2.5%–3.5% of the gross turnover of the hotels situated on native land is paid to landowners. Another disincentive emerges from the landowners' insistence that tourists employ members of their own villages where appropriate as first priority. Another issue facing the tourism industry and potential investors is the ongoing conflict between the role of the NLTB and the land-owning units, whereby landowners have sought hefty compensations

[9] However, there is concern among Fijian garment manufacturers that if Australia signs a bilateral free trade agreement with China, they would be further disadvantaged (Hannan 2005).

[10] These include hotel aid and investment allowances, carry forward of losses, accelerated depreciated allowances, relaxation of work permit rules and duty concessions. There has also been a series of property developments from residential to commercial, all part of a 10–15 year development plan. This includes the expansion of Port Denarau marina, retail and commercial centres and additional golf holes. The sellout of new residential areas in Fairway Palms, Mariners Beach, the Cove, and Marina Point is encouraging and the newly released Sovereign Quays and Paradise Point as freehold residential sites are fast developing.

from operators. The authors argue that the lack of security of tenure from the NLTB has led to several cases of illegal takeover or demands for higher rent from existing hotel owners. `

The ICT Industry

While much needs to be done to remove the supply side constraints in tourism and other sectors in the economy, there is, however, an exciting new service industry underway in Fiji. This is the offshore back-office and call-centre industry, which can swiftly create thousands of jobs. Call centres are basically a business process outsourcing centre where people are employed to handle paper work, enquiries, account matters, credit card transactions, pay rolls, transcription services, content conversions, and the renewal of insurance policies. At a higher level, this includes giving quick advice using computers and telephones – all services that businesses all over the world can have done for them abroad far more cheaply than in their own countries.

Currently, there are two call centres operating in Suva. They are run by Quest, a subsidiary of the Australia New Zealand group and by an American giant business, Affiliated Computer Services. The latter company has moved its branch from Mexico to Suva and is expecting to draw new business from Pacific Rim countries and the US. There are big plans for expansion and the call centres located in Fiji are ideal as Fiji's daytime overlaps with the working hours in the two client sources, America and Britain. Most of the staff are currently University of South Pacific part-time students studying for accountancy, business management and computer science degrees. After graduating, about 45% of them have become full time employees. An essential for hosting these centres is having good English speakers, and Fiji has a comparative advantage in this – and its efforts to improve its telecommunications system are in the right direction.

For instance, the telecommunications industry is under review for privatisation as noted in the 2007 Budget and there are plans to develop an E-commerce Bill to ensure that the interests of suppliers and buyers engaged in transactions over the Internet are adequately protected. In January 2007, the Kalabu Tax Free Zone was declared an ICT zone where ICT operators are allowed to enjoy a tax holiday for 10 years. The University of South Pacific is also getting into ICT in a big way with its F$29 million facility, the Pacific Information and Communication Technology. ICT use has been recognised in fisheries (with a satellite tracking system, the location of a boat and the number of fish being caught can be noted), tourism (advertising of hotel and resort areas) and education (electronic library) services.

CAUSALITY LINKS TO GROWTH

This section examines the causal links between the various sectors of the Fiji economy and their impacts on economic growth. There are a few ways of investigating causal links. The pioneering work of Granger (1969) was first extended by the use of Sims' (1972) forward and backward causality tests. This led to the estimation of first, the bivariate, and then the multivariate ECM, which enabled the examination of short- and long-run causality relationships. However, there are some problems with the multivariate ECM for the use of causality interpretation.

First, in an ECM the significance and sometimes the signs of the coefficients that provide information on causality are known to be sensitive to the number of variables as well as the choice of the normalising cointegrating vector. While the latter task is meant to be based on economic theory, often, due to the lack of it, normalisation[11] is done on an *ad hoc* basis and not necessarily supported by sound economic theory. The second problem is that for higher dimensional systems, the causal variables must be adequately involved in the cointegration, but often sequential strategies are not carried out to examine sufficient cointegration in the vector ECM (Giles and Williams 2000). Third, and more importantly, it has been argued by Toda and Phillips (1993) and Zapata and Rambaldi (1997) that standard Granger causality tests have non-standard asymptotic properties, and thus the use of the F-test based on a VAR or ECM is not valid if the variables in the VAR are integrated or cointegrated. The issue is more complicated given the pre-testing distortions associated with the prior test for cointegration such as unit root tests or if the stability and rank conditions are not fulfilled when there is more than one cointegrating vector in a multivariate model.

Thus, an improved testing procedure developed by Toda and Yamamoto (1995) is used here to study the inter-industry linkages in the three growth sectors. This procedure uses the modified Wald test for restrictions on the parameters of the first k lags in a VAR ($k + d_{max}$) where k refers to lag length and d_{max} is the maximum order of integration that occurs in the system. The reason why this works is that the distributions of test statistics with non-stationary time series are singular and by over-parameterising the VAR, one can avoid singularity and obtain test statistics with the usual asymptotic distributions (Dolado and Lütkepohl, 1996). Here, a model is estimated to identify causality links between the aggregate economy, agriculture, manufacturing and services sectors.[12] We hypothesise that there is a relationship between aggregate economic growth, and the agriculture, manufacturing and services sectors. The empirical model for estimation is the following 4-equation VAR model:

$$\begin{bmatrix} DAgg_t \\ DAgric_t \\ DManu_t \\ DServ_t \end{bmatrix} = \begin{bmatrix} A_{10} \\ A_{20} \\ A_{30} \\ A_{40} \end{bmatrix} + \begin{bmatrix} A_{11}(L) & A_{12}(L) & A_{13}(L) \\ A_{21}(L) & A_{22}(L) & A_{23}(L) \\ A_{31}(L) & A_{32}(L) & A_{33}(L) \\ A_{41}(L) & A_{42}(L) & A_{43}(L) \end{bmatrix} \times \begin{bmatrix} DAgg_{t-k} \\ DAgric_{t-k} \\ DManu_{t-k} \\ DServ_{t-k} \end{bmatrix} + \begin{bmatrix} \varepsilon_{1t} \\ \varepsilon_{2t} \\ \varepsilon_{3t} \\ \varepsilon_{4t} \end{bmatrix} \quad (2.1)$$

where Agg, Agric, Manu and Serv represent real GDP of the aggregate economy, agriculture, manufacturing, and other sectors, respectively; D is a difference operator; k represents number of lags; A_{i0} are the parameters representing intercept terms; $A_{ij}(L)$ are the polynomials in the lag operator L; and ε_{it} are white-noise disturbances that may be correlated.

The optimal lag length is chosen by minimising the values of the Akaike Information and Schwartz Bayesian Criteria. To gain efficiency through cross equation residuals (that is, by assuming the multivariate error vector has a non-zero diagonal covariance matrix), Zellner's seemingly unrelated regression is used to obtain estimates of the VAR coefficients (Charemza and Deadman 1992). Taking a VAR model with two lags as an example and looking at Equation (2.1), a given variable does not Granger-cause X if, and only if, all the coefficients

[11] This procedure is to detect if there is a cointegrating relationship between a selected number of variables in a multivariate setting.

[12] The services sector includes utilities, construction, commerce, hotels and restaurants, transport, communication, finance, insurance, property services, business services, and other private services.

of $A_{1j}(L)$ are equal to zero. Conversely, *X* does not Granger-cause the variable if, and only if, all the coefficients of $A_{j1}(L)$ are equal to zero. Therefore, in a model with two lags, the hypotheses to be tested are:

$$H_0: a_{1j}(1) = a_{1j}(2) = 0 \tag{2.2}$$
$$H_0: a_{j1}(1) = a_{j1}(2) = 0 \tag{2.3}$$

where in equation (2.2), $a_{1j}(i)$ are the coefficients of the given variable in the first equation and $a_{j1}(i)$ are the coefficients of *X* in the jth equation in the VAR model of the first equation.

The annual data used covers the period of 1970 to 2002 on real GDP, agriculture value added, manufacturing value added and services value added and were obtained from the World Bank (World Development Indicators database). All variables are in constant 2000 Fiji dollars. The empirical results are tabulated in table 2.5. A *p*-value of less than 0.05 implies that the null hypothesis (that the right hand side variable does not Granger-cause the left hand side variable) is rejected at the 5% level of significance. The Granger causality results indicate that there is one-way Granger causality running from agricultural sector growth to aggregate economic growth. However, there is weak evidence (at the 10% level of significance) supporting the possibility of a bidirectional causal relationship between aggregate economic growth and agricultural sector growth. The remainder of the results indicates that there is no causality in any direction between aggregate economic growth, manufacturing sector growth and services sector growth. These results suggest that despite the declining share of agriculture in national output, it still remains a significant contributor to economic growth.

Table 2.5. Inter-Industry Causality Links

Direction of Causality	*p*-value	Result
Agric → Agg	0.001	Reject
Manu → Agg	0.867	Do not reject
Serv → Agg	0.800	Do not reject
Agg → Agric	0.100	Do not reject
Agg → Manu	0.859	Do not reject
Agg → Serv	0.499	Do not reject
Agric → Manu	0.163	Do not reject
Manu → Agric	0.637	Do not reject
Agric → Serv	0.085	Do not reject
Serv → Agric	0.779	Do not reject
Manu → Serv	0.503	Do not reject
Serv → Manu	0.392	Do not reject

Notes:

1. A → B refers to the null hypothesis that A does not Granger-cause B.
2. The above results report *p*-values based on the χ^2 statistic.

The results also show that there are no significant linkages between manufacturing, agriculture, and the services sectors. This implies, for example, that the tourism sector, which is a significant component of the services sector, sources very few inputs from the agricultural sector. Hence, the rapid growth of the services sector in recent years has had minimal impact on the agricultural sector. This situation is due to the fact that the tourism industry is mainly urban based, whereas the agricultural industry is mainly rural based. Therefore, to achieve broad-based growth, there is a need for policies that encourage industries to set up in the rural areas. With the declining importance of agriculture, labour could be diverted from agriculture into tourism and manufacturing.

However, to facilitate such a transition, there is a need for an improvement in basic education and skills training, as tourism and manufacturing require more specialised skills compared to agriculture. Although the manufacturing sector, for example, is currently labour-intensive, over time there would be a need for it to move up the value-added chain, which underlines the need for an investment in skills training.

To promote future broad-based growth, there is a need for fiscal and other incentives targeted at other industries apart from manufacturing. This is what Bhagwati (1984) referred to as the 'splintering effect', where service industries grow due to the increased production of manufactured goods. Also, with increasing specialisation, or technological progress allowing for standardisation of services or relatively lower transactions costs, manufacturing industries may choose to contract out their 'in-house' services, thereby increasing the link between the manufacturing and the services sector.

To further explore the extent to which the agriculture, manufacturing, and services sectors contribute to Fiji's economic growth, we re-specify Equation (2.1) in order to test the export-led growth hypothesis. The export-led growth hypothesis postulates that export expansion, especially of manufactured goods, is a key factor in promoting economic growth. Several arguments have been advanced to justify the export-led growth hypothesis. First, it has been suggested that exports could be a catalyst for income growth, especially in small domestic markets where sustained demand growth cannot be maintained.[13] From the supply side, export growth could promote economic growth by increasing total factor productivity (TFP) in a number of ways. Firstly, growth in exports could enhance specialization in sectors where a country has a comparative advantage, leading to a reallocation of resources to the more efficient export sector.

Secondly, export growth could enhance productivity through increased economies of scale. Thirdly, export growth could affect TFP through dynamic spillover effects on the rest of the economy. Fourthly, export expansion may indirectly affect growth by providing the foreign exchange that allows for increasing levels of capital goods imports, which can stimulate output growth by raising the level of capital formation.

There is currently a vast empirical literature that explores the link as well as direction of causation between exports and economic growth. Overall, the conclusions are mixed and contradictory, at best. Thus, the debate on the nexus between exports and economic growth is far from settled. The variables in the model are the real GDP of the aggregate economy, agricultural exports, tourism exports, and other exports. The following 4-equation VAR model was estimated. The data were obtained from the Fiji Department of Statistics and covers the period 1970 to 2002. The exports data were in current prices and were deflated using the GDP deflator. The empirical results are reported in table 2.6.

[13] See Siliverstors and Herzer (2007) for an extensive review of export-led growth studies.

$$\begin{bmatrix} DAgg_t \\ DAgricexp_t \\ DTourexp_t \\ DOtherexp_t \end{bmatrix} = \begin{bmatrix} A_{10} \\ A_{20} \\ A_{30} \\ A_{40} \end{bmatrix} + \begin{bmatrix} A_{11}(L) & A_{12}(L) & A_{13}(L) \\ A_{21}(L) & A_{22}(L) & A_{23}(L) \\ A_{31}(L) & A_{32}(L) & A_{33}(L) \\ A_{41}(L) & A_{42}(L) & A_{43}(L) \end{bmatrix} \times \begin{bmatrix} DAgg_{t-k} \\ DAgricexp_{t-k} \\ DTourexp_{t-k} \\ DOtherexp_{t-k} \end{bmatrix} + \begin{bmatrix} e_{1t} \\ e_{2t} \\ e_{3t} \\ e_{4t} \end{bmatrix} \quad (2.4)$$

where Agg, Agricexp, Tourexp and Otherexp represent aggregate economy's real GDP, agricultural exports, tourism exports, and other exports, respectively; and all other variables are as defined in Equation 2.2.

From the first row of table 2.6, it can be seen that the null hypothesis that agricultural exports do not Granger-cause aggregate economic growth is rejected at the 5% level of significance. However, it can also be seen that the null hypothesis that aggregate economic growth does not Granger-cause agricultural exports cannot be rejected. Therefore, there is one-way Granger causality running from agricultural exports to aggregate economic growth.

Similarly, for tourism exports, there is one-way causality running from tourism exports to aggregate economic growth and no reverse causality. However, in the case of other exports, there is no evidence of causality in either direction. Also, it is observed that there are no causal links between tourism and agriculture. However, there is weak evidence of bi-directional causality between tourism exports and other exports. These results support the earlier findings that agriculture and tourism are the main drivers of aggregate economic growth in Fiji. They also highlight the lack of (or weak) linkages between the tourism, agriculture and other sectors.

Table 2.6. Test Results for the Export-Led Growth Hypothesis

Direction of Causality	*p*-value	Result
Agricexp → Agg	0.041	Reject
Tourexp → Agg	0.011	Reject
Otherexp → Agg	0.800	Do not reject
Agg → Agricexp	0.813	Do not reject
Tourexp → Agricexp	0.223	Do not reject
Otherexp → Agricexp	0.093	Do not reject
Agg → Tourexp	0.132	Do not reject
Agricexp→ Tourexp	0.113	Do not reject
Otherexp → Tourexp	0.056	Reject
Agg → Otherexp	0.632	Do not reject
Agricexp → Otherexp	0.112	Do not reject
Tourexp → Otherexp	0.052	Reject

Notes:

1. A → B refers to the null hypothesis that A does not Granger-cause B.
2. The above results report p-values based on the χ^2 statistic.

POLICY IMPLICATIONS

Fiji's post-colonial industrial policies were based on an import substitution strategy, providing assistance to manufacturers, imposing high levels of tariff protection, protecting domestic competition using quotas and licenses, offering virtually no incentives for export production, and imposing tight controls on foreign investment. However in the early 1980s, Fiji embraced the IMF and World Bank recommendations on structural adjustment policies such as substantial deregulation of the labour and product markets along the lines of the Washington consensus.

As a result, 1984 saw the beginning of the move away from an inward-looking strategy to outward-looking policies such as improving competitiveness and export performance. But the real impetus for changes in the policy direction came about after the military coups of 1987. Tax-free factories and export-processing zones were the driving force of Fijian exports.

Since 1989, Fiji has adopted a phased program to eliminate quantitative import barriers such as import licensing requirements and quantitative restrictions, as well as reducing tariffs. For example, of the 46 items under license control at that time, only one item (lubricants and hydraulic fluids) was still subject to import licensing by 1996. In 1996, Fiji became a member of the WTO and currently it accords most-favoured nation treatment to all its trading partners. Fiji has preferential access (duty free and unrestricted access) for its manufactured goods under the SPARTECA, a non-reciprocal agreement between Australia (for most products except for sugar), New Zealand and 14 South Pacific Forum island countries. This came into effect in January 1981. After the 1987 coups, a trade agreement among the Melanesian Spearhead Group Countries (Papua New Guinea, Solomon Islands, Vanuatu and Fiji) was signed on July 1993 – but nothing has come out of this as it was more a political move by the then prime minister, Sitiveni Rabuka whose objective was to obtain support from Vanuatu and the Solomon Islands who objected to the coup.

However, a more effective trade agreement is PICTA, which from April 2003 allows for free trade among the Forum island countries through the progressive reduction and elimination of tariffs by 2012. The PACER with Australia and New Zealand came into force on 3rd October 2002 and this is expected to provide further assistance for trade facilitation for Fiji via the provision of technical assistance and capacity building. As we show in Chapter 9, a reduction in import barriers should lead to increased exports and imports – tax on imports is effectively a tax on exports because import barriers raise the input prices for exporting industries.

The fact is that Fiji has not been able to diversify its merchandise export base to a great extent, relying mainly on the export of sugar and, since 1987, on garments. In general, the progress of trade reform has been slow. For instance, the Minister of Finance announced in 1998 that nominal tariffs would be reduced to 22.5% by 2002 – but that did not happen. Also in 1999, Fiji committed to lowering its non-protective tariffs to 10% but, at the same time, it was announced that protective tariffs would be raised to 35%! The government has also imposed discretionary import quotas on a number of goods that are perceived to compete with local goods. Duncan *et al.* (1999) note that successive governments have rolled back trade reforms and have been inconsistent in setting tariffs.

The move towards outward-oriented policies saw reforms continuing in the early 1990s. There were reductions in industry protection to open the domestic economy to international competition (import tariffs were cut by about one-third between 1990 and 1995) and export incentives were provided through the development of tax-free schemes. The introduction of the Duty Suspension Scheme from 2000 allowed exporters to import inputs duty free. In August 2001, the Reserve Bank of Fiji introduced an export credit ratio policy, which required banks to lend a minimum of 5% of their average deposits to eligible exporters of goods and services.

What is now required to accelerate Fiji's economic growth is a strategy to diversify the country's merchandise export base, in particular the non-sugar agricultural sector. As we show in the causality analysis, there are currently few linkages between the agricultural and manufacturing sectors. Increasing the development and processing of agricultural produce could rectify this situation. Such a strategy would not only strengthen the links between the agricultural and manufacturing sectors, but also create greater employment and output opportunities. A move in this direction would set the pace for the accelerated development of agro-industrialisation, which involves the inter-related activities of production, processing, transport, storage, financing, marketing and distribution of specific agricultural produce. To promote agro-industrial development, there would need to be a suite of complementary policies to encourage agribusiness development and rural development.

To further boost exports growth, and hence economic growth, there is a need for fairer WTO trading rules. Historically, WTO rules have provided a weak discipline on agricultural trade and this practice continues for reasons related to the Uruguay Round on agricultural agreements. The agreement institutionalized a new definition of subsidies tailored to the interests of the US and the EU, the strongest negotiating parties. These countries are always strongly represented in terms of the numbers of skilled negotiators, compared to teams from the LDCs who are short on expertise.

What is required is a new set of rules that take the simple step of insisting on the economic principle that agricultural exports should reflect the costs of production. The World Bank and IMF, whose boards are dominated by the US and the EU, have been preaching and pressuring developing countries to cut their import tariff rates as part of the trade liberalisation and structural adjustment policies. World Bank and IMF loans are conditional on a country committing to implementing such policies. However, the evidence points to a case of double standards, as the advanced countries are not obligated to implement similar policies. In late 1999, the IMF strongly opposed the protection given to the domestic sugar industry in Mozambique, but it backed down after a huge public protest in Mozambique.

CONCLUSION

Fiji's economic growth performance since independence has been inconsistent and patchy, at best. Prospects for sustained economic growth have been undermined by political instability arising from military coups in 1987 and an attempted coup in 2000. The latest coup in December 2006 does not bode well for Fiji's short-term growth prospects. Since 1995, Fiji's ranking on the HDI has fallen. The political turbulence caused by the coups, coupled with poor macroeconomic management, has had an adverse impact on both savings and investment (including FDI), which have followed a declining trend since 1987.

Although Fiji is still predominantly an agricultural-based economy, the share of tourism in national output and exports has been rising for some time. Like other small island nations, Fiji faces the challenges of a small domestic market, a narrow resource base and remoteness from the major international markets. The loss of the EU sugar preferences and the non-renewal of land leases pose a major threat to the country's development prospects since both situations imply a loss of thousands of jobs.

The analysis in this chapter confirms the fact that despite the declining share of agriculture in GDP, it remains a significant contributor to economic growth and employment. The analysis also concludes that agricultural and tourism exports are the main drivers of economic growth. For a long time, Fiji has relied on the sugar industry and, lately, the garment industry. While there has been a move towards an outward-oriented trade policy as opposed to the import-substitution policies of the immediate post-independence era, the pace of reforms has been slow and the measures implemented have been incomplete.

The main conclusion arising from the analysis in this chapter is that Fiji will need to increase productivity in the agricultural sector and diversify its export base in order meet the shortfall in national income from the loss of sugar preferences. This calls for institutional reforms and the development of appropriate policies to remove the supply-side constraints that prevent local producers from responding effectively to favourable movements in the terms of trade. The empirical analysis also established the lack of significant linkages between the two growth leading sectors: tourism and agriculture. The fact that the tourism sector imports most of its food inputs could, *inter alia*, be due to the fact that the local produce is not of a sufficient standard and that the supply may be considered unreliable. The challenge for the government is to put in place measures to assist farmers to grow agricultural produce that meets international standards and to establish a reliable industry.

One serious supply-side constraint in both the agricultural, tourism and manufacturing sectors is the lack of skilled labour. It is suggested that the government should fund the training of workers in basic skills, especially the displaced workers from the agricultural sector so that they can be absorbed into other industries. Such practical training would also enable some of these workers to establish their own businesses.

However, for such a transition to be successful, the government would need to set up a complementary program to provide them access to credit. Skills training is also required to improve value adding in the manufacturing and tourism industries. It was also noted that one area with the capacity to create new jobs is the establishment of call centres. However, the prospect of establishing more call centres in Fiji depends on the availability of sufficient numbers of well-educated workers and on a favourable domestic investment climate.

The fisheries sector is one area whose vast potential remains to be tapped. The major constraint in this area is lack of sufficient domestic investment. Other constraints include lack of supporting infrastructure, such as fishing wharves and electricity for refrigeration and processing in rural areas.

Although Fiji is disadvantaged by its remoteness from major exports markets, it was noted that value adding for fisheries could be enhanced by targeting niche markets for processed fish products such as smoked, flavoured and prepared fillets. The government could attract investment into this sector by adopting a policy package that includes tax incentives, financial assistance for local producers and infrastructure development schemes.

In conclusion, the point is re-emphasised that global trade reform needs to be a two-way street for the benefits to be maximised for the entire world. We have noted that developing countries are required by aid donors to fully liberalise their economies while some advanced countries have not done so. We show in later chapters that unilateral trade liberalisation is not the best option for Fiji for maximising national income and welfare. The best outcome is achieved through global trade liberalisation. This underlines the urgent need to move the current trade talks forward with the view to removing tariff and non-tariff barriers worldwide.

Chapter 3

The Sugar Industry

Introduction

Sugar became the principal export from Fiji as early as 1883. Despite its importance to the economic and daily life of Fiji, surprisingly little has been written, in an integrated form, about the industry's development and performance to date. Thus, the next few chapters attempt to remedy this omission. This chapter begins with a discussion on the global sugar market and producers, in particular, the EU sugar regime and preferences given to ACP countries as well as the ongoing EPA negotiations.

The next section provides a historical perspective of Fiji's sugar industry followed by the issues related to the political economy of the industry such as the problems of the land tenure system and ethnic issues in sugar production, as well as the various institutions involved in sugar production. Lastly, the performance and structure of the sugar industry is reviewed to set the stage for the following chapters.

The Global Sugar Market

Worldwide, about 121 countries produce sugar but from two different crops. Sugarcane, a giant tropical grass, is the source of over two-thirds of global production and is grown throughout the developing world, as well as in the US, Japan and Australia. The remainder comes from sugar beet, a temperate root crop grown mainly in Europe, the US and Japan.

Sugar is among the most traded commodities with exports accounting for over one quarter of global production – but it also has one of the most distorted global markets. The sugar trade conjures up images of the colonial era when the West Indies exported cane sugar to meet European demand. That image has been reversed. Europe is now the biggest exporter of white sugar to the rest of the world, despite having one of the highest costs of production. Such absurdity is made possible by fixed prices and hefty subsidies to Europe's large-scale farmers and agribusinesses. Europe's exports of 700,000 tons of sugar in 1970 have grown to an average of 5.3 million tons over 2001–03, which is about 14% of the world market share. The top five cane producers – India, Brazil, China Thailand, and Mexico – account for another 42% (Oxfam 2004).

The US has long played opposite to Europe with its own protectionist regime. For instance, Groombridge (2001) notes that the US government spends close to €1.7 billion each year buying and storing excess sugar to maintain the artificially high domestic prices, and that only 12% of US sugar consumption is met through imports. The US has long conducted a policy that has a major impact upon the global trade in sugar since the 1980s. The US also supports the price of corn, which has become a substitute for sugar in the form of fructose corn syrup. The US sugar regime protects fewer than 20,000 workers, of whom only 3,000 would be likely to lose their jobs if reform were undertaken – and yet, the sugar program costs nearly US$2 billion a year in higher prices (Oxfam 2004). Sugar has always been such a sensitive and important product that it was even left out of the US and Australia free trade agreement that came into effect on January 2005 – interestingly, this led the Australian government to unveil an A$441 million rescue package to assist the nation's struggling sugar industry.

Besides the US and the EU, the Japanese sugar market is also subject to massive state intervention and subsidies. Nevertheless, there are other cost-effective exporters who are not subject to such actions and they include Brazil, India, Thailand, Australia, South Africa, Columbia and Cuba.

The EU Sugar Regime

The EU sugar regime – launched in 1967 under the Common Agricultural Policy – keeps the sugar industry in business by first guaranteeing farmers a high price for selling their sugar beet to processors, and then guaranteeing sugar processors a high price for selling their refined sugar. The result is that European sugar costs three times more than the world market price. This is only made possible by hidden export subsidies, raised through levies on farmers and processors – levies they can afford because of the high price they receive for their sugar.

The EU justifies the sugar regime as an investment in rural development, but Europe's sugar farmers only constituted 4% of all EU farmers in 2001 (Raworth 2002), and this figure is unlikely to have changed significantly given that the sugar regime encourages large-scale farming. Yet another claim of the sugar regime is that the use of sugar beet is of environmental benefit – which is rather unclear. In fact, the Department of Environment Food and Rural Affairs (2002) reports that when sugar beet is harvested in the UK, the soil caught in the roots removed from the land amounts up to 350,000 tons a year. In self-defence, the sugar beet lobby points to the wildlife attracted to this spring-grown crop, such as the stone curlew, lapwing and skylark. But these environmental benefits are side effects of the policy and not its deliberate aim.

One hidden impact of the EU sugar regime is that it encourages inefficient resource use in Europe. For instance, every €1 in export sales generated by sugar costs the EU €3.30 in subsidies (Oxfam 2004). Also, it costs well over 50% more to produce sugar from beet than from cane – and the EU is among the world's highest cost sugar producers. For example, it costs Europe around €673 to produce one ton of white sugar compared to €286 for competitive countries such as Brazil, Columbia, Malawi, Guatemala and Zambia (Raworth 2002). This destroys the ability of some of these low-cost, less-developed producers to reap the potential benefits of comparative advantage, thereby curtailing the possibility of generating much-needed foreign exchange. It is rather unfortunate that these economies are heavily dependent on sugar production.

It is not surprising that the high guaranteed prices via heavy subsidies lead to excessive production of sugar beet in the EU, which is then dumped at lower prices in the world market. Thus, not only are world prices artificially depressed, but this undercuts LDC exports. Cuba, for example, announced that almost half of its sugar mills were closing down because of depressed export prices (*The Times*, 8 June 2002).

Finally, the EU's practice of subsidising refined white sugar has led several countries to have a high degree of dependence on exports of raw sugarcane. This has limited the opportunities for developing countries to add value to their commodity exports and create their own white sugar brands. In fact, big agro-industries in the EU refine the sugar imported from the developing countries and export it back to these very same countries. In addition, when world sugar prices collapsed in 1998, Europe's sugar-based confectionary exports – such as Cadbury's chocolate – were subsidised to match the low level of sugar prices. This seriously challenged the viability of Swaziland's value-adding sweets and chocolate industry (which took ten years to build) and, since then, production has fallen by 30% (Raworth 2002).

The EU's distortionary sugar policy has hardly changed and has evaded reform at every turn in negotiations in 1992, 1995, and 2000 – even though a 'peace clause'[1] was signed under the Uruguay Round Agreement due to expire at the end of 2003. But before that, in July 2003, Australia and Thailand joined Brazil and filed for a dispute settlement panel at WTO to determine whether the EU sugar production and export subsidies are legal under the existing trade treaties. Although the EU managed to block the creation of an investigation panel for quite a while eventually, in April 2005, the WTO upheld its judgment that EU sugar policies were illegal.

While it is certain that the EU will undertake reforms in the sugar industry, the nature and timetable of the reform process is unclear at this stage. But reform will need to be handled gradually in order to minimise market instability and to ensure that shifts in supply do not create sudden spikes in the world price of sugar – this could lead to sugar being replaced by high fructose corn syrup in soft drinks and processed foods. The future shape of the world sugar market will need to be considered, including possible changes in market structure and, if appropriate, the use of international cooperation mechanisms to stabilise prices and monitor competition.

Perhaps more than any other sector, the EU sugar regime demonstrates why reform cannot be treated solely as a domestic EU affair. This is because of the EU's position as a major global producer, exporter and importer and the fact that decisions taken in Brussels will have major ramifications, not just for a large group of poor countries, but also for millions of desperately poor people. That is why the EU needs to display a sense of international responsibility commensurate with its market power. Beyond Europe, other changes are needed, including sugar regime reform in the US and Japan to ensure that the excess production of sugar is removed and world prices are not kept artificially low.

[1] Without this 'peace clause', countries would have greater freedom to take action against the EU.

THE EU SUGAR PREFERENCES

First, it is useful to understand the history and actual negotiation as part of a set of unique characteristics that have defined EU sugar preferences to the ACP countries since 1975. It all began during the Ottawa Conference in 1932, when the UK offered its colonies and members of the Commonwealth trade preference for their commodities in its internal market. Sugar featured prominently in this system of trade preference that was created in large measure to assist the UK as well as Commonwealth producers during the Great Depression. But it was not until after World War II (in December 1951) that the UK proposed the Commonwealth Sugar Agreement to assure a guaranteed supply of sugar to the domestic market after almost decades of depression and war.

The sugar protocol expired at the end of 1974 and under the terms of the Lancaster House Agreement, the UK had made clear and specific commitments to the ACP countries to produce an alternative arrangement upon accession to the Treaty of Rome. Thus, negotiations over the protocol occurred in 1974 and early 1975, just when sugar prices reached their highest levels during the 20th century.

At the same time, negotiations were occurring over the entry of the UK into the EC and in order to expedite British entry, the EC accepted 1.3 million tons on the EC market – and this figure has essentially been maintained in addition to linking the countries of the EC to their former colonies. The timing of this coincided with the EC internal sugar policy being renewed by 1975.

Also, there was a combination of extremely bad harvests in Cuba and the USSR as well as in the EC. Sugar consumption was unexpectedly high in Europe combined with a shift back to sugar consumption in the US resulting from the reported cancer risks of artificial sweeteners. These forces together created the most rapid increase in the price of sugar and exerted substantial pressure on the EC to arrive at a solution that was a very generous agreement on prices to benefit the ACP producers. This led to the conclusion of the Lome Convention on 1st February 1975.[2]

As part of the sugar regime, raw cane sugar is imported from 17 of the 77 ACP countries[3] (plus India), restricted by quotas but purchased at the high EU price. The commitment is to purchase about 1.3 million tons and there is also an annual import allocation of between 200,000 and 350,000 tons of sugar under the Special Preferential Sugar arrangement whereby the ACP countries receive about 85% of the guaranteed price of the sugar protocol. The refining of the raw sugar into white sugar is primarily undertaken in the UK, Portugal and France. This preferential access has recently been of great value to those ACP countries in terms of stable export earnings in the face of depressed world markets.

However, the exports of these selected 18 ACP countries only accounted for about 8% of total EU production in 2001 (European Commission 2002). Among the lucky 18, almost 80% of the benefits accrue to just five of them – Mauritius, Fiji, Guyana, Swaziland and Jamaica – none of which are classified as LDCs. Of the rest, only four are LDCs with preferential access – and their combined share of benefits is just 4% in total (NEI 2000).

---

[2] Incidentally, Grynberg (1993) notes that the benefits from the Lome Convention are far more significant than the Commonwealth Sugar Agreement.

[3] ACP countries under the sugar protocol are: Barbados, Belize, Congo, Côte d'Ivoire, Fiji, Guyana, Jamaica, Kenya, Madagascar, Malawi, Mauritius, St Kitts and Nevis, Swaziland, Tanzania, Trinidad and Tobago, Uganda, Zambia and Zimbabwe.

There is no relationship between the size of income transfer under the sugar preferences and the consideration of the state of economic and social development or the contribution of agriculture to GDP in the heterogeneous ACP countries. For example, Mauritius has the highest quota allocation although it has the third highest per capita income and has one of the highest indicators for health, education and infrastructure development. In contrast, Zambia, Tanzania, Congo and Madagascar have the smallest per capita quotas yet have particularly poor social and economic indicators.

Nevertheless, some compensation was seen in 2000 when preferences were set out under the Cotonou Agreement[4] (which grew out of the original Lome Agreement, 1975–2000). This was an 'Everything But Arms' (EBA) initiative adopted on 28th February 2001 to provide tariff and quota-free access to its market for all products except armaments from 49 least developed countries. The EBA initiative included full access to the EU sugar markets, promising increased valuable exports for the four LDCs that already had quota-limited access (Malawi, Madagascar, Tanzania and Zambia). It also created new opportunities for other LDCs such as Sudan, Ethiopia, Mozambique, and Senegal, which were locked out of Europe. While it is not exactly clear on what basis countries were chosen for preferential treatment, there was some understanding that at the time of creation of the EU, only the EU member countries' colonies were considered.

By the time the EBA initiative was launched in 2001, vested European interests had successfully lobbied to slash back the deal on sugar. Instead of open access, sugar-producing LDCs were granted very restricted quotas that would incrementally increase until 2009 when unrestricted access was promised. To make up for the EBA sugar imports, Europe has cut the ACP quota access to existing countries under the Special Preferential Sugar Arrangement – this amounts to literally trading one group of developing country against another, while only marginally cutting back the EU's own sugar beet production.

Whatever the case, under the 2000 Cotonou Agreement, which expired at the end of 2007, sugar preferences will be fully withdrawn and new trading arrangements between ACP countries and the EU – known as the Economic Partnership Agreement (EPA) – will enter into force by 1st Jan 2008 and expire in 2018 (or at the very latest in 2020).

The EU-ACP EPA

The EPA is to create a free trade agreement (FTA) between the two regions and is a response to continuing criticism that the non-reciprocal and discriminating preferential trade agreements offered by the EU are incompatible with WTO rules. Guiding principles underlying the EPA are to be the following (Bilal and Van Hove 2002):

- *Development:* The agreements are to be oriented towards facilitating sustainable development and reducing poverty in ACP countries.
- *Reciprocity:* All trade restrictions between the parties are to be progressively removed, leading to a free trade area. This is in marked contrast to the current non-

[4] This was between 77 ACP countries and the EU-15 and was signed on 23rd June 2000.

reciprocal arrangement. ACP countries would have to open their markets for EU exports in order to keep or attain preferential access to EU markets.

- *Regionalism:* The EU sees increased regional integration within groups of ACP countries as a step toward greater integration in the world economy, and is planning agreements with ACP regional groups rather than individual countries.
- *Differentiation:* The EPAs are to include a strong component of special and differential treatment, taking into account differing circumstances and stages of development of ACP countries.

While these general principles hold some promise for ACP countries, there are risks involved as well. In particular, reciprocity of preferential access across a whole range of products will lead to trade diversion, as some of the trade between non-EU and ACP countries will be diverted to the EU. As a result, new or additional distortions may be introduced to ACP economies. However, by September 2007, there was a strong indication that negotiations would not be completed before the end of 2007, although since September 2002, six groups[5] within the ACP region have started negotiations with the EU on key sectors of their economies.

It is also unclear if the suspension of the Doha Round has implications for the progress and content of EPA negotiations. For instance, how would the new ACP-EU trade regime be adjusted if the WTO rules were to be modified later? Also, the outcomes of the EPA negotiations will set the precedent for any agreement (and the concessions will be amplified) when Fiji negotiates with Australia and New Zealand under PACER once the EPA is complete.

In addition, there is yet to be any agreement on the transition period and product coverage for reciprocal market access as well as on how to deal with development issues – although the need to identify specific national level projects to enable each ACP country to adjust and benefit from the EPA has been accepted. The EPA Newsletter (4th April 2007), however, notes that the offered full-market access to ACP in negotiations has a phase-in period for rice and sugar to protect the balance in the EU market. This is while internal reforms in EU are underway and, from 2015, ACP sugar would be duty and quota free. The EU's offer indicates that the EPA need not be tied to the equivalent openness from ACP countries and the ACP can retain the right to protect sensitive products where the removal of import duties could threaten local producers. The discussion on rules of origin[6] has not seen any headway yet, and this area is a major concern for the ACP countries.

In general, the ACP countries view EPAs as a necessary evil and tend to agree that it benefits the EU more than it does them (Hoestenberghe and Roelfsema 2006). Hoestenberghe and Roelfsema further argue that EPAs will not increase ACP countries' access to the EU

---

[5] They are West Africa, Central Africa, Eastern and South Africa, the Caribbean, South African Development Community and the Pacific.

[6] These rules are used to ensure that it is the ACP countries that benefit from access to EU markets and do not just become a transit channel for exports from third countries without benefit to local industry. But the smallness of the countries can limit local sourcing possibilities and face restriction from sourcing materials from low-cost locations in Asia. Thus, the large ACP countries stand to benefit due to exploitation of economies of scale. However, Brenton (2003) reports that there is no evidence that strict rules of origin over the past 20 years have stimulated the development of integrated production structures in developing countries. The strict rules constrain the ability of firms in least developed countries to integrate into global production networks and, in effect, act to dampen the location of any value-added activities in these countries.

market by much. The EPA negotiations are between 25 EU countries and six groups of ACP countries, with the EU countries having a combined GDP of US$13,000 billion in 2005. Among the ACP countries are 39 of the world's least developed countries. The smallest group, the Pacific Islands, has a combined GDP of only US$9 billion – 1,400 times smaller than the EU.

Thus, the EPA as a trade agreement between unequal trade partners is a concern (Oxfam 2006b). In addition, a comprehensive agreement with the EU on any one product could reduce the ability of the Pacific states to achieve their individual national goals given the differences in size, wealth and resource endowment among them.

In any case, in compliance with WTO rules, the EU is committed to smoothing the transition of the ACP countries because of the EU sugar reform and the implementation of the EPA by providing a total of F$1,400 million (€650 million) over an eight-year period. But there is concern that the emphasis on trade will re-orientate the focus of aid – or make aid conditional on market access for EU products – as funds may be shifted to achieve the goal of trade adjustment, if and when the EU accepts to do so (Hoestenberghe and Roelfsema 2006).

At the same time, there is a need to monitor the use of EU funds as they may well be unused or abused if implementation is not efficient due to lack of expertise in doing so – thus, resource mobilization is a long-standing problem. In addition, corruption in the civil service has dogged every government in Fiji since independence.[7] On the downside, the receiving country, Fiji, is concerned about EU bureaucracy involved in the approval and distribution of funds. It is unclear how closely the EU will be overseeing the disbursement of funds and to what extent the Fijian government will be given the right to approve or disapprove the use of funds itself.

The implementation the EPA itself is expected to be costly for ACP countries, with losses in tariff revenue and employment. Milner (2006) conservatively estimates that total adjustment costs – such as compensation for loss of tariff revenue, employment and production, and support for the export development of ACP countries – could be about €9.2 billion. The EU has a history of providing development assistance to ACP countries, covering areas such as health, education, water and sanitation and roads. This support is channeled through the European Development Fund and disbursed in five-year cycles. In response to ACP concerns about the costs of EPAs, the EU has agreed to increase the amount pledged under the next funding cycle for 2008–2013 to €22.7 billion. However, even before the EPAs came onto the scene, it was estimated that €21.3 billion would be needed merely to fund the costs of the EU's existing aid portfolio.[8] But Oxfam (2006b) warns that deeper scrutiny suggests that this assistance may be more illusion that reality – it highlights the poor track record of the EU in its 5-year financing cycle of the European Development Fund assistance package.

Table 3.1 shows that since 1975, the percentage of total allocation disbursed from 1975 to 2007 has declined from 43% to about 25% in the last five-year period. The EU has further suggested that the aid to compensate ACP countries for the costs of implementing the EPAs would come from the development fund for the next cycle of 2008–2013. If this is the case, then it is questionable if any new funds are being set aside – or does it mean that existing

[7] The F$200 million scandal at the National Bank of Fiji, the F$16 million scam at the Ministry of Agriculture and allegations of abuse within the Fisheries department and the Public Works Department have all led to a massive decline in public confidence in all governments and politicians (see *The Fiji Times* 13 July 2004).

[8] The ACP Council of Ministers Meeting at Port Moresby in May 2006.

funds would be diverted away from other areas such as health, education and rural development? (Oxfam 2006b). The ACP governments have called for a separate EPA financing facility so that the EU can be held to its promise and funds clearly tracked – but, to date, this has not been agreed upon.

Furthermore, the lesson is that existing schemes (such as the EU's Special Framework for Assistance from 1999–2009 to facilitate preference erosion from the EU's banana regime) have been subject to strict and often inconsistent conditionality on the use of the funds. This has led to delays in payments and frequent changes to the schemes, and to a constraint on investment decisions (LMC International and Oxford Policy Management 2003). Thus, there are many concerns surrounding the EPA negotiations and the development assistance package.

Table 3.1. European Development Funds (million euros)

Assistance Package Period	Funds allocated	Disbursements
1975–1980	3390	1454.4 (43%)
1980–1985	5227	2041.6 (39%)
1985–1990	8400	3341.6 (40%)
1990–1995	12000	4417.9 (37%)
1995–2000	14625	2921.6 (20%)
2000–2005	15200	4239.0 (28%)

Note: Figures in parentheses denote the percentage of allocated funds that were actually disbursed.
Source: Milner (2006).

Fiji's Sugar Industry

This section starts with a brief discussion on the sugarcane crop followed by a historical perspective of Fiji's sugar. The latter sets the stage for reviewing the political economy surrounding the sugar industry related to land and ethnic issues and the way various institutions operate in the vertically integrated sugar industry.

The Sugarcane Crop

Sugarcane is a giant tropical grass whose leaves trap the sun's energy through photosynthesis and converts it to sucrose (sugar) more effectively than any other crop. Sugar made in this way is stored as a juice in the plant's fibrous stalks. Sugarcane is a sub-tropical crop that grows well in warm, sunny weather and well-drained soil with at least 1,500 mm of rain a year. Immediately after harvesting, fine, relatively cool weather retards the plant's growth and increases sugar content.

Sugarcane is a unique crop for cultivation. It is propagated by planting sections of the stalk known as seed cane. Once the first crop, called plant can, is harvested (this involves the cutting of plant shoots such as stems and leaves), the plant will grow back from the portion of the stalk left under the ground. The subsequent crops are known as ratoon crops and, thus, do not require replanting; they rely only on fertilizer, thereby cutting costs. However, this does not necessarily give cane of good quality and is unable to match the harvesting of seed cane.

On average, a plant crop and three to four ratoon crops are obtained from one planting so that each field is usually planted every five to six years. Planting is one of the most important farm operations because it determines the performance of a cane block (that is, plant crop and up to four ratoon crops), depending on the type of cane plant. A successful crop depends upon the optimum execution of a number of factors: land preparation; planting time; planting material; planting operation; soil moisture; fertilizing and cultivation; and the climate.

The climate is said to impact on sugarcane in several ways as it determines the processes of yield accumulation and the amount of sugar produced. More specifically, the amount and distribution of rainfall before and during the harvest season markedly influences sucrose content (CCS). Higher CCS tends to be associated with lower rainfall. Second, climatic conditions control the development and spread of fungal diseases, insects, pests and weeds, which can restrict crop growth. Third, rainfall also sets the potential for runoff and deep drainage with possible environmental impacts associated with the movements of nutrients and pesticides. Fourth, rainfall variability indirectly influences the harvesting and scheduling of cane supply during the harvest season.

In Fiji, sugarcane is harvested once a year and the crushing season usually commences in June/July and ends in December. As the season length increases, the average sugar content across the season declines with the flowering of sugarcane. Sugar content is optimum if harvesting is done between July and October but season length can be affected by climatic conditions and ratooning characteristics of late-cut cane. Sugarcane in Fiji is grown for between 12 and 16 months before being harvested and loaded manually by "harvesting gangs" made up of 10–15 farm labourers.

While raw sugar is the main product obtained from sugarcane, the by-product molasses[9] is also used as feed for livestock. Unlike other sugarcane producers such as Brazil and Australia, who are increasingly involved in producing ethanol for fuel from bagasse (another by-product of cane milling), Fiji only uses bagasse for fuel in the mills. Fiji also does not produce rum, the alcoholic product made by distilling fermented sugarcane juice molasses.

HISTORICAL PERSPECTIVE OF FIJI'S SUGAR

Initially, cotton was Fiji's chief crop but a twist of fate led Fiji to cut cane rather than pick cotton. The end of the American Civil War saw the cotton trade recovering in that country, and Fiji was left without a market for its cotton production. It was Ratu Seru Cakobau, the then paramount chief of Bau, who encouraged settlers in Fiji to grow sugarcane, an indigenous plant.[10] Thus, settlers took up planting this labour-intensive crop. However, as demand grew, it became necessary after 1879 to import indentured workers from India on the model previously used in Mauritius and the West Indies. Indians were then contracted to work for a fixed term of five years for the economic well-being of the European plantation

[9] Molasses is a heavy, dark liquid discharged by the centrifugals after no more sugar can be separated from the cane.

[10] Thomas Williams, the great missionary observer, writing of conditions before 1856 in Fiji said, "Sugar canes, with but imperfect attention, already flourishes and was grown for chewing."

owners and the Australian sugar-milling company, the Colonial Sugar Refinery (CSR) Company Limited, after which they would be entitled to return to India or given the opportunity to stay in Fiji. The importation of Indian labour was stopped in 1916 and the indenture system was discontinued in 1920 because of the continuing opposition from the Indian authorities and from pressure groups in Fiji. While pay was minimal and conditions appalling, the poverty from which most of the Indian migrants came from was far worse and of the 60,000 that were dispatched to Fiji, only 40% opted to return at the end of their contracts.

Following the termination of the indenture system, the industry was faced with a serious shortage of labour and intense competition among planters and wide fluctuations in sugar prices led to a gradual concentration of ownership – by 1925, CSR had effectively established a monopoly over production, milling and cultivation. After the Eve Commission of 1960, CSR's milling interests were transferred to South Pacific Sugar Mills, a Fiji incorporated public company with nominal local shareholding – the bulk of the shares remained with CSR.

Under this threat, the CSR introduced a system of contract growing of cane by small tenant farmers. Thus, tenants were given small plots of land, averaging 11 acres, for the production of cane and other subsistence crops. But there were disagreements on the terms of a new sugar contract (the first drawn up in 1960 by Sir Malcolm Trustam-Eve) and it was not until 1970 that the Indian farmers received economic justice from Lord Denning who in his award on a new cane contract, the *Contract of General Application*,[11] ensured that the money from sugar sales were shared equitably – the growers receiving 65% and the millers 35%.[12] This was a major victory for the growers. CSR could not see profitable operations on this basis and soon left in March 1973.

The Birth and Operation of the Fiji Sugar Commission

Also in 1970 Fiji became independent and, with the withdrawal of CSR, the government saw the need to take over the milling operations, thus became the majority shareholder owning 68% of the shares (the remaining shares are held by organizations and individuals in Fiji) in the nationalised sugar industry, giving birth to the Fiji Sugar Corporation (FSC) in April 1973. There were no changes to the sugar industry structure for many years thereafter and the three major institutions that deliberated on industry matters were the Independent Chairman's Office, a Sugar Board and a Sugar Advisory Council.

However, the growers were persistent in their demands for a change that would give them a greater role in industry decisions. These demands finally led to the new structure that was given legal status by an Act of Parliament in 1984. The new institutions established were the Sugar Commission of Fiji, the Sugarcane Growers Council, the Mill Area Committee and the Sugar Industry Tribunal. The Sugar Commission of Fiji is the body responsible for the

[11] The conditions include each farmer having a separate but identical contract with FSC with provisions covering the sale and purchase of cane, harvesting and delivery, burnt cane, crushing operations, advances, storage, marketing and sale of sugar and division of proceeds.

[12] This formula for division of proceeds has always been a bone of contention between the millers and the growers – this is discussed in chapter 6.

overall coordination of the activities in the industry and is funded from sugar industry proceeds. The Board, however, has representatives from the other institutions.

The relationship between the FSC, the millers and the cane growers was governed by a sugarcane contract. Eventually, under the Sugar Cane Industry Act 1984, the cane contract was replaced by the Kermode Master Award, a standard document with a continuing life but with provisions for review of the terms and conditions if so required. Unlike the earlier contracts, this award has no expiry date, thus growers are spared the trauma and uncertainty that they had previously endured every 10 years.

The contract also sets out the harvest quota for each farm. The harvest quota is the amount of cane that will be bought each year from the farm by FSC. This regulation of cane to be purchased is based on the yield of sugar from cane, milling capacity and market commitments. However, since 1980, harvest quotas have not been imposed as cane sugar production has not exceeded the limits of milling capacity and available market outlets. The sections on delivery and transport in the contract spell out FSC's responsibility for the provision of rail transport and all related facilities. The clause on advances regulates the Corporation's obligation to make interest-free advances to growers for the cost of seed cane required for planting, purchase of fertilizer and harvesting and delivery costs. The contract also contains penal provisions for burnt cane supplied to the mills to discourage the burning of cane.

Once sugar is extracted at the mill, the FSC receives and manages the proceeds of sugar and molasses to make payments to growers at the time specified in the contract. As the price of cane is not known until all the season's sugar has been sold, the FSC is supposed to pay growers in four installments as proceeds are received.

The Political Economy of the Sugar Industry

It is perhaps not surprising that the importance of sugar to Fiji has attracted much political attention and power play within the institutions that operate in the sugar industry. This association has intensified since the military coups of 1987, when indigenous Fijian political domination was asserted militarily. Conflicts in the industry are thus closely affected by national political considerations related to land and ethnicity. This necessitates an understanding of the political economy of the sugar industry – but it also complicates any attempt to study the sugar industry in detail. The next subsection outlines the role and institutional aspects of the various "sugar daddies" that help the functioning of the sugar industry; the second subsection deals with land and ethnic issues.

The Sugar Daddies

The Sugar Commission of Fiji is responsible for the overall coordination of the activities in the industry. Growers, the FSC, the Mill Area Committees and the Sugar Industry Tribunal are represented in this body that has a total of about 20 representatives. Given that the Commission is answerable to many parties, it tries to be neutral and objective in its decisions amidst the politics surrounding its operations. The chairman has powers over growers, such as minimum tonnage requirements, and constituting gangs and making them efficient through rationalisation. However, he has neither the mandate nor expertise to look at the FSC's operational facilities whether at the factory level, the rail network, the supply of cane or acceptance and delivery or the processing of cane to extract sugar.

The FSC is the largest public company in Fiji (about 68% is owned by the government, 17% by Fiji National Provident Fund and 9% by Fijian Holdings Ltd.). It owns and operates all four of Fiji's sugar mills, the railway systems and the research centre. The mills alone employ about 4,500 workers at the height of the crushing season and the FSC is the largest private sector employer in Fiji. Although the FSC is a publicly-owned monopoly, since 1997 (except in 1999) it has been making losses – its accumulated losses stood near F$60 million at the end of 2003.[13] It has been argued that this is due to the concealment of the FSC's inefficiency and mismanagement and that the reported profit levels before 2000 have been at the expense of improving mill efficiency and investment in sugarcane farming research (Prasad and Narayan 2004).

The FSC has, however, defended its position[14] on the types of investments and improvements undertaken – but a question remains as to the effectiveness of these actions. Also, the FSC feels that there needs to be changes in the Master Award to correct anomalies as it has to absorb an unreasonably high proportion of costs, when these could be more equitably shared by the industry. For instance, a "user-pay" rail system should be instituted as in other countries, the miller, who is not for example responsible for transporting cane to the mills receives 35% share that allows sufficient funds for future capital investment. Another example provided was that the Sugar Cane Research Centre's operations costs is currently 75% funded by the FSC, although the FSC receives only 28% of the sugar proceeds. The FSC has further argued that effectiveness of its operations hinges on sugarcane production, which refers to the growers, and that they cannot remain complacent given the loss in EU sugar subsidies.

The growers, on the other hand, are not satisfied with the FSC's operation[15] of the rail transport system and harvesting schedules. They complained that FSC is more interested in catering to large commercial farms where harvesting and rail transport is concerned. The rail system is in dire need of rehabilitation due to poor maintenance. According to the Master Award, the FSC is to provide farmers with essential food items such as rice and sugar and these functions too have been inefficiently handled.

Thus, the FSC and the growers are embroiled in lot of blame pushing and this could be due to a number of reasons. First, the growers and millers are two different groups with quite different objectives. Second, a majority of the growers are small-scale farmers and, thus, farming behaviour is not strictly what one would expect from a business enterprise. Third, the unresolved issue of the land tenure system, detailed in the next section, does not help the situation. Fourth, as sugar cane is the mainstay of the economy, it is a futile ground for politics related to gathering support from the farmers as seen by the numerous organisations which have been set up to protect farmers, so to speak.

---

[13] It has been reported that the government has lent the FSC F$8.5 million a year from 1998 to 2002 and this was to be written off. In 2005, F$54 million of loans from the government to the FSC was written off (FSC Annual Report 2006).

[14] These have been gathered in various reviews on the sugar industry and from personal interviews with FSC officials in 2004.

[15] This view was obtained from the survey on 677 farmers in 2004.

For instance, the Sugarcane Growers Council was established to represent the cane growers and to protect and further their interests. It is funded by levies imposed on the growers and the philosophy of the council is to provide a range of services to the growers to improve their economic growth and social well-being. This is because their viability determines the growth of the sugar industry to a large extent.

The National Farmers Union was established in 1978 and claims to have more than 4,000 members; it also works towards protecting the rights and interests of farmers. The general secretary, Mahendra Chaudhury, is the leader of the Labour Party and was ousted as prime minister in May 2000 after being elected in 1999.

And lastly, there is the Fiji Cane Growers Association set up by the National Federation Party in 1992 for the same purpose. This organisation is being used by the National Federation Party to counter the influence of the National Farmers Union on farmers, which is seen as an influence that converts into votes for the Labour Party. In 2005, the commencement of the crushing season was affected by calls for a harvest boycott by the National Farmers Union and some years ago, the National Federation Party led two other harvest boycotts.

There is an immense power struggle between the institutions involved in the sugar industry, all of which make it difficult for effective sugar reform. For instance, the Sugar Industry Tribunal is involved in the determination of disputes in the industry among growers. In general, it would like to be less restricted on how it operates and keeps itself informed, especially on operational matters.[16]

The Sugar Commission of Fiji, on the other hand, would like to take on a more active role in public relations to effectively promote the importance of sugar. The chairman was disappointed that he was not consulted by the 2004 Indian Mission, which undertook a comprehensive study on sugar reform in Fiji. The chairman of the Sugarcane Growers Council, too, was not consulted about the Indian Mission, which was to be the backbone of reform, and was undertaken within only 10 days. In addition, there have been numerous occasions when representatives from the various institutions would not attend important meetings, as they were dissatisfied with the way things were operating at different levels.

LAND POLICY AND ISSUES

Land in Fiji is a highly politicized matter given its importance for sugar and agricultural crop production as well as ethnicity. The latter is due to the fact that more than 85% of the land was placed under protective policies, referred to as "native land" (that is, owned by native Fijians), by the colonial administration. This land could be leased but not freely bought or sold. However, most of the agricultural farming is undertaken by the Indian Fijians on leased land. Although controversy over land-lease has been a long-standing problem since the 1960s, the current debate on the non-renewal of land leases began in the mid 1990s and has continued without resolution.

Land in Fiji is one of three types as seen in table 3.2. Freehold land constitutes about 7% of the total land area and it is highly coveted since it represents the best form of tenure in Fiji. Also, the early settlers picked out this land, and is the most accessible, best drained, flattest and most fertile land. The state has control over 6% of Fiji's land area (this is about 162,000 acres) after land in schedules A (native land that reverted to the state after the extinction of the clan that owned it), and B (state land over which no Fijian has claimed ownership) were converted to native land in 2002. Native land, constituting 87%, is further divided into two major categories: reserve and non-reserve. While the former is set aside for the support and maintenance of the native landowning unit, the latter may only be leased with the consent and approval of the majority of the landowning unit.

Table 3.2. Categories of Land Ownership in Fiji (%)

Type of Ownership	Total Area[a]	Total Area[b]
Native Land	82.38	87
Crown land (owned by the state)	9.45	6
Freehold (owned by individual of all races)	8.17	7
Total	100	100

Note: [a],[b] After conversion of schedules A and B to native land in 2002.
Source: Based on Ward (1995).

Prasad (2006) warns that the share of communally-owned land is likely to increase to 90% if native Fijians continue to receive support for the purchase of freehold land. This policy is driven by genuine concern for the long-term interests of indigenous Fijians, but is not necessarily in the economic interests of the nation.

To simplify and stabilise the process of leasing land, the government created the Native Land Trust Board (NLTB) in 1940 under the Native Land Trust Act. The NLTB controlled customary-held land and dealt with the landowners and tenants. It was under no obligation to consult the landowners about the renewal or issuance of leases. This practice has contributed to the conflict over land. In addition to issuing and renewing leases, the NLTB collects rents, takes 25% of the rent income for administration and pays heads of the landowning units 22.5% of the gross rent collected. The rest is divided among the members of the landowning unit, who may number from a few hundred to more than a thousand. Thus, the returns to individual landowners vary considerably. The powers of the NLTB were, however, retained under the Agricultural Landlord and Tenant Act (ALTA) introduced in 1976.

Two aspects of the ALTA have contributed to land conflict. One is the fixed rental amount of 6% of the unimproved capital value with a mandatory assessment of the land value every five years. Another is that all leases granted under ALTA since 1st September 1977 were to be held for a minimum of 30 years without an automatic renewal clause. The lease-holders before this date were entitled to a single extension of 20 years under ALTA. This meant that a majority of the leases have expired since 1997, with the native Fijian landowners generally unwilling to renew them and the tenants, who were mainly Indo-Fijians, were left in strife.

But the political leaders were not interested in trying to solve the problem. For instance, the Rabuka government clearly stated in its reform agenda that the Constitution review was a priority over the ALTA matter. This postponement had disastrous consequences as, inevitably, the land issue took on an ethnic dimension and became a source of conflict – a

[16] This was indicated in a personal communication in July 2004.

politically charged process of land-lease negotiations began as a contest between landowners, the NLTB and the farmers. An official pronouncement[17] reads:

> Fijians collectively own more than 83% of total land area in Fiji. The question people must ask is how is that even though they are the biggest landowners in Fiji, they are the poorest as shown in the household income survey. ... In the cane belt, the Indian tenants reap the full benefits ... but Fijian Landowners do not share that windfall income ... it has been estimated that out of every $100 earned on cane farms on Fijian-owned land, $70 goes to the tenant farmer, $28 to Fiji Sugar Corporation and a mere $2 to the landowner.

As the Minister of Information of the then Interim Government, Inoke Kubuabola put it: "As the Fijians see it, the cane growers have used their considerable political muscle to lever themselves into an extremely privileged position".[18] The Fijians were then encouraged by the party in power to farm their own lands instead of renewing the land leases to Indian Fijians.

Table 3.3 shows that, by 2005, some 5,845 agricultural leases have expired, of which about 75% of them are sugarcane leases and a vast majority of the tenants are Indo-Fijians. The insecurity and risk with regard to land leases has led to falling confidence in the sugar industry and this has implications for depressed farm investments and poor access to credit.

Table 3.3. Number of Land Lease Expiry by Year

Year of Expiry	Agricultural Leases	Sugarcane Leases (Area in hectares)	Indo-Fijian Leases
1997	45	27 (232)	27
1998	189	129 (1463)	120
1999	231	168 (1962)	158
2000	1828	1215 (8838)	1113
2001	1808	1542 (8337)	1494
2002	479	325 (2912)	310
2003	645	466 (3240)	435
2004	332	231 (2390)	216
2005	288	244 (2490)	228

Source*:* World Bank (1995) and Reddy and Naidu (2001).

In addition, in the absence of renewal, the farmers can be required to vacate the land on expiry – and since farmers often build their house on the same land, this has caused many of them great hardship. In fact, the Government of Fiji (2006) reports that up until 2004, no land was provided by the NLTB for the government to resettle evicted cane farmers or other citizens whose ALTA leases expired in the 1997–2004 period – but since 2004, a total of 3,000 acres has been provided by the NLTB for re-housing evicted citizens. However, according to the Ministry of Sugar and Land Resettlement, only about 200 evicted farmers have benefited from this scheme, which has been seriously under-resourced. The resettled

[17] Government statement of its 'Blueprint for the Development of Indigenous Fijians and Rotumans' printed in *The Times*, 27 Feb 2001.

[18] See The *Post* 7 Feb 2001.

farmers, on the other hand, reported[19] that the land given to them was not suitable for cane farming, which is what they were familiar with and would rather cultivate. Others indicated that they were unable to do much with an alternative livelihood as they had not been sufficiently compensated for the cane production on their evicted land, or that the resettlement grant had yet to be paid by the Ministry.

Structure and Performance of the Sugar Industry

Cane farming in Fiji is characteristically a family-owned, farmer-operated enterprise and this feature has remained intact over the past three-quarters of a century. It distinguishes the Fijian sugar industry from those of many other sugar-producing countries where production is on plantations owned by the millers (and to a lesser extent by independent growers) but on relatively large farms. In Fiji, on the other hand, the independent growers produce nearly all the sugarcane on farms averaging 4.5 hectares. McGregor (2006) reports that more than half of the commercial farms are less than 5 ha and 19% could be described as medium-sized or larger as seen in table 3.4.

Table 3.4. Commercial Farm Size

Farm Size	Percentage of Farms (%)
1 to 3 ha	33
3 to 5 ha	23
5 to 10 ha	25
10 to 100 ha	19

Source: McGregor (2006).

About 250,000 people, or one in three people in Fiji, derive their income from this industry as it has always been labour-intensive – thus, it has a large multiplier effect of 2.23 (also said to provide 60% of cash income in Fiji's agriculture), which is even more favourable than the tourism industry (Government of Fiji 2005). The industry's main focus is on producing sugar for export to the EU, US and Japan (figure 3.1), with small amounts consumed domestically and in the Pacific region.

In 2005, there were about 20,400 registered cane growers, of whom about 75% were Indo-Fijians and 24% natives. It must, however, be noted that about 3,500 of them are 'non-performing' farmers who produce less than 10 tons of cane (Government of Fiji 2006a). In addition, the FSC reports that over 8,000 farmers use less than half their farm land to grow sugar with an average yield of 24.6 tons/ha – another 4,000 farmers, who use just over 50% of their land, produced 40 tons/ha (Government of Fiji 2005).

[19] Fieldwork interviews with resettled cane farmers in Navua area near Suva.

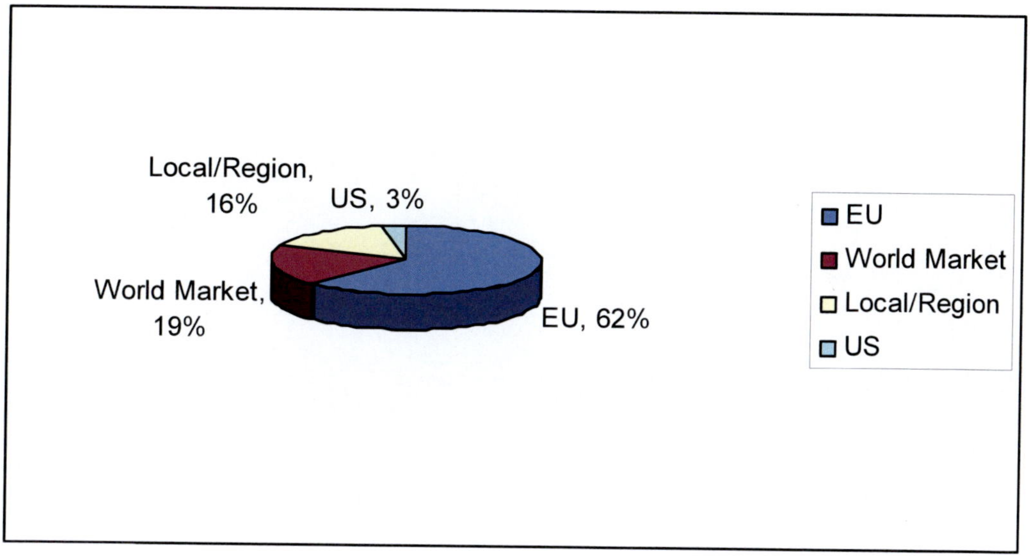

Source: Government of Fiji (2006).

Figure 3.1. Key Destinations for Fiji's Sugar, 2005.

There are, however, about 5,000 best-performing farmers with an average production of 61 tons/ha and this group will be targeted for planned increases in productivity and production (*ibid.*). It is inevitable that the erosion of sugar preferences leads to the rationalisation of sugar production, such that land under sugarcane cultivation is close to 65,000 ha – although the cane lease contracts total up to 184,431 ha of land. There is concern that the unused land area is not being effectively used for other crop production.

Figures 3.2 and 3.3 show trends in cane production and the cane area harvested. The overall production of sugar varies drastically from year to year, partly due to the considerable variability in weather conditions such as cyclones and droughts. The cane area harvested, on the other hand, has increased by about 30% in the last 30 decades due to the boost given by the EU's preferential treatment.

As a result, new farmers entered cane farming and marginal lands, which were initially considered unsuitable for sugarcane production, were brought into production by the existing farmers (Grynberg 1993). The economic viability of the new land is more marginal, requiring greater physical and financial inputs, such as irrigation, fertilizer, soil conditioners and higher transportation costs, to maintain productivity and profitability. However, there has been a decline in production since 1995.

In table 3.5, it can be seen that the sugar yield from cane is a matter of concern as it indicates that more cane is required to produce the same amount of sugar. Essentially, the TCTS ratio (the quantity of cane required to produce a unit of raw sugar) is dependent on three factors: cane quality, efficiencies of the milling operations (recovery) and the quality of raw sugar produced. Although the first factor is related to farm production, cane quality can deteriorate if harvested cane is not quickly transported to the mills to be crushed; the latter is a component of the operations of the FSC, as are the other two factors.

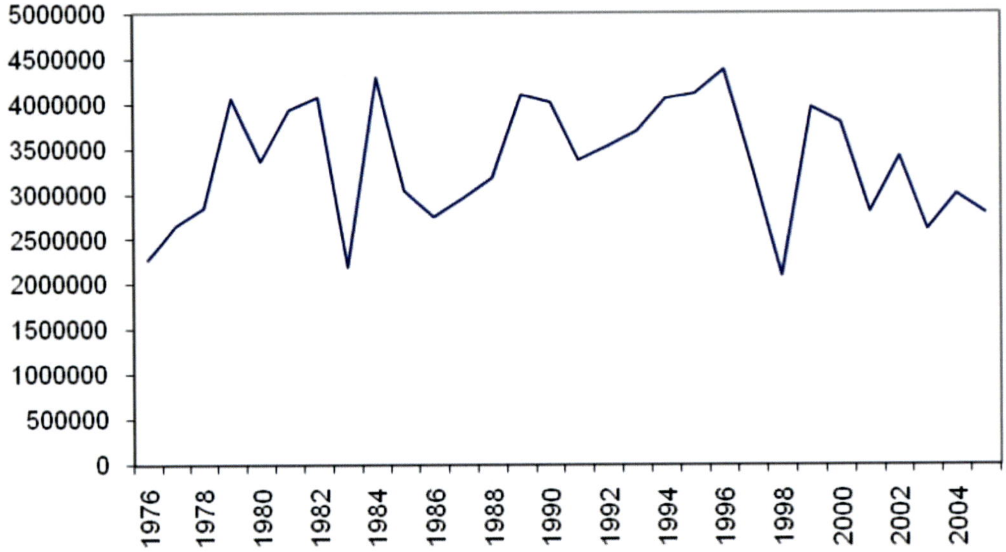

Figure 3.2. Cane Produced (tons).

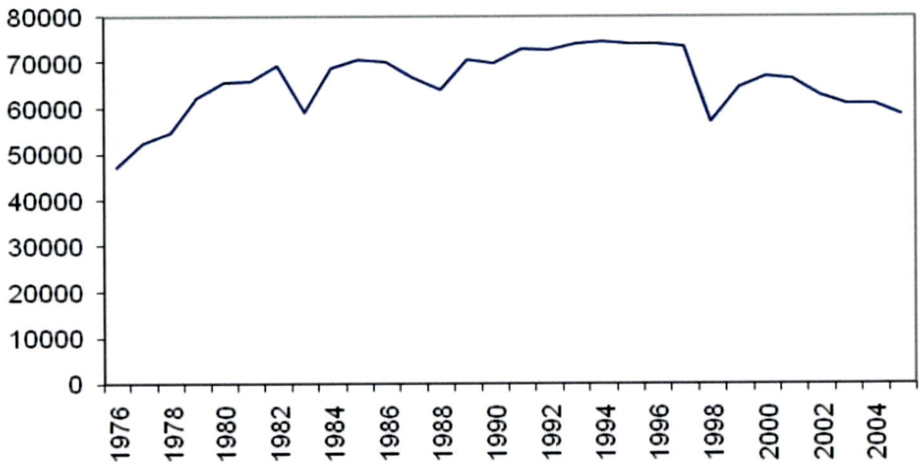

Figure 3.3. Cane Area Harvested (hectares).

However, the TCTS ratio, which is generally regarded as an overall efficiency indicator for the whole industry, is below the target of 8.0 as recommended by the Sugar Technology Mission (2004) and this was long considered a reasonable level in any season (Hemraj 1982).

The cane yield, on the other hand, appears to have risen until the mid 1980s, after which there is, in general, a falling trend (although there may be slight variations within the four mills). This reflects deterioration in performance at the field level and, in part, can be explained by the increased use of marginal land and the entry of farmers who may be inefficient producers, but were attracted by high EU prices in the past. For mill operations, Pure Obtainable Cane Sugar (POCS) is an indicator of the sugar recovery rate in the factory, and here, too, cane quality has decreased. The five-year average POCS for 2001–05 was 11.68%. It had recorded as low as 9.95% in the 2000 season, whereas the average for 1991–

95 was 12.51% and 12.9% for 1976–80. In general, figure 3.4 shows a general downward trend in POCS over time.

Table 3.5. Average Trends in Cane and Sugar Yield

Period	Cane Yield (tons/ha)	Sugar Yield (TCTS)
1970-74	51.24	7.88
1975-79	53.13	7.91
1980-84	53.92	8.42
1985-89	50.86	8.43
1990-94	51.50	8.61
1995-99	51.32	9.37
2000-05	48.89	10.12

Notes:

1. Cane yield is measured by the amount of cane produced per harvested area.
2. Sugar yield is measured by the TCTS, which is the quantity of cane required to produce a unit of raw sugar.

Source: Sugar Cane Research Centre Annual Reports.

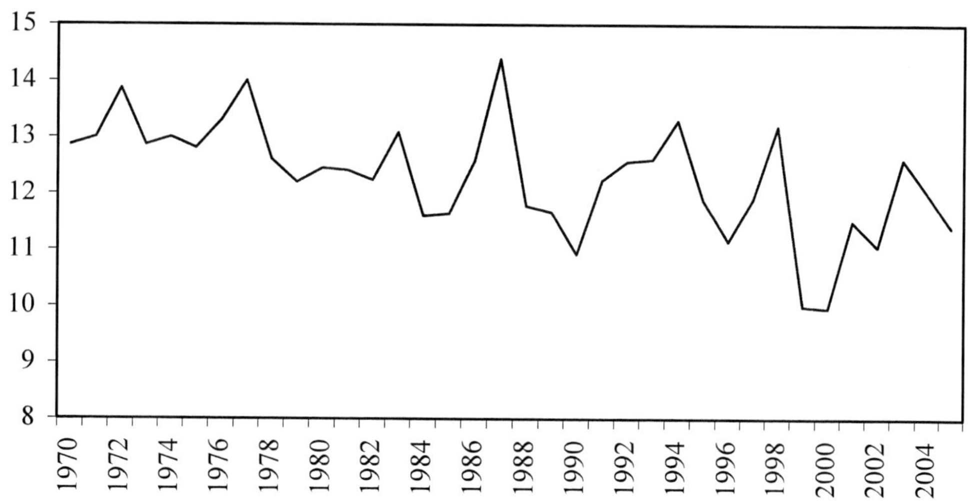

Figure 3.4. Trend in Pure Obtainable Cane Sugar (percent).

One unique feature of the sugar industry lies in the tight vertically-integrated nature of operations, whereby efficiency in farm production, milling and processing, as well as marketing, determine the viability of the sugar industry. Thus, successive consultants' reports over the past 15 years have detailed chronic inefficiencies at various levels of operation within the industry. In general, the Government of Fiji (2006) lists the following factors that explain the failure to rectify these deficiencies:

i. Excessive complacency of both cane growers and millers resulting from the over-generous subsidy regime, leading to a failure to reinvest in production to sustain competitiveness and output levels.
ii. The prospect (since 1997) and the reality of non-renewal of land leases affecting predominantly Indian cane farmers, while at the same time landowners (native Fijian farmers) have been slow to fill the gap.
iii. Perceived inadequate returns to cane cultivation, harvesting and transportation as well as sugar milling.

CONCLUSION

Although sugar is one of the most protected industries in the developed countries, Fiji together with the 18 other ACP countries were given high price subsidies for the import of raw sugar. This has, however, been both a blessing and a curse – with the withdrawal of sugar preferences in 2007, Fiji needs to get on with sugar reform, a process that has been delayed mainly due to lack of political will and consensus among the stakeholders. Given that sugar is the mainstay of the Fiji economy, it is no surprise that there are quite a number of institutions responsible for sustaining the viability of this important industry. While the involvement of these organisations is necessary to safeguard the interests of diverse stakeholders in the industry, it also makes it difficult to achieve consensus on various issues for the betterment of this industry.

The economic importance of sugar in the country makes a fertile ground for political activity and a pathway to power. This situation is complicated by the ethnically divided community and the land issues associated with ownership, as the Indian farmers are often the tenants on land owned by native Fijians. In reality, the political economy of sugar operates on more than one level. At the national level, there is the interrelated issue of ethnicity and land; at the industry level, there are tensions between the sugarcane growers (or farmers), the mill workers, and the mill management.

Within the Cane Growers Council, there is a struggle for power between several farmers' associations that have evolved to act as a basis for mobilisation for election to the management board of the council. These unions are aligned to different political parties claiming to look after the cane farmers. Thus, efforts to reform the sugar industry in the wake of challenges arising from the global context will inevitably involve restructuring at all levels.

Chapter 4

PRODUCTIVITY OF CANE FARMERS

INTRODUCTION

The withdrawal of sugar subsidies by the EU became imminent from 1986 when agriculture was brought within the ambit of the General Agreement on Trade and Tariffs, and particularly since December 1994 following the EU's commitment to limit the value of export subsidies at the conclusion of the Uruguay Round. Thus, to some extent, Fiji was quite prepared to face the music. This is reflected in the many (but futile) attempts to consider sugar reform based on various inquiries and consultancies. In 1981, the Fijian government commissioned the consultancy firm Brooker Agriculture International Limited to conduct one of the earliest reform studies. This was followed by at least three other major reports.[1]

However, none of these reports focused on farm efficiency at the micro level. To date, Reddy and Yanagida (1999) is the only study on Fiji that has attempted to fill this gap. But their study uses the parametric approach to estimate the stochastic production frontier and only discusses technical efficiency. This chapter is an improvement over their study in the following ways: First, in addition to the parametric approach (which allows for non-neutral shifts in the production frontier unlike earlier studies), a non-parametric approach given by the Data Envelopment Analysis (DEA) is used for robustness.

Second, measures computed include overall technical and scale efficiency as well as input-specific technical efficiency. Although important, the latter is often not given enough attention in most efficiency studies. Third, the list of factors influencing technical efficiency is extended to include off-farm income, distance from mill, and means of cane transportation. These, together with data on farmers' perceptions of problems and attitude towards cane farming and the operation of sugar institutions, shed light on where Fiji's sugar industry is heading and the extent of its viability in the global market. Thus, a more holistic approach to policy making is adopted here for a comprehensive understanding of the need for reform.

The rest of the chapter is organised as follows: the next section provides an overview of the key issues facing sugarcane farms, while section three details the farm level survey undertaken and the variables used.[2] The fourth section sets out the theoretical framework

---

[1] These include the reports from Landell Mill International (1991), Fiji Sugar Corporation (1997) and the Sugar Technology Mission (2004).

[2] The chapter draws on Mahadevan (2008a, 2008b).

underling the parametric and non-parametric models and the empirical results are discussed in the following section. Finally, the determinants of technical efficiency are investigated and the policy questions are discussed in section six, while section seven concludes.

KEY ISSUES FACING CANE FARMERS

One major concern has not only been Fiji's declining cane yield but also that it is far lower than other sugar-producing countries. The average cane yield is 47 tons/ha over 2001–05 compared to about 52 tons/ha in the decades of the 1970s and '80s. While this may not appear drastic, table 4.1 paints a grim picture of poor of Fiji's global competitiveness, which matters in the wake of the erosion of SU sugar subsidy.

Table 4.1. Competitiveness of Fiji's Sugarcane Yield

Country	Partial Productivity (tons/acre)
Fiji (1997–01)	19.6
Mauritius (1997–98)	31.9
Queensland, Australia (1999–01)	35.4
Hawai (1997–99)	43.8
Lousiana State, USA (1999)	31.3

Source: Reddy (2003).

Fiji's low cane yield is partly due to the labour-intensive production chain of cultivation, harvesting and manufacture of raw sugar. By international standards, this is far from being cost effective. It raises serious questions on the ability of Fiji's sugar industry to survive with such low productivity in the absence of the EU's sugar subsidy and the competitive global market. In fact, some of the Hawaiian sugar plantations have closed due to changes in trading arrangements and increasing production costs. Even among the 20 ACP sugar producers, Fiji has the second lowest cane yield and the lowest sugar yield per harvested hectare (Quarase 2004). More recently, in 2003, cane output in Fiji, which is around 50 tons/ha, compares unfavourably with Australia's production at 120 tons/ha.

As stated earlier, another reason for the low cane yield in Fiji is the poor land quality and insecurity. Poor land that is unsuitable for cane production cannot be expected to produce a high cane yield. Table 4.2 shows that only 16% of the land is suitable for agriculture and with improvements made to land quality, another 43% of land can be used for farming.

However, land improvements are costly and often not undertaken by farmers as it squeezes their profit margin. First, if farmers do make such improvements, they have to pay higher rent to the NLTB because of the higher cane yield made possibly by the improvements.

Second, the incentive to invest in land improvement is low because of the low profit earned by farmers, averaging about F$30–40 per ton of cane with an average total cost[3] per ton of cane ranging from F$20–F$26 (Government of Fiji 2006a). Third, without access to

[3] This includes input costs (such as planting, land preparation, purchase of fertilizer and weedicide), harvest, transport, roads and drainage fee, and land rental).

reasonable credit facilities, no grower has the financial capacity to make the necessary improvements. The farmers already have high levels of debt.

Table 4.2. Fiji's Land Use Classification in 1978

Class of Land	Type of Land	Percentage of Total Area
First	Suitable for agriculture	16
Second	Suitable for agriculture only after improvements are made	43
Third	Suitable for agriculture only after advanced drainage and soil conservation	35
Fourth	Unsuitable for agriculture	6
Total		100

Source: Fiji Ministry of Agriculture and Forests (1978).

Over 70% of the growers live perpetually in debt, and a significant proportion of their cane income is deducted at source for various debt-servicing schedules (Fiji Development Bank 2003). And if there is uncertainty about the renewal of the lease, banks will be hesitant to lend, as land is the collateral basis for market credit. One remedy for the absence of collateral has been the use of micro credit, where the credit to an individual is guaranteed by a peer group, enabling the lender to spread the risk – but micro-financing has not been successful in the PICs (Conroy 2006).

As stated earlier, the land tenure system is one of the major unresolved issues adversely affecting sugarcane production. The FSC statistics in table 4.3 show that only 62.5% of expired leases in the cane belt have been renewed. Where leases are renewed, the costs of taking up the new lease are often high, even for native cane farmers. These official costs include a high NLTB contract offer and biannual rental payments and the unofficial costs faced by mostly by non-native farmers, including the indeterminate goodwill payments (reportedly around F$1000 per acre), which are regulated by local customs and not officially regulated nor even legally permitted (Government of Fiji 2006a).

Table 4.3 shows that between 1997 and 2005, only 10% of the expired cane leases were renewed to sitting tenants while 90% were renewed to new tenants. To some extent, the low renewal ratio is partly due to the slow response of the government to the processing of land-lease applications. For example, out of a total of 1,062 applications for renewal as at the end of December 2003, only 449 applications were processed. However, the motivation for offering leases to new tenants is reflected in the willingness of the new tenants to pay 'goodwill' (which is a one-off payment made to the landowner) whereas the sitting tenants are less likely to make such payments.

In Fiji, land politics is closely related to ethnic politics. Although native Fijians own some 87% of total land, the sugar industry at the farm level comprises about 25% native Fijians and 75% Indian Fijians. The lack of participation by the indigenous population in the commercial agriculture sector has long been a concern to the government since the 1959 Spate Report and 1960 Burns Report. Both reports recommended that the way forward for Fijian economic prosperity was to establish a "community of independent farmers" free from the "burden of obligations" related to the communal way of living in the villages. The socio-cultural constraints of the Fijians have long been argued to hamper effective cane production

(Watters 1969, Rutz 1978, Kurer 2001). In fact, a leading high chief, the Tui Ba, has been reported to say that "... [Fijian] landowners may be able to do sugar cane farming for a few years only, after which the land will become bushland".

Table 4.3. Cane Lease Expiry by Ethnic Group and Mill

Mill	Number Expired	Issued to Sitting Tenants			Issued to New Tenants			Total Issued Leases		
		Fijian	Indian	Total	Fijian	Indian	Total	Fijian	Indian	Total
Lautoka	2026	10	123	133	522	550	1072	532	673	1205
Rarawai	1014	4	60	64	414	299	713	418	359	777
Labasa	1323	–	77	77	443	218	661	443	295	738
Penang	157	4	1	5	82	20	102	86	21	107
Total	4520	18	261	279	1461	1087	2548	1479	1348	2827

Note: The above is recorded for the year ended 31st Dec 2005.
Source: Sugar Commission of Fiji (2006).

However, Kingi and Kompas (2005) argue that a centralised management system incorporating communal land ownership and formal groups within the native Fijians has resulted in higher technical efficiency in sugarcane performance. Table 4.4 shows results from primary and secondary data on cane yield productivity disparities among the ethnic groups by various studies, all of which reinforce the view that Fijians are less productive than Indians.

The inability of ethnic Fijians to raise their efficiency significantly will further reduce average farm efficiency as more ethnic Fijians enter into sugarcane production while Indian Fijians move out as their leases expire. However, these are only partial productivity measures, and the empirical model used in this chapter is able to indicate the levels of overall and input specific technical efficiency, allowing a more detailed study of the performance of both types of farmers. This is especially important given the impending withdrawal of EU sugar prices, which will result in inefficient farmers leaving the industry.

Table 4.4. Cane Yield Differentials (tons/acres) Among Ethnic Groups

Year	Sample Size	Ethnic Indians	Ethnic Fijians
1985	2596	20.36	17.55
1987	2609	20.45	17.28
1989	2645	22.82	17.90
1994*	784	22.36	19.29
1996**	397	24.36	18.82
2003***	677	21.48	16.31

Sources: Data from FSC (1989).
* Data from World Bank survey on Seaqaqa sugar project (Kurer 2001).
** Data from survey (Reddy 1998).
*** Data from this survey.

The Survey

The data for the empirical investigation were obtained from a survey carried out in 2004 in the Nadi catchment located in the western part of Viti Levu. The sample comprised 677 farmers randomly selected from the records of the FSC. Table 4.5 provides the definition of variables used, while table 4.6 gives some descriptive statistics. Approximately 31% of the sample farmers were indigenous Fijians and 69% were Indo-Fijians. On average, the latter has almost twice the length of farming experience than the indigenous farmers. While 64% of the latter own their land, in general, they also had access to better quality land than the Indo Fijians. On average, farmers were 52 years old and had about eight years of education. The average area of cane land cultivated was 8.4 acres with most of the sample farmers (84%) being full-time farmers, although 71% had an alternative source of income.

Table 4.5. Definition of Variables

Variable	Definition	Measurement
Production frontier model		
Y	Sugar cane harvested	Tons
LAN	Land area under cane crop	Acres
LAB	Total labour including hired labour	Hours
BULL	Bullock labour	Hours
TRACT	Tractor use	Hours
FERT	Quantity of fertiliser applied	Kilograms
WEED	Quantity of weedicide used	Litres
OTHER	Land rent, drainage fee, etc.	Fijian $
Inefficiency model		
EXP	Farming experience	Years
AGE	Age of farmer	Years
EDU	Years of schooling	Years
DIST	Distance from mill	Kilometres
SIZE	Farm Size	1= area > 20 acres 0= area ≤ 20 acres
ETHN	Farmer's ethnicity	1 = Indian, 0 = native
FSTAT	Farming status	1 = full time, 0 = part time
TRANS	Means of transporting cane to mill	1 = lorry, 0 = rail
FSTAY	Farmer lives on farm	1 = yes, 0 = no
OFFINC	Farmer has off farm income	1 = yes, 0 = no
OWN	Owns land	1 = yes, 0 = no
CLASS	Class of land	1 = flat, 2 = gentle, 3 = quite steep, 4 = steep

Theoretical Models

Here, both parametric and non-parametric models are used to obtain efficiency measures as a check on robustness. Although the former is based on the chosen functional form, the advantage lies in its ability to statistically validate the model. At the same time, to overcome the imposition of the functional form, a non-parametric model is used and it does require *a priori* specification of the functional form. As accurate input prices were difficult to obtain, it was decided that the production frontier would be estimated for empirical investigation.

Table 4.6. Some Descriptive Statistics

Variable	Native Fijian	Indo-Fijian	Total sample
		Mean	
Area of cane farm in acres	7.09 (4.7)	8.92 (7.2)	8.39 (6.7)
Age of farmer	48.8 (13.2)	52.22 (12.3)	51.12 (13.2)
Years of farming experience	14.2 (10.2)	30.68 (14.1)	25.45 (14.2)
Years of schooling	8.44 (2.9)	8.32 (3.4)	8.36 (2.9)
Distance from mill (km)	14 (5.660	18 (4.31)	20 (5.22)
		Percentage of farmers	
Full-time farming	88.7%	81.5%	83.5%
Stay on farm	73.7%	100%	91.7%
Have alternative income	61 %	79 %	71%
Cane transport by lorry	55.8 %	60 %	57.4 %
Own land	64.3%	16.4%	31.5%
1st class land	20.2%	16.8%	17.9%
2nd class land	46.9%	26.5%	32.9%
3rd class land	25.8%	50.4%	42.7%
4th class land	7.1%	6.3%	6.5%
Sample size	213	464	677

Note: Standard deviation in parenthesis.

In this section, in addition to farm-specific (also known as overall) technical efficiency measure, input-specific technical efficiency, as well as scale efficiency measures, are computed. While the parametric model provides estimates of the first two types of TE, the non-parametric Data Envelopment Analysis (DEA) computes overall TE and scale efficiency and the latter does not require input prices with the use of DEA. Technical efficiency reflects the ability of a farm to reduce inputs to obtain a given output level, and the scale efficiency index indicates the type of returns to scale experienced by each farm. This provides information on whether the farm should increase or decrease its input use to reach its optimal output level, which has the lowest cost of production.

The Parametric Production Frontier Model

The parametric model estimated is that of the random coefficient stochastic frontier model set out in Kalirajan and Obwona (1994). The frontier concept emphasizes the idea of maximality which it embodies, and represents the 'best practice' technique. The generalized version of the frontier model can be written as:

$$\mathrm{Ln}\, Y_i = \gamma_{1i} + \sum_{j=1}^{n} \gamma_{ij}\ \mathrm{Ln}\, X_{ij} \tag{4.1}$$

where i represents number of farms; j represents number of inputs used; Y = output; X = inputs; λ_{1j} = intercept term of the ith farm; and λ_{ij} = actual response of output to the method of application of the jth input used by the ith farm.

Since intercepts and slope coefficients can vary across farms, we can write:

$$\gamma_{ij} = \bar{\gamma}_j + \mu_{ij}$$
$$\gamma_{1i} = \bar{\gamma}_1 + v_{1j} \qquad (4.2)$$

where $\bar{\gamma}_j$ is the mean response coefficient of output with respect to the jth input; μ_{ij} and v_{1j} are random disturbance terms; and:

$$E(\gamma_{ij}) = \bar{\gamma}_j,\ E(\mu_{ij}) = 0,\ \text{Var}(\mu_{ij}) = \sigma_{uit} \text{ for } j = t \text{ and zero otherwise.}$$

Combining equations (4.1) and (4.2):

$$\text{Ln } Y_i = \bar{\gamma}_1 + \sum_{j=1}^{k} \bar{\gamma}_j \text{ Ln } X_{ij} + \sum_{j=1}^{n} u_{ij} \text{ Ln } X_{ij} + v_{1i} \qquad (4.3)$$

Following Aitken's generalised least squares method suggested by Hildreth and Houck (1968) and the estimation procedure by Griffiths (1972), the farm input-specific response coefficient estimates of the above model can be obtained.[4] The highest magnitude of each response coefficient and intercept given by γ^* form the frontier coefficients of the maximal production frontier. The potential output of the industry can be realized when the best practice techniques are used and this is given by:

$$\text{Ln } Y^*_{it} = \gamma^*_1 + \sum_{j=1}^{k} \gamma^*_j \text{ Ln } X_{ijt} \qquad (4.4)$$

Based on the above, the model to be estimated is:

$$\text{Ln } Y_i = \beta_0 + \beta_1 \text{Ln LAN}_i + \beta_2 \text{Ln LAB}_i + \beta_3 \text{Ln BULL}_i + \beta_4 \text{Ln TRACT}_i + \beta_5 \text{Ln FERT}_i + \beta_6 \text{Ln WEED}_i + \beta_7 \text{Ln OTHER}_i + u_i + v_i \qquad (4.5)$$

The Cobb-Douglas production function represented by equation (4.5) was found to be a better fit of the data than the more flexible translog production function.[5] Using the frontier estimates, the maximum potential output can be calculated and the ratio of observed output to

[4] It is done by first obtaining the variance covariance matrix obtained from the estimation of equation (4.3) and then the unknown error term can be obtained as an approximation using the minimum square rule.

[5] The null hypothesis that all pairwise translog relationships between the seven input variables are zero could not be rejected by the likelihood ratio test while the null hypothesis that the coefficients of the Cobb-Douglas production function sum to one was not rejected at the 5% level of significance.

potential output gives the overall or farm-specific TE measure for the farm. The above estimation was undertaken using the TERAN software developed at the Australian National University.

THE NON-PARAMETRIC DEA PRODUCTION FRONTIER MODEL

Data Envelopment Analysis involves the use of linear programming methods to construct a non-parametric piece-wise surface (or frontier) over the data from which efficiency measures are then calculated relative to this surface. One advantage, as argued by Gong and Sickles (1992), is that DEA is more appealing than the parametric model as inefficiency is likely to be correlated with the inputs. However, DEA is not free from drawbacks either. For instance, since DEA is deterministic, it does not allow for statistical tests typical of the parametric approach. Also, DEA attributes all the deviations from the frontier to inefficiencies, a frontier estimated by DEA is likely to be sensitive to measurement errors or other noise in the data, but the latter are assumed to be non-existent. An attempt is made, however, to check for such sensitivity in section 4.6.

Here, we follow the output-orientated efficiency of Fare *et al.* (1994) using the input distance function to consider how much inputs can be proportionally reduced without changing output quantity. For the ith farm, data is represented by the vectors x_i and y_i of inputs and outputs. Here, we consider K inputs and only one type of output given by cane production. We further define all the data to be represented by X which is the K by N matrix of inputs for N farms; and Y denotes the 1 by N output matrix. Although the input-orientated variable returns to scale DEA frontier can be computed, here, constant returns to scale are considered in order to compare the technical efficiency measures with the Cobb-Douglas production frontier model. The DEA frontier is defined by the solution to N linear programs (solved once for each farm in the sample) of the form:

$$\begin{aligned} &\text{Min}_{\phi\lambda}\ \phi, \\ &\text{such that} \quad -y_i + Y\lambda \geq 0, \\ &\phi\, x_i - X\lambda \geq 0, \\ &\lambda \geq 0, \end{aligned} \tag{4.6}$$

where ϕ is the input distance function, λ is a N x 1 vector of constants, $\phi \leq 1$, and ϕ-1 is the proportional decrease in inputs that could be used by the ith farm, with output quantity held constant. Note that $1/\phi$ defines a TE score, which varies between zero and one. The value of ϕ is then solved for each farm using Coelli's (1996a) DEAP Version 2.1 program to compute technical and scale efficiency indices.

EMPIRICAL RESULTS

First, the input response coefficients obtained from the parametric model and the overall and input-specific TE estimates obtained are discussed. Then the overall TE estimates are compared with those obtained from the non-parametric model followed by the scale efficiency measures.

Table 4.7 shows the stochastic frontier coefficients that define the maximum possible cane output if technical efficiency of production is 100% – that is, if farms use the best practice technique combined with the inputs and existing technology.

Table 4.7. Stochastic Frontier Estimates

Variables	Frontier Coefficients	Range of Actual Response Coefficients
Constant	3.89 (0.131)*	2.67 to 3.89
Land	0.71 (0.031)*	0.63 to 0.71
Labor	0.13 (0.022)*	0.10 to 0.13
Bullock hours	0.065 (0.008)*	0.057 to 0.065
Tractor hours	0.024 (0.012)*	0.019 to 0.024
Fertiliser use	0.084 (0.015)*	0.071 to 0.084
Weedicide use	- 0.015 (0.008)**	-0.019 to -0.015
Other expenditure	0.017 (0.014)	0.011 to 0.017

Notes:

1. Figures in parenthesis are standard errors.
2. * and ** mean the coefficient is significant at the 5% and 10% levels of significance respectively.

At the outset, the validity of the modelling of equation (4.5) as a random coefficient specification for the present data was examined by the Lagrange multiplier test procedure suggested by Breusch and Pagan (1979). The test results indicate that the likelihood ratio test statistic of χ^2 (8) value of 25.81 was significant at the 5% level, thereby supporting the modeling process. It was also found that all the input coefficients of the production frontier were significant at the 5% level except for other expenditure incurred by farmers, although weedicide use was weakly significant at the 10% level. One reason for the negative impact of weedicide on cane output could be due to the lack of knowledge in how much to use or the timing of use as these determine the effectiveness of weed control on cane. The other expenditure variable is insignificant, and this is possible as a cursory look at the data did not reveal any distinct pattern between the observed huge variations and cane production itself. For instance, land rent does not necessarily reflect area leased for farming. Some farmers paid little rent for large plots depending on when the lease was signed, while others had different arrangements with their landowner to share cane proceeds and thus pay less rent.

Table 4.7 also shows that the range of actual response coefficients of inputs for individual farms is quite substantial. These variations indicate that the methods of application of different inputs vary among farms and, consequently, individual contributions of inputs to output differ from farm to farm.

EFFICIENCY MEASURES FROM PARAMETRIC MODEL

The farm-specific overall technical efficiency measures are tabulated in frequency form in table 4.8. While the efficiency measures range from 0.63 to 0.93 for the total sample, there are considerable differences in the performance of the two ethnic groups. The Indo-Fijians are, on average, 10% more efficient than their native counterparts. With the latter, about 25% of the farmers fall in the lowest and highest efficiency category, while about 60% of the Indo-Fijians produced at least 76% of the maximum possible output. Overall, the total sample performance shows that farmers will be able to increase output by about 25% if they used farm inputs and technology efficiently.

Table 4.8. Frequency Distribution of Farm-Specific Technical Efficiency from Parametric Model

Efficiency Level (%)	Number of Native Fijian Farms	Number of Indo-Fijian Farms	Total Sample
61 –65	37	15	52
66 –70	14	69	83
71 –75	96	85	181
76 –80	10	183	193
81 –85	36	59	95
86 –93	20	53	73
Mean Efficiency	71.2	81.8	74.7

In most previous efficiency studies, the notion of technical efficiency encompasses the efficiency of total factor employment without being capable of identifying inefficiency of each individual input. Kopp (1981) explains that such measures treat the contribution of each input equally and thereby mask any differences in efficiency that might be attributed to particular factor inputs. Thus, the idea of technical inefficiency should be extended to a more disaggregated level, *viz.* input-specific technical efficiency (Kumbhakar 1988).

The random coefficient production frontier model adopted here enables the measure of not just the overall efficiency, but also input-specific efficiency measures as reported in table 4.9. It is rational to argue that, depending on which farm uses which best practice technique with which input, production coefficients would vary from farm to farm and hence result in variations in input-specific efficiency. Although some farms are able to use some of the inputs with 100% efficiency, this does not mean that it is the same farmer who uses all the inputs most efficiently.

The results show quite high levels of input use efficiency, but labour and tractor use are relatively less efficient. First, tractors are not commonly used except on large farms that make it worthwhile or conducive for use. Second, most farmers do not own tractors, and those who hire them have difficulty doing so as there is a shortage – others share them when they are able to hire tractors. Thus, there is little opportunity for farmers to learn to use them effectively, and this was further hampered by unfavourable weather conditions. In contrast, bullocks are commonly used as 73% of farmers own them, and learning by doing gains over time has positively impacted on the way in which animal power is being used. Nevertheless, improvements can still be made to cane output if farmers use about 10% less of bullock hours.

Labour is the least efficiently used input. One reason could be that self-employed labour may not necessarily be well used, as individuals do not pay themselves for labour services. Another reason is that 84% of the farmers are full-timers and, thus, may take their time to farm in a more leisurely manner. On the other hand, fertiliser use has the highest mean efficiency. But the number of farmers using land more efficiently is more than those using fertiliser efficiently.

Table 4.9. Frequency Distribution of Input-Specific Technical Efficiency from Parametric Model

Efficiency	Number of Farms				
Measure (%)	Land	Labour	Bullock	Tractor	Fertiliser
75–79	-	87	-	203	-
80–84	-	412	-	346	50
85–89	98	56	373	17	76
90–94	341	20	199	47	402
95–99	201	67	76	13	83
100	42	35	29	51	66
Mean Efficiency	92.4	80.6	89.5	82.7	93.7

Note: Weedicide and other expenditures have not been included as their frontier coefficients were less significant than the above inputs as seen in table 4.7.

All the farmers were on average input-using land such that 92.4% of the maximum possible output was being obtained. This was to gain as much as possible from the then existing high EU sugar prices. It was also found that 72% of the 98 farmers who were operating at the relatively low end of the land efficiency measure had less than three years before their land lease expired and, thus, had possibly less incentive to use the land efficiently for cane production.

It must be noted that native farmers generally used land, bullocks and tractors less efficiently than their counterparts (evidence not shown to conserve space). First, it is possible that since a majority of natives own their land, they do not have to grapple with the uncertainty that the Indians face and, thus, are less careful about land use. Furthermore, while native Fijians on average work on smaller farms (see table 4.6), a closer look at the survey data showed that almost 40% of them – compared to 24% of the Indians – farmed less than 10 acres of land. The smaller scale of production may adversely affect the incentive to improve efficiency or make it uneconomical, for instance, to use tractors. With bullocks, only 36% of native farmers owned them while 64% of Indian farmers owned theirs. Thus, it is likely that the Indian farmers were able to learn to use bullocks more effectively, and were able to use them when they needed to rather than the natives who have to hire or borrow them.[6] It is also

[6] As explained with tractor use, farmers who did not own bullocks faced the same problem and the timing of bullock use on farms is crucial for maximising cane output in terms of land preparation. Additionally, Kingi

true to say that, on average, the native Fijian's lack of experience does not put them in good stead with input use (the survey shows that they only have half the 30 years of farming experience that the Indians have).

EFFICIENCY MEASURES FROM NON-PARAMETRIC MODEL

Both the overall TE and scale efficiency measures are reported as a frequency distribution in tables 4.10 and 4.11. Table 4.10 shows that a majority of the farms (about 52%) are experiencing increasing returns to scale – which means that they should expand output by increasing the use of their inputs to achieve economies of scale. However, constant returns to scale are evident for 84 farms, indicating that they are using correct levels of inputs relative to other farms in the sample. Decreasing returns to scale hold for 242 farms, indicating that these farms would be better off not to increase input levels as this would further increase scale inefficiency.

The last column in table 4.10 indicates that there is no distinct correlation between scale efficiency and high technical efficiency. This is reinforced in the last column of table 4.11 as well. Farms that are scale efficient may not necessarily be operating on the frontier and, in fact, of the 22 farms that are fully technically efficient, only 3 are using the correct level of inputs. In addition, table 4.11 shows a mean technical efficiency level of 71.8% – which means that, on average, the current level of output can be produced using 28% less inputs than are applied by farmers. Also, about 40% of the farms are operating at less than 70% technical efficiency and a quarter of the farms fall under the 70%–79% level.

Table 4.10. Frequency Distribution of Scale Efficiency from Non-parametric Model

Returns to Scale	Number of Farms	Mean Technical Efficiency (%)
Increasing	351	67.4
Constant	84	68.6
Decreasing	242	75.1

Table 4.11. Frequency Distribution of Farm-Specific Technical Efficiency from Non-parametric Model

Efficiency Level (%)	Number of Farms	Number of Scale-Efficient Farms
< 50	12	1
50–59	45	4
60–69	284	10
70–79	187	35
80–89	67	22
90–100	82	12
Mean Efficiency	71.8	

and Kompas (2005) report that native farmers are also subject to requests from families to donate their bullocks to village ceremonies.

In general, the parametric and non-parametric models do not differ greatly in the farm-specific TE estimates. The mean TE under the former was lower (71.8%) than the latter (74.7%) and this is expected as DEA assumes no noise, and as all random errors are considered as the efficiency measures, thereby producing lower TE estimates.

DETERMINANTS OF TECHNICAL EFFICIENCY

In this section, two types of analyses are undertaken on farm-specific TE, one using the estimates from the parametric and the other the estimates from the non-parametric model. Different variables are also used in the two models to determine the impact on TE and provide variety in the analysis.

The Parametric Efficiency Model

Here, the TE estimates obtained from equation (4.5) is measure is used as the dependent variable in a separate ordinary least squares regression to investigate empirically the significance of the influence of various factors as seen in equation (4.7).[7] An interactive term, EDU*EXP, has been included to minimise possible multicollinearity between the two variables.

$$\text{Transformed TE} = \alpha_0 + \alpha_1 \text{Ln EXP} + \alpha_2 \text{Ln EDU} + \alpha_3 \text{Ln (EDU*EXP)} + \alpha_4 \text{ETHN} + \alpha_5 \text{FSTAT} + \alpha_6 \text{OWN} \quad (4.7)$$

As the TE measure is bounded between 0 and 1, a Tobit regression was attempted, but the estimations failed the test for satisfactory functional form. Thus, the TE measures were transformed to Ln TE - Ln (1-TE) in order to comply with standard normal assumptions of the error term in a multiple regression equation. Due to the above transformation of TE, the regression coefficients have no direct interpretation, but it is possible to calculate the elasticity value from the estimated coefficient if the independent variables are logged.[8] The estimations in table 4.12 did not suffer from functional form misspecification and were easily corrected for heterosceadasticity using the White's (1980) method. The R^2 was also reasonable for a cross-sectional study as it ranged from 0.68 to 0.74.

In the total sample, the positive and significant coefficient on ethnicity indicates that Indian farmers use resources and technology more efficiently than the natives. This is also apparent in the discussion earlier on input use. It is, however, a worrying trend if native farmers do not try hard enough to improve their farming techniques and, at the same time, when more natives without experience attempt to farm their lands after their tenant's lease expires.

---

[7] Alternatively, as in some stochastic frontier estimations (Coelli *et al.* 1998), the factors affecting TE can be included indirectly within the specification of equation (4.5).

[8] Equating TE/1-TE to the antilog of the estimated coefficient value and solving for TE gives the elasticity value of the variable's effect on changes in TE.

As expected, land ownership is a significant factor in affecting efficiency. In the total sample, the owner-occupied farm efficiency is higher than the tenant farms. The significant negative impact of land tenure security on farm productivity has been widely studied (Feder and Onchan 1987; Barrows and Roth 1990). This is confirmed by the survey finding as 73% of the farmers conceded that, due to the land issue, they would not hesitate to burn cane to ensure maximum income with little or no regard to the short-term effects on sugar recovery at the mills or the long-term effects of burning on their farm productivity.

Table 4.12. Determinants of Technical Efficiency from Parametric Model

Variable	Native Fijians		Indo-Fijians	Total Sample
Constant	2.18** (1.04)	2.04** (0.88)	1.962** (0.993)	1.893** (0.912)
Ethnicity	-	-	-	0.018** (0.007)
Stay on Farm	-	1.22* (0.412)	-	-
Experience	0.017*** (0.009)	0.11*** (0.006)	0.013* (0.004)	0.004** (0.002)
Education	0.051** (0.026)	0.17** (0.008)	0.081** (0.041)	0.012** (0.005)
Experience *Education	0.008 (0.007)	0.005 (0.006)	0.005** (0.002)	0.003** (0.001)
Farming Status	1.306*** (0.712)	-	1.48** (0.751)	1.125** (0.408)
Land Ownership	0.91*** (0.578)	0.78*** (0.445)	1.03* (0.258)	0.93** (0.371)

Notes:

1. Figures in parenthesis are standard errors.
2. ** and *** means the coefficient is significant at the 1%, 5% and 10% level of significance respectively.

Land improvement measures such as soil conservation and reducing soil tillage or intercropping were not high on the farmers' priorities as they are costly investments given the uncertainty of farming their land beyond the lease period. It is, however, not surprising that land ownership is weakly significant for the native Fijian sample when compared to the Indian sample, as 64.3% of the native farmers own their land and do not need to pay rent – hence the incentive to get more output is not that high.

The experience factor is also less significant in the sample of native farmers. This not only reflects the lower average farm experience of the native farmers (see table 4.6), but the average age of native farmers is 49 years which means that they started farming when they were quite old. Thus, they can be expected to be relatively less receptive to and more conservative in adopting new technologies and better practices. On the other hand, *a priori*, more years of formal education is seen to increase efficiency for both types of farmers as they can be better exposed to improved farming techniques (such as soil conservation, fertilizer and weedicide application, the use of new and higher cane yielding cane varieties) as well as extension services.

However, the interaction term of experience and education is only significant for the Indian farmers, indicating that with more experience and education, the marginal increase in efficiency is certainly positive. However, with native farmers, the more educated they are, the less willing they are to work hard on the farm – possibly because they shun hard work or expect to earn more given their level of education. Indian farmers, on the other hand, have often helped out on their family's farm since they were young, even when at school, and thus have a higher level of commitment to farming.

Relative to farming status, full-time farmers performed better than part timers, but this was stronger in the sample of native Fijians. This is because the natives of the rural farming community are often known to live in their respective villages. They either travel to farm their land or help their tenants with an arrangement to share proceeds with the tenant while being "full time" farmers. In fact, only 71% of full-time native farmers stayed on their farms. The highly significant coefficient when the FSTAY dummy was used in the regression (in place of FSTAT) corroborates with the findings of Kingi and Kompas (2005).

The Non-Parametric Efficiency Model

With the TE estimates from DEA, it was possible to use a linear Tobit analysis to identify factors associated with efficiency improvement in the model below:

$$\text{TE} = \alpha_0 + \alpha_1 \text{AGE} + \alpha_2 (\text{AGE})^2 + \alpha_3 \text{EDU} + \alpha_4 \text{ETHN} + \alpha_5 \text{FSTAT} + \alpha_6 \text{OFFINC} + \alpha_7 \text{CLASS} + \alpha_8 \text{TRANS} + \alpha_9 \text{DIST} + \alpha_{10} \text{SIZE} \quad (4.8)$$

All definitions of the variables in the above equation are given in table 4.5.[9] The results of the censored Tobit model of equation (4.8) are presented in table 4.13. The variable $(\text{AGE})^2$ was added as TE was found to show a significant quadratic relationship with the variable AGE.[10]

The R^2 of 0.84 was also reasonable for a cross sectional study of 677 farmers. Lastly, to test the sensitivity of the DEA results to measurement error for the observations that defines the frontier, all 12 of the most efficient data points were removed before re-running the DEA and re-estimating the determinants of TE. With only two exceptions, the signs of the estimated coefficients remained the same with small changes in their magnitudes. More importantly, the shape of the age-efficiency relationship remained intact and, thus, it is unlikely that measurement error on the frontier substantially affected the results.

The results show that efficiency increases with age and then eventually decreases. This is consistent with what would be expected. The older the farmer, the more experienced he is in cane farming and using traditional cane varieties – but at the same time, farmers closer to retirement may be less motivated, more risk averse and, therefore, less efficient than younger farmers. Younger farmers tend to have a higher probability of adopting technology than older framers and an ability and willingness to bear risk. Thus, targeting younger and older farmers for extension activities could increase their levels of technical efficiency relative to middle-

---

[9] It is inappropriate to do a similar analysis for scale efficiency as the value of the index on its own is not representative of increasing or decreasing returns to scale, but where the farm is located on the frontier is what determines the nature of returns to scale.

[10] To further check on the appropriateness of the quadratic specification, the model was re-estimated using a series of dummy variables (for young, middle-aged, and older farmers using various age cut-offs for the categories)

aged farmers. The significance of the education coefficient shows that, with better education, the farmer generally responds more readily to new technology or the adoption of good farming techniques (such as crop management, protection and improvement related to soil conservation, and applications of fertilizer and weedicide).

Table 4.13. Determinants of Technical Efficiency from Non-Parametric Model

Variables	Parameter
Constant	3.455 (1.23)*
Age	0.015 (0.006)*
Age^2	- 0.012 (0.005)*
Education	0.172 (0.071)*
Ethnicity	0.413 (0.208)*
Full-time farming	0.085 (0.036)*
Having off-farm income	- 0.009 (0.004)*
Land class	- 0.002 (0.001)*
Cane transport by lorry	0.137 (0.059)*
Distance from mill	0.0326 (0.016)*
Farm size greater than 20 acres	0.056 (0.022)*

Notes:

1. Figures in parenthesis are standard errors.
2. * means the coefficient is significant at the 5% level.

The positive and significant coefficient on ethnicity indicates that Indian farmers use resources and technology more efficiently than the native farmers. In fact, Kurer (2001) has expressed concern that the transfer of land to Fijian landowners after expiry would encourage the influx of inexperienced and under-capitalised Fijian farmers.[11] Since colonial times, the Indian Fijians were the ones who farmed sugarcane and, thus, have more experience than the natives.

In terms of farming status, full-time farming increases efficiency as it allows for more effective learning by doing gains. But full-time farmers may have an alternative source of income, as the data reveals that 60% of full-time farmers have off-farm income. If this income is substantial, farming may be a secondary interest and, thus, adversely affect the incentive to improve efficiency. On the other hand, this additional income may be used to buy farm implements or hire labour for farming, thereby increasing efficiency. The positive and significant coefficient on off-farm income shows that the latter is not the case. This is in part due to land insecurity and the uncertain prospects facing the sugar industry due to the withdrawal of EU's price subsidy.

in place of age and the square of age. The resulting graphs approximated the inverted U-shaped curve fairly closely, indicating that the quadratic specification was robust.

[11] It is also unclear how effective the Farming Assistance Scheme that commenced in 2000 to help incoming landowners with farm management courses has been. One criticism of another government scheme, the Rural Farming Assistance implemented in 2002, has been the slow delivery of assistance to farmers in terms of land preparation, purchase of seed material and basic farm equipment (*Fiji Times* 14 May 2004).

The farm-size dummy coefficient shows that efficiency gain for the large farms is significantly higher than that for small and medium–sized farms. Since larger plots of farmed land are more amenable to better and more effective use of inputs and technology, amalgamating land leases may be necessary. This also makes farms more economically viable for loans.

The coefficient on land class is negative (the higher the land class, the greater the slope of the land) and significant. Flat land reduces cultivation costs and increases the response rate from fertilizer use and efforts to minimise soil erosion from sloping land, thereby raising the efficiency of land use and cane output. Data on soil fertility was, however, unavailable to permit a better measurement of land quality.

The negative coefficient on mill distance shows that the further way the farm is from the mill, the lower is the efficiency. This is partly related to problems of the FSC transporting harvested cane in time to the mill due to the poorly run government rail system. The rail network has steadily and significantly deteriorated because of under-investment in maintenance: the locomotives are old, face high repair bills and, hence, frequently breakdown (Davies 1998, Sugar Technology Mission 2004). Farmers also alternatively transport their cane by lorry. The coefficient of the transport dummy on lorry use indicates that road transport does help improve technical efficiency due to better control over the timing of cane pick up and delivery to the mills.

Conclusion

Empirical evidence on cane farm production shows that, on average, farmers produce about 27% (taking the average between the parametric and nonparametric models) below their maximum possible output. This is because they do not use inputs and technology efficiently. An even greater concern is that native farmers on average produce 10% less cane than Indian farmers. One can expect that the market could resolve the issue of who should remain in the industry based on efficiency and competitiveness but this may not foster the social objective of the Fijian government to increase ethnic Fijian participation in the sugarcane industry.

However, a reasonable compromise can be made on this objective by encouraging native Fijians to be involved in alternative crop farming in line with the six-year long Alternative Livelihood Project in Fiji that began in 2006. This project is funded by the Asian Development Bank, the Fiji government, and other local institutions. It is timely to channel available labour into these new crops, especially if cane cultivation is new to them as well. With the loss of EU sugar prices, it would be best if the market were catered for by efficient producers. Crop diversification would help growers minimise the risks associated with any increase in price variability as a result of the liberalisation of sugar policies.

The econometric evidence also pointed to the need to increase farm size by amalgamating land leases. This would enable economies of scale in output and allow better use of inputs and technology for improved efficiency performance. Large farms are more commercially viable in a competitive environment. This would, however, mean that many of the current small farm households might face difficulties – but given the high possibility of facing eviction after the lease expires, this would be an opportune time to form large plantations. These farmers could, however, be employed for a stable wage to work on the farms or to possibly work on a share of cane proceeds that would make it sufficiently attractive for them to be employees.

One advantage of large-scale farming is that it is more economically viable, which makes it easier to obtain loans from financial institutions to invest in farm inputs. Also, with fewer small-scale farms, extension visits by research officers would be more feasible and easier to monitor.

The sugar reform process has also highlighted the need to increase cane yield from the present 48.7 tons/ha to 62.9 tons/ha to enhance the sustainability of the sugar industry (Government of Fiji 2006a). This requires cane farmers to embrace "best practice" related to soil preparation, planting of seed cane, fertilisation and drainage. Thus, government intervention – in the form of allocating more funds for research in crop management and protection and improvement, as well as extension and farm advisory service (this was dismantled by FSC in 2001 due to financial constraints) – needs to be of high priority. While all these measures are necessary they are, however, not sufficient as improvements in milling, transport and processing also need to be undertaken simultaneously for the optimum performance of the sugar industry.

Chapter 5

The Lack of Soil Conservation on Cane Farms

Introduction

It has already been established that Fiji's cane yield is well below that of the other sugar producers such as Australia, Brazil, India and the ACP sugar producers. This is, in part, due to the labour-intensive nature of Fiji's sugar production. The low cane yield has also often been attributed to land issues such as land quality, land degradation and land insecurity.

Recent evidence in Fiji suggests that the problem of land degradation in particular is worsening.[1] Soil loss measurements by Fiji's Ministry of Agriculture, Sugar, and Land Resettlement indicates that the agricultural productive base in many sugarcane areas is running down at a rate well above what is regarded as economically acceptable (Leslie and Ratukalou 2002). The main form of land degeneration is soil degradation, which occurs from widespread and indiscriminate burning particularly, but not exclusively, in the sugarcane growing areas. Other causes of soil degradation include deforestation, overgrazing, and the expansion of sugarcane and other crops such as dalo and yagona onto marginal land. Although soil depletion has worsened, the majority of farmers still will not put in conservation improvements without financial help (*ibid.*). Fiji is too small and too vulnerable for such problems to be ignored for any length of time.

Despite the seriousness of these land related problems in Fiji, there have been no formal studies to examine:

1. The impact of these issues within the framework of technical efficiency in cane production. That is, what is the effect of soil erosion on cane output and what has it cost cane farmers and the sugar industry? If soil conservation were undertaken, does the extent or type of conservation measure significantly affect cane output?
2. The factors that affect the perception of the soil erosion problem, and the extent of soil conservation effort on cane farms.

The rest of the chapter is organised as follows. First, the environmental impacts of Fiji's sugar industry expansion and, in particular, the problems of soil erosion on cane farms are discussed. The next section sets out the hypotheses and theoretical model for the empirical

[1] Land degradation consists of soil, biological, physical and chemical degradation.

investigation of the first question above.[2] This is followed by the discussion of empirical results and farming practices to shed light on policy options for soil conservation. The next section looks into the empirical investigation of the second question above to provide more direction in soil conservation policy.[3]

ENVIRONMENTAL IMPACT OF SUGAR INDUSTRY EXPANSION

While the preferential EU sugar price helped develop Fiji's economy, it increased Fiji's reliance on sugarcane production to the point of neglecting the environment. Although there are a number of environmental provisions and requirements in the sugar protocol under the Lomé agreement, none of them were put in place in Fiji. This was due to the absence of appropriate institutional regulatory mechanisms and the weak powerless nature of the environment institutions in Fiji (Kumar and Prasad 2004). Although the National Environment Strategy was issued in 1993, it was only after a decade that the Sustainable Environment Bill was drafted in 2004 and to date, it is yet to be enacted.

The growth of the sugar industry generated two sets of environmental consequences. On the input side (cane farms), more land, including progressively marginal land, was brought into cultivation, and land was intensively used. On the output side (sugar processing at mills), waste products of various types were not well managed. We discuss the latter first before focusing on the former, which relates to the issues investigated in this chapter.

Environmental Damage due to Mill Operations

Several studies have indicated that sugar-mill effluents are a source of river pollution (Tamata *et al.* 1996, FSC Report 2002, APO 2003). For each season, the four mills draw up at least 38.3 million metric tons of water from rivers and nearby creeks for cooling purposes (FSC Report 2002). As there is no closed circuit cooling, the used water is discharged with extra heat and other impurities back into the water outlets, affecting plant and animal life. When mill equipment fails – and this is, unfortunately, frequently – sugar, as well stale juice, gets into the water and these add to water treatment costs.

Solid waste, such as bagasse and mill mud, is also indiscriminately dumped at and around the mills. The burning of bagasse produces a considerable volume of ash, and when bagasse is not used in the boilers of the mills (as in the Labasa and Rarawai mills), they have to be stored – and, thus, the FSC incurs a cost. In 2002, there was 783,158 tons of bagasse, 63,000 tons of mill mud and 62,653 tons of dry ash. Due to insufficient equipment to handle this waste, ash and dust released from bagasse burning pollutes the air and is a health risk to mill workers and the public alike (APO 2003). The sugar mills also produce strong odours from blocked drains, bagasse stockpiles, mill mud, and wastewater treatment ponds – causing complaints from people (FSC 2002). It is imperative that the FSC takes serious consideration of such environmental impacts by ensuring the effective functioning of mill equipment,

[2] This section draws on Mahadevan (2008c).

[3] This section draws on Asafu-Adjaye (2008).

installing and upgrading effluent handling facilities. They must also explore diversification projects for their solid wastes to avoid pollutants from entering the natural water systems and disrupting the ecosystem.

Farm Level Environmental Damage

One major source of farm-level environmental damage comes from the use of marginal land. This causes soil degradation due to the replacement of the natural soil cover by sugarcane, and the greater use of additives to boost soil nutrients. Fertilizers and pesticide applied to soil that is depleted both physically and nutritionally is a waste of resources. Also, excessive pesticide and fertilizers leads to land degradation, a serious consequence of which is more severe impacts from natural disasters and increased vulnerability to droughts and flooding. The cost of natural disasters is conservatively estimated at an average of F$20 million per annum (Swami 2004). In Fiji, sugarcane is grown at the edge of rivers and streams leaving no riparian vegetation. This means that there is no buffer between streams and agricultural systems to perform a filtering function to reduce the concentration of nutrients, pesticides and other sediments. Thus, run-offs containing valuable agricultural resources – such as topsoil and fertilizers – freely enter the water bodies with an impact on riparian, fresh water and marine environments.

Soil Erosion

As early as mid 1980, Fiji recognised the problem of soil erosion in their Ninth Development Plan 1986–1990 in the following way:

> "Soil erosion is considered to be the most serious environmental problem in areas of steepland cultivation, due to overgrazing or over-stocking, uncontrolled burning of grassland and cane trash, steepland logging, construction of new roads, land excavation for subdivision, and uncontrolled bush clearing for cultivation".

In 2001, the expansion of the sugar industry led to 4,377 farmers planting cane on 16,107 ha of steep land (that is, land with a slope of 16°–20°) and 982 farmers were cultivating 4 400 ha of very steep land with a slope of 21° and above (Kumar and Prasad 2004). By world standards, land with slopes greater than 8° would be considered unsuitable for growing sugarcane without unacceptable damage to the environment (Galletly and Swartz 1974). Morrison (1992) – the only comprehensive study that applied the Universal Soil Loss Equation to estimate the extent of soil erosion in Fiji per year – found that sugarcane farms with an 8° slope have a soil loss of 37 tons/ha.

In Fiji, the Agriculture Ministry's Land Use Section restricts cane cultivation on slopes of 11° and above, although the FSC and NLTB have allowed cultivation on slopes as steep as 21° and above (Leslie and Ratukalou 2002), motivated by Fiji's high dependence on the sugar industry. Expanding use of such marginal land not only increases the loss of bio-diversity through mono-cropping, but also the surface run-off from steep land. Run-off is much greater than for flatter lands, and results in higher soil erosion than would otherwise have been.

A minor drought appears to be a major drought because the topsoil on steep lands has been washed away. There is a narrowing of the soil profile such that a minor drought effect spreads down slope and becomes more intense with much lower yields in comparison with yields ten years ago (Gawander 1998). Unfortunately, the natural geographical erosion rate in Fiji is high because of its landscape, lithology and uneven topography (Leslie and Ratukalou 2002). In fact, as early as 1974, Galletly and Swartz (1974) found the calculated soil erosion index of Fiji to be very high – 700 for the dry zone and 800 for the wet zone – compared to world standards that averaged between 200 and 400. The authors cautioned that when the soil erosion index exceeds 500, extreme care is required in the use of land, irrespective of soil type.

For a sugar growing area, Liedtke (1989) found the rate of soil loss to be 22–80 tons/ha/year on slopes 5°–20° for the month of February 1983 – and it is worth noting that this was an exceptionally dry month. In another sugarcane area, Clarke and Morrison (1987) recorded a soil loss of 8–14 cm when the first crop was harvested, and this represents losses equivalent to about 100 tons/ha/year. Although less than satisfactory in terms of land quality, the Seaqaqa area was the last area to be developed for sugarcane in the 1970s and Gawander (1998) reports that 50 cm of soil was lost from sections of the soil in Seaqaqa from 1986–92; this amounted to a soil loss of 200–300 tons/ha/year.

In a review of four catchment areas in Viti Levu (the western side of Fiji), the Japanese International Corporation Agency (1998) estimated total soil loss to be between 1.1 million tons and 9.3 million tons per annum in the four areas. This is equivalent to a topsoil loss of 2.2–5.4 millimetre per annum. The dredging costs alone due to soil erosion were estimated at F$2.5 million. Compared to the 1992 study undertaken by the International Union for Conservation of Nature, the total soil loss in the 1998 Japanese study has increased by about 35% over time.

SURVEY RESULTS ON SOIL EROSION AND CONSERVATION

Table 5.1 shows some results from the survey questions on soil erosion. It shows that 45% of the farmers undertook some form of soil conservation. Efforts towards this was greater at the beginning of their leases, but very little was done towards the expiry of the lease when land was used very intensively. Thus, long-term soil conservation measures that are more expensive but more effective are not a permanent feature. There is also a wide variation in the land types (related to slope and need for modification to render land suitable) owned by farmers, with about 49% of them farming quite steep and very steep land. The worrying fact is that 52% of farmers are grappling with severe soil erosion and 25% face moderate soil erosion. To help reduce the soil erosion problem, 64% of the farmers have drains installed to help remove excess water, 45% have undertaken some form of soil conservation measure, and 53% have attended a soil conservation program. Appendix 5.1 explains the types of conservation effort undertaken.

Table 5.1. Survey Results on Soil Erosion and Conservation

Variable	Percentage of farmers
Flat land	17.9
Gentle land	32.9
Quite steep land	42.7
Very steep land	6.5
Have drains installed	64
Attended soil conservation program	53
Undertake one of the soil conservation measures stated below	45
Type of soil conservation adopted	
Planting of vetivar grass	11
Contour planting and trash conservation	7
Contour planting	10
Trash conservation	7
Traditional conservation	10
Perception of Farmers	
Low level of soil erosion	23
Moderate soil erosion	25
Severe soil erosion	52
Sample size	677

IMPACT OF SOIL EROSION AND CONSERVATION

Both parametric and non-parametric models are used to obtain technical efficiency measures as a check on robustness. Here, as was done in the previous chapter, the constant returns to scale DEA is considered to compare the technical efficiency measures with the Cobb-Douglas stochastic production frontier model. In this chapter, the latter model is estimated using the different version of the stochastic production frontier set out in Coelli *et al.* (1998) to provide a different flavour to the model adopted earlier.

The Stochastic Production Frontier Model

The generalised version of the frontier model allows for a non-negative random component in the error term to generate a measure of technical inefficiency, or the ratio of actual to expected maximum output, given inputs and the existing technology. The specification can be expressed formally by:

$$Y_i=f(X_i, \beta, t)e^{vi-ui} \qquad (5.1)$$

where Y_i is output, X_i is a vector of inputs and β is a vector of parameters to be estimated.

The error term v_i is assumed to be independently and identically distributed as $N(0,\sigma^2_v)$ and captures random variation in output due to factors beyond the control of farms, such as variations in the weather. The error term u_i captures technical inefficiency in production, assumed to be firm-specific and follows a half-normal distribution. A higher value for u implies an increase in technical inefficiency. If u is zero, the farm is perfectly technically efficient. Following Battese and Coelli (1995),

$$u_i = \delta_0 + z_i\, \delta \tag{5.2}$$

defines an inefficiency distribution parameter for z_i, a vector of firm-specific effects that determine technical inefficiency and where δ is a vector of parameters to be estimated. The technical efficiency (TE) of the ith firm can be defined as:

$$TE_i = \frac{E(Y_i \mid u_i, X_i)}{E(Y_i \mid u_i = 0, X_i)} = e^{-u_i} \tag{5.3}$$

for E, the expectations operator. The measure of technical efficiency is thus based on the conditional expectation of equation (5.3), given the values of $(v_i - u_i)$ evaluated at the maximum likelihood estimates of the parameters in the model. This expression equals

$$E\left[\exp(u_i) \mid v_i - u_i\right] = \frac{1-\phi(\alpha_a + \gamma(v_i - u_i)/\sigma_a)}{1-\phi(\gamma(v_i - u_i)/\sigma_a)} \exp\left[\gamma(v_i - u_i) + \sigma_a^2/2\right] \tag{5.4}$$

where $\sigma_a = \sqrt{\gamma(1-\gamma)\sigma^2}, \sigma^2 \equiv \sigma_u^2 + \sigma_v^2, \gamma \equiv \sigma_u^2/\sigma^2$ and $\phi(\cdot)$ is the distribution function of a half normal random variable.

A value of γ closer to zero implies that much of the variation is due to random stochastic effects, whereas a value of γ closer to one implies differences mainly in the technical efficiency across firms. Based on the above, the following Cobb-Douglas model is estimated using the FRONTIER 4.1 program (see Coelli 1996b).[4]

$$\begin{aligned} Ln\, Y_i = {} & \beta_0 + \beta_1 Ln\,\text{LAN}_i + \beta_2 Ln\,\text{LAB}_i + \beta_3 Ln\,\text{BULL}_i + \beta_4 Ln\,\text{TRACT}_i + \beta_5 Ln\,\text{FERT}_i \\ & + \beta_6 Ln\,\text{WEED}_i + \beta_7 Ln\,\text{OTHER}_i + \beta_8\,\text{EROSION}_i + u_i + v_i \end{aligned} \tag{5.5}$$

for the ith farm and the technical inefficiency model as specified in equation (5.2) is:

$$\begin{aligned} u_i = {} & \alpha_0 + \alpha_1 Ln\text{AGE} + \alpha_2\, Ln\text{EDU} + \alpha_3\,\text{EXT} + \alpha_4\,\text{OFFINC} + \alpha_5\,\text{SOIL} \\ & + \alpha_6\,\text{OWN} + \alpha_7\,\text{LANTYPE} \end{aligned} \tag{5.6}$$

[4] The null hypothesis that all pairwise translog relationships between the input variables are zero could not be rejected by the likelihood ratio test while the null hypothesis that the coefficients of the Cobb-Douglas production function sum to one was not rejected at the 5% level of significance.

where SOIL represents land quality measured by four different proxies in the last 4 rows in table 5.2.

The estimates for the above equations are obtained simultaneously using the maximum likelihood function derived in Battese and Coelli (1995). All definitions of the variables in equations (5.5) and (5.6) are found in table 4.5 except for EROSION, EXT and SOIL, which are found in table 5.2.

Table 5.2. Definition of Variables

Variable	Definition	Measurement
EROSION	Extent of soil erosion	1 = low 2 = moderate 3 = severe
EXT	Attended soil conservation program	1 = yes, 0 = no
LANTYPE	Type of land Marginal land unsuitable for agriculture Problem soil needing lots of attention Land requiring some minor conservation First class returns on farming	 4 = very steep 3 = quite steep 2 = gentle 1 = flat
DRAIN	Drains installed	1= yes, 0 = no
CONSTYPE	Type of conservation adopted Traditional conservation Trash conservation Contour planting Contour planting and trash conservation Planting of vetivar grass	 1 = least effective 2 3 4 5 = most effective
CONS	Undertake soil conservation	1 = yes, 0 = no
COMP	Composite index Very steep land without drainage Quite steep land without drainage Gently steeped land without drainage Flat land without drainage Very steep land with drainage Quite steep land with drainage Gently steeped land with drainage Flat land with drainage	 1= least effective 2 3 4 5 6 7 8 = most effective

Note: See Appendix 5.1 for explanation on types of soil conservation measures adopted.

An attempt is made to rank the types of conservation measures (CONSTYPE) to see if this matters in improving TE (see Appendix 1). As soil is lost during clearing and rainfall, there is potential for run-off and deep drainage with a possible environmental impact associated with the movements of nutrients and pesticides. Farmers have, however, been long encouraged to plant rice as it acts as cover crop during the rainy season and before cane is replanted (Fiji Sugar Cane Research Centre Annual Report 2002/03). But rain also disrupts harvesting, which under wet conditions can cause loss of cane stool, soil structural damage and soil compaction. Thus, contour banks and trash conservation are important to help reduce soil erosion, although both make it difficult to harvest.[5] The report also found that total soil loss was greatest (at 17.0 ton/ha) from plots that had furrows running up and down hill – followed by contour planting at 10.1 ton/ha. In contrast, the total erosion from contour with vetivar hedgerow plots with cane was only 7.6 tons/ha.

The second issue is our attempt to construct a composite index relating land types to drains in place. With land types, flat land was observed to be good for farming – but flat land is not necessarily good for farming without drains in place for several reasons (James ed. 2004). First, is the physical effect of water logging cane roots; and second, a temperature effect of water logging which can cause burning and scalding of roots. It is important to get rid of excess water by having drains as this allows well-drained soils to be worked to a good tilth for soil cultivation. Therefore, to better capture the combined effects of land type and effort to install drains, we constructed a simple composite index (COMP) as an interactive term of the two variables and ordered in ascending numbers representing greater effectiveness. Thus, the order (of 1 to 8) would start from the poorest land types without drainage followed by those with drainage – that is, very steep land without drainage would be represented by 1, quite steep land without drainage would be ordered 2, and so on. Hence, the most effective type – denoted by number 8 – would be for flat land with drainage.

The composite index is, however, not without its limitations. First, it is unable to incorporate soil fertility measures, as data for that do not currently exist for Fiji. Second, the application of herbicides and fertilizers and the use of high-yielding varieties can help overcome some negative effects of soil erosion to produce cane efficiently. Third, conservation effort of various types, as stated in table 5.1, can also reduce some of the adverse effects of land type and drains not in place. But an attempt to incorporate conservation effort is a complex and unmanageable task as such an index increases the subjectivity inherent in the composite index.

Empirical Results

The estimated parametric production function's input shares are given in table 5.3 where all the input coefficients are significant at the 5% level, except for other expenditure incurred by farmers. This is similar to the results in table 4.7. The estimate of γ, which is the ratio of the variance of farm-specific performance of TE to total variance of output, is statistically significant at the 1% level. This implies that the variation in TE among sample farmers is not due to statistical chance factors, but principally to individual TE differences.

The technical efficiency measures for the sample using parametric and nonparametric approaches with and without soil erosion are reported in table 5.4. By and large, the inclusion of the environment variable results in lower TE measures (under both approaches) and the difference in the mean (as well as the minimum efficiency) is significant at the 5% level.

Thus, it is important to ensure that the TE measures are not inflated due to the neglect of soil erosion in production efficiency. On average, the parametric approach, with soil erosion as an input, provided a TE measure of 69.4% – which means that it is possible to increase output by about 30% if inputs and technology are used efficiently. As expected, the mean efficiency scores from the DEA frontier are less than those obtained from the stochastic

[5] Another disadvantage of contour banking is the inevitable reduction in the area available for farming.

frontier because DEA attributes any deviation from the frontier to inefficiency. However, the differences between the efficiency measures of the two approaches are not statistically significant at the 5% level, thus providing robustness to the TE measures obtained for further empirical investigation in relation to policy making.

Table 5.3. Maximum Likelihood Estimates of Model

Variables	Parameters	Coefficients
Production frontier model		
Constant	β_0	1.916 (0.271)*
Land	β_1	0.58 (0.066)*
Labor	β_2	0.21 (0.059)*
Bullock hours	β_3	0.083 (0.023)*
Tractor hours	β_4	0.019 (0.004)*
Fertiliser use	β_5	0.041 (0.019)*
Weedicide use	β_6	0.032 (0.011)*
Other expenditure	β_7	0.029 (0.019)
Soil erosion	β_8	0.106 (0.043)*
Variance parameters		
	σ^2	0.053 (0.018)
	γ	0.901 (0.079)
Log likelihood		89.75
Mean efficiency	0.694	
Total sample	677	

Notes:

1. Figures in parenthesis are standard errors.
2. * and ** means that the coefficient is significant at the 5% and 10% level respectively.

Importantly, table 5.4 can be used to obtain a crude estimation of the impact of soil erosion on output with a monetary value of that loss. The mean TE differences between both the measures that have and have not used soil erosion indicates a loss of 6.8% (7.3%) in TE from the parametric (non-parametric) approach, providing an average TE loss of about 7%. As the total cane produced in 2003 was 2,600,000 tons, soil erosion is seen to result in a loss of 241,060 tons of cane, which is about 9.3% of cane produced. This amounts to a loss of US$8 million in cane output while the industry loses US$12 million in sugar sales.[6]

[6] This is based on data of cane price of F$60/ton paid to growers, a ton of cane to a ton of sugar ratio of 8.89, and sales for local consumption and export (ratios obtained from ex-post data) priced at F$440/ton and F$832/ton, respectively.

Table 5.4. Comparison of Technical Efficiency Measures (%)

	Parametric Approach		Non-parametric Approach	
Efficiency	Without soil erosion variable	With soil erosion variable	Without soil erosion variable	With soil erosion variable
Mean	76.2	69.4	74.8	67.5
Maximum	92.4	91.6	100	100
Minimum	46.8	37.2	44.3	36.4

Correlation between Independent Variables

Before discussing the determinants of technical inefficiency, it is necessary to discuss the correlation matrix of the independent variables that will be used in the regressions to minimise multicollinearity in the estimations. Table 5.5 helps identify the variables that can be appropriately used in the same regression to avoid multicollinearity. Often, age and education can be expected to be negatively correlated but this is not high for this sample of farmers.

There also appears to be little correlation between farmers who have off-farm income and those who own land. It is, however, not surprising – especially where dummy variables are concerned – as there is little correlation in terms of an increase or decrease that can be accurately picked up, even if there is a close relationship between them. For instance, older farmers could adopt conservation because they have more experience, or they could be less willing to bear the risk of investing in soil conservation due to their shorter planning horizons. Also, younger farmers may be more educated and have a better ability to obtain and understand information about efficiency and soil conservation effort, and therefore be more involved with innovative farming practices.

Determinants of Technical Efficiency

For the sake of brevity and because similar results were obtained, the regression estimations with the DEA-generated TE measures are not reported. The estimates in table 5.6 however need to be interpreted with caution as a negative sign on a coefficient indicates that an increase in the value of the variable results in a decrease in inefficiency as represented by u_i in equation (5.6). Various models have been estimated to provide different types of information on land quality and the choice of variables in the regressions are dictated by the correlation relationships in table 5.5. At the outset, it must be noted that there were no problems with functional form misspecification and autocorrelation, but some of the models were corrected for heteroscedasticity (as can be expected with a cross-sectional sample) using White's (1980) procedure.

The R^2s obtained for the model estimations ranged from 0.79 to 0.83, which is reasonably good for a cross-sectional study. The consistency in the signs and significance of coefficients on the first five variables in table 5.6 across all the models show that the results are sufficiently robust and conclusive for interpretation. Studenmund (2000) further explains that if such consistency is not affected by the omission and addition of the variables and there are reasonably high R^2s (as found here), then there is little need to worry about spurious results.

Table 5.5. Correlation Matrix of the Independent Variables

Variable	AGE	EDU	OFFINC	OWN	LANTYPE	EXT	DRAIN	CONS	CONS TYPE	COMP
AGE	1									
EDUC	-0.138	1								
OFFINC	0.020	0.011	1							
OWN	-0.007	0.032	-0.079	1						
LANTYPE	-0.025	0.075	0.040	-0.044	1					
EXT	-0.058	0.001	-0.040	0.017	-0.036	1				
DRAIN	0.131	0.126	-0.089	0.146	0.205	0.128	1			
CONS	0.014	0.201	-0.115	0.257	0.113	0.206	0.107	1		
CONSTYPE	0.251	0.151	-0.066	0.185	0.169	0.103	0.188	0.139	1	
COMP	0.108	0.095	0.182	0.112	0.201	0.225	0.243	0.056	0.301	1

Table 5.6. Determinants of Technical Inefficiency

Variable	Model 1	Model 2	Model 3	Model 4	Model 5
Age	-0.101 (0.025)*	-0.112 (0.029)*	-0.206 (0.031)*	-0.153 (0.047)*	-0.147 (0.035)*
Education	-0.092 (0.016)*	-0.103 (0.019)*	-0.086 (0.018)*	-0.079 (0.012)*	-0.096 (0.024)*
Off farm income	0.713 (0.227)*	0.625 (0.208)*	0.704 (0.189)*	0.669 (0.192)*	0.735 (0.216)*
Own land	-1.506 (0.612)*	-1.317 (0.458)*	-0.993 (0.374)*	-1.087 (0.404)*	-1.224 (0.537)*
Type of land	0.854 (0.301)*	0.903 (0.413)*	1.125 (0.458)*	1.034 (0.399)*	0.951 (0.446)*
Extension program	–	-0.778 (0.331)*	–	–	–
Drains installed	-0.953 (0.359)**	–	–	–	-1.141 (0.408)**
Undertake conservation	–	–	–	-0.704 (0.256)*	-0.852 (0.306)*
Type of conservation	-0.694 (0.436)	–	-0.882 (0.551)	–	–
Composite index	–	–	-0.564 (0.213)*	-0.603 (0.227)*	–

Notes:

1. Standard deviation in parenthesis.
2. * and ** means the coefficient is significant at the 5% and 1% levels respectively.

It can be seen that age and education positively impact on technical efficiency since older farmers are experienced and hence more knowledgeable about cane farming. The more educated the farmer, the better exposed and understanding he has in the adoption of good farming practices related to cane varieties, soil conservation measures, and the appropriate usage of fertilizers and weedicide. The class of land, on the other hand, deters efficiency improvements because higher-class land indicates it is more sloping, which raises cultivation costs and reduces the response rate from fertilizer application.

With regards to land tenure, the owner-occupied farm efficiency is higher than that of tenant farms. Clearly, the land uncertainty issue needs to be resolved urgently if farm efficiency is to be improved for the viability of the sugar industry. Coupled with the erosion of sugar prices, farmers are extremely concerned about the future of cane farming. These same concerns explain the negative and significant coefficient found for off-farm income. As the alternative source of income increases, technical inefficiency increases because farming becomes a secondary interest in that the returns on cane farming are not sufficient enough to invest in improving land productivity by undertaking soil conservation measures.

The coefficient on land type is positive (the greater the slope of the land, the higher the technical inefficiency) and significant. Flat land reduces cultivation costs and increases the response rate from fertiliser use. It also increases effort to minimise soil erosion from sloping land, thereby raising the efficiency of cane production.

Next we turn to the variables that measure land quality and soil conservation efforts. Model 2 shows that farmers who have attended soil conservation programs provided by extension services are more aware of the various aspects of farming practice. Examples of what they learn include the following: the importance of soil moisture and hence trash conservation; the installation of run-off and control measures to carry run-off water at low velocities to grasses waterways; trash retention to suppress weed growth and reduce the likelihood of soil compaction; and the appropriate use in the amount as well as timing and method of applying fertilizer.

In particular, it is evident from models 4 and 5 that farmers who practiced any one of the five types of soil conservation measures (CONS) outlined in table 1 are more technically efficient. However, TE is not affected by the type of conservation measure used as seen by the insignificance of the coefficient on CONSTYPE in models 1 and 3. This could be because the variable is unable to capture the extent and how effectively or correctly the method is actually used on the farm.

The coefficient on DRAINS is negative, as expected, and improves TE significantly in models 1 and 5. Finally, the coefficient on the composite index is highly significant at the 1% level (as seen in models 3 and 4), reinforcing the hypothesis that a combination of land type and drainage is a crucial factor in improving TE.

Willingness to Adopt Soil Conservation

This section examines factors that affect cane farmers' adoption of soil conservation measures. It contributes to the existing literature in the following ways. Most of the previous soil conservation studies treat adoption of soil conservation as a binary choice decision in which a farmer either adopts a recommended technology or not. Here, we consider a range of adoption possibilities, including traditional and other types of soil conservation. We also take into account the fact that a farmer's perception of the soil erosion problem and the amount of conservation effort are determined simultaneously. The endogeneity of the perception variable is accounted for by using appropriate estimation methods.

Hypotheses and Conceptual Model

Following Ervin and Ervin (1982), we hypothesise that the decision-making process to adopt soil conservation measures begins with a perception of the erosion problem seen in figure 5.1. The degree of this perception depends on the farmer's personal characteristics (such as age, education, conservation attitudes), and the physical characteristics of the land (such as slope). The effect of age on adoption of soil conservation is not clear. On the one hand, older farmers could adopt conservation because they have more experience. But, on the other hand, they could be less willing to bear the risk of investing in soil conservation due to their shorter planning horizons. Also, younger farmers may be more educated and therefore more involved with innovative farming practices and, consequently, will be more aware of erosion problems and solutions.

Higher education levels are hypothesised to be associated with improved knowledge about conservation measures and the productivity effects of erosion. As shown in the diagram, institutional factors, such as extension education, may also assist in heightening awareness of the soil erosion problem. Once the farmer has perceived the erosion problem, he/she decides to adopt a soil conservation practice(s). This decision is affected by personal, institutional, physical, and economic factors. For example, the higher the level of education, the more information and awareness the farmer has regarding the costs and benefits of soil conservation – therefore the more likely he/she is to adopt a given practice. Institutional factors such as extension programs and the possibility to share costs may persuade farmers to adopt particular measures.

The perceived extent of actual or potential physical erosion on the farm may also persuade a farmer to choose a particular measure. Economic factors – such as net farm income, off-farm income, risk aversion, discount rate/planning period, debt status, and land tenure – may either inhibit or enhance a farmer's inclination towards adopting soil conservation. For example, a high level of debt or low net farm income will tend to reduce the probability of adopting a capital-intensive measure, while lack of secure tenure will reduce incentives for investing in conservation measures.

The final step in the process is the determination of soil conservation effort. The choice of soil conservation effort is affect by the four factors outlined above. Personal factors such as education and farming experience affect the proper application and maintenance of soil conservation practices. The choice of how much effort to apply also depends on the physical characteristics of the land such as slope and farm size. However, because measures that are more efficient in reducing erosion are more expensive, we hypothesise that conservation effort will be more significantly affected by the economic factors.

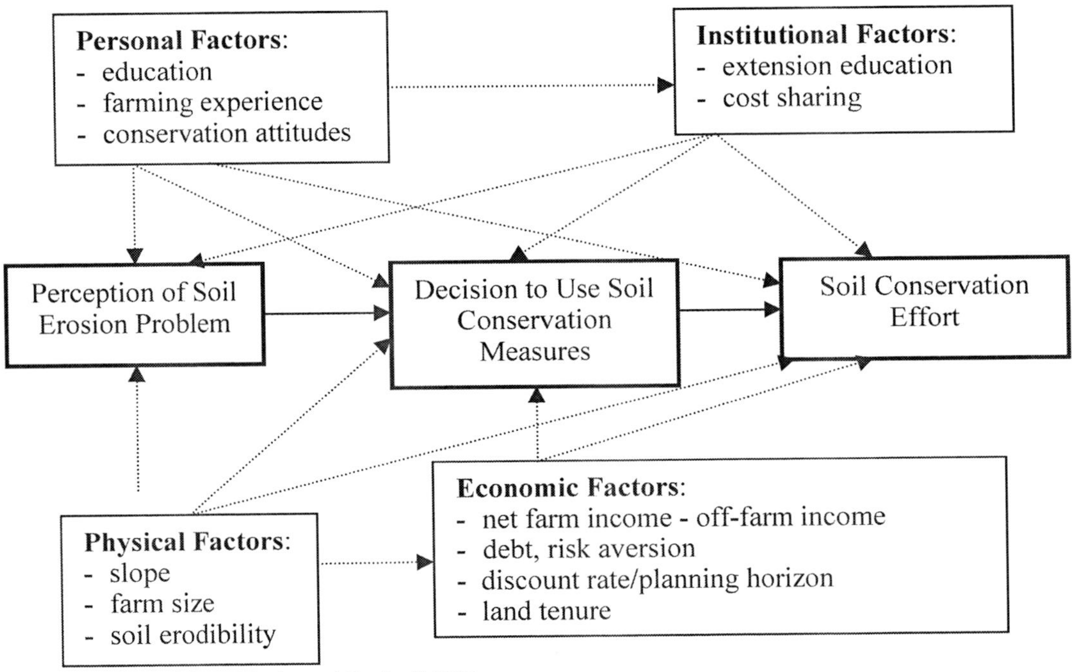

Source: Adapted from Ervin and Ervin (1982).

Figure 5.1. The Decision to Use Soil Conservation.

Empirical Model and Variables

In the past, analytical models such as probit and logit models have been used to analyse farmers' adoption decisions – but a farmer's decision to use a particular technology is not necessarily binary (i.e. yes/no) but may be multivariate in nature. As has been pointed out by Lynne *et al.* (1988) and Dorfman (1996), using a binary dependent variable could lead to the loss of useful economic information contained in the interdependent and simultaneous adoption decisions. In this chapter, we use an extension of the tobit model to analyse the soil conservation behaviour of the sample farmers.

We assume that farmers respond to their circumstances within a utility-maximising framework. Let U_{i1} represent the perceived utility from adopting a soil conservation measure, while U_{i0} represents utility from the traditional farming practice. Also, let X_i represent the set of socioeconomic, institutional, and physical factors which influence the adoption decisions of farmer *i*. Although not directly observable, the utility function of a given farmer (*i*) from using a given measure (*j*) can be written as:

$$U_{ij} = G_i(X_j) + e_{ij}; \quad j = 1,0; i = 1, \dots, n \tag{5.7}$$

where G_i is a farm-specific function, e_{ij} is a disturbance term with zero mean and constant variance, and 1 represents adoption of a soil conservation measure and 0 represents non-adoption.

The ith farmer adopts, that is $j = 1$, if $U_{i1} > U_{i0}$. Assuming that G is linear, we can express the underlying stochastic model by the following relationship:

$$Y_j = X_j'\beta + \varepsilon_i \text{ if } X_j'\beta + \varepsilon_i > 0; \quad i = 1, \dots, n \tag{5.8a}$$

$$Y_i = 0 \text{ if } X_j'\beta + \varepsilon_i \leq 0 \tag{5.8b}$$

where Y_j is the dependent variable, X_j' is a vector of independent variables, β is a vector of coefficients, and ε_{ij} are independently and identically distributed error terms assumed to be normal with zero mean and constant variance σ^2.

Rather than frame the expected utility of adoption as a binary choice, we use a censored regression model that implies continuous choice over some predetermined interval, thereby allowing us to consider a range of adoption possibilities. Let Y^*_j be a latent variable that depends linearly on the explanatory variables:

$$Y^*_j = X_j'\beta + \varepsilon_i \tag{5.9}$$

The observed Y_j is determined from Y^*_j using the rule:

$$Y_i = \begin{cases} 0 \text{ if } Y_i^* \leq \gamma_1 \\ 1 \text{ if } \gamma_1 < Y_i^* \leq \gamma_2 \\ 2 \text{ if } \gamma_2 < Y_i^* \leq \gamma_3 \\ . \\ . \\ \text{M if } \gamma_\text{M} < Y_i^* \end{cases} \tag{5.10}$$

where the γ_i's are threshold values.

It follows that the probability of observing a given value of Y (e.g. $Y = 1$) is given by:

$$P(Y_i = 1 | X_i, \beta, \gamma) = F(\gamma_2 - X_i'\beta) - F(\gamma_1 - X_i'\beta) \tag{5.11}$$

where F is the cumulative distribution function of ε.

In censored regression models, a change in X_i in has two effects: an effect on the mean of Y, given that it is observed, and an effect on the probability of Y being observed (McDonald and Moffitt, 1980). Therefore, the regression coefficients cannot be interpreted as the effect on Y of marginal changes in X_i.

In order to test the hypothesised relationships outlined in the decision-making process in figure 5.1, we construct two variables to measure the three components of the decision-making process. That is, perception of the soil erosion problem, the decision to use a soil conservation practice and soil conservation effort. To measure perception of the soil erosion problem (*PERCEP*), the respondents were asked to indicate the extent of soil erosion on their land. Possible responses to this question (and their values) are low (1), moderate (2), and severe (3).

To measure the second and third components, the respondents were presented with a hypothetical scenario in which the government proposes to introduce a program of planting vetiver grass strips on farmers' land to reduce soil erosion. It was pointed out that although the grass would reduce the planting area, it would increase the harvest in the long run as the land became more fertile due to less soil erosion. The respondents were then asked whether they would participate in the program. The possible response to this soil conservation decision was either a yes (1) or no (0). If the farmer agreed to participate in the program, he/she was then asked to indicate how many vetiver grass strips they would volunteer to plant on their land (*EFFORT*).[7] Ideally, measurement of soil conservation effort should be related to either physical units of conservation or expenditures on soil conservation practices. However, this type of information required more detailed data, which was not feasible to incorporate into the survey given time and resource constraints.

From the conceptual framework described in figure 5.1, it can be seen that a farmer's perception of the erosion problem and the decision to adopt a conservation measure are interrelated. That is, it seems very likely that farmers' perceptions are driven by their experience, and hence determined simultaneously with the variable *EFFORT*. Thus, the variable *PERCEP* is endogenous and hence simultaneously determined with the *EFFORT* variable using the two-stage approach. In the first stage, we estimate *PERCEP* as a function of the independent variables listed below in equation (5.12) and in the second stage, a predicted value of *PERCEP* ($PERCEP^*$) is used as an independent variable in the *EFFORT* equation. The following models are therefore estimated.

$$PERCEP = f(AGE, EDU, EXPER, ETHN, EXTN, DIST) \qquad (5.12)$$

$$EFFORT = f(PERCEP^*, FINC, FSTAT, OWN, LAN, CLASS) \qquad (5.13)$$

The independent variables are as defined in table 4.5 except for *FINC*, which represents the net farm income of farmers and was found to be F$1759 on average for the sample.

Empirical Results

The above estimations are tabulated in tables 5.7 and 5.8 where it can be seen that the key variables affecting perception of the soil erosion problem are personal characteristics such as age, experience, ethnicity, exposure to extension education, and distance from a research station. An interaction variable for age and education is included to account for the high correlation between these two variables.

The coefficient on age is positive and highly significant. This implies that when we control for key variables – such as farming experience, educational attainment, ethnicity, and extension – the age of a farmer is important in his/her ability to perceive the effects of erosion. Also, we see that the coefficient on experience is also significant. Therefore, as expected, older and more experienced farmers are more likely to perceive the erosion problem. The coefficient on education is positive but not statistically significant, while the

[7] The mean number of strips in the sample was found to be 2.91. For the analysis, the number of strips divided by the farm area was used.

interaction variable for age and education is also not significant. Therefore, educational attainment can be considered as less important in affecting perceptions of the soil erosion problem in this case.

Table 5.7. Regression Estimates for the Perception of the Soil Erosion Problem

Variable	Coefficient	*z*-Statistic	*p*-value
AGE	0.0235	4.2122	0.0000
EXP	0.0388	3.3588	0.0008
EDU	0.0107	0.2468	0.8051
*AGE*EDU*	-0.0007	-0.7885	0.4304
ETHN	-0.4633	-3.1923	0.0014
EXTN	0.6297	2.3337	0.0196
DIST	-0.0651	-7.8226	0.0000
Log-likelihood	870.86		
Wald χ^2 statistic	327.0		

The coefficient on ethnicity is statistically significant. Bearing in mind that this a dummy variable with "0" representing indigenous Fijian farmers, the negative coefficient implies that when we control for key intervening variables such as experience, education, age, and extension, Indo-Fijian farmers are more likely to perceive the soil erosion problem better than indigenous Fijian farmers. This result is unsurprising given that the former have more farming experience than the latter.

Extension education has a significant positive effect on perception of the soil erosion problem, confirming the findings of previous studies. Contrary to expectations, economic factors (net farm income, farming status, and land ownership), as well as physical factors (land size cultivated and class of land) did not exert any significant influences on perception of the soil erosion problem and were omitted in the final model. Finally, *DIST* is significant in that farmers who live closer to a research station are more likely to be perceptive of the soil erosion problem due to the benefit of the demonstration effect. A Wald χ^2 test for the null hypothesis that all the independent variables in the model are jointly zero gave a test statistic of 327.0 with a *p*-value of 0.000, convincingly rejecting the null hypothesis. Therefore, all the variables significantly contribute to the fit of the model.

Table 5.8 presents results for soil conservation effort (equation 5.13) once the adoption decision has been made. Looking first at the *EFFORT* equation, it can be seen that the coefficient on the perception variable has the expected positive sign and is highly significant. This implies that the more perceptive the farmer, the more likely he (or she) is to make a greater conservation effort. As expected, net farm income has the expected positive sign and is statistically significant. The coefficient on farming status is also significant, implying that full-time farmers are more likely to make greater conservation effort than part-time farmers.

The coefficient on land ownership (*OWN*) is positive and significant, confirming that security of tenure affects a long-term investment such as soil conservation. We may conclude from this that farmers with smaller plots are unlikely to undertake soil conservation on account of the higher short-term opportunity cost of investing in such measures.

Table 5.8. Regression Estimates for Soil Conservation Effort

Variable	Coefficient	z-Statistic	*p*-value
PERCEP[*]	0.4786	10.6149	0.0000
FSTAT	0.4475	6.2386	0.0000
FINC	0.0001	3.1565	0.0016
OWN	0.0700	1.0268	0.3045
CLASS	-0.1439	-5.1167	0.0000
Log-likelihood	-537.69		
Wald χ^2 statistic	220.48		

Finally, as expected from theory, the coefficient on class of land is positive and highly significant, implying that farmers cultivating the more marginal land are expected to maker greater soil conservation effort, *ceteris paribus*. A Wald χ^2 test for the null hypothesis that all the independent variables are jointly zero gave a test statistic of 220.48 with a *p*-value of 0.000. Therefore the model variables significantly predict conservation effort.

CONCLUSION

In general, there is a lack of environmental concern in Fiji among policy makers and the community at large. Policy makers were always more concerned about income and employment generation, which is reflected in the national and sectoral development policies and plans. And due to the uncertainty of lease renewal and cost of affordability, farmers were unwilling to invest in soil conservation measures to improve cane yield.

The cost of soil erosion in terms of cane output was, however, found to be significant, resulting in a loss of US$8 million worth of cane output to farmers while the industry lost US$12 million in sugar sales. With soil conservation, while the type of method adopted does not affect efficiency, farmers' participation in soil conservation programs offered by extension education, as well as drains installed to reduce soil erosion, improve efficiency significantly.

Unfortunately, the strong indication is that soil conservation efforts have a long way to go in Fiji and will not be addressed soon. First, one major problem facing environmental management in the country is the institutional weakness in implementing and enforcing environmental legislation. Currently, the ADB is focusing its efforts to assist the government and incorporate this aspect in its future loans – but, to date, progress is very slow.

Second, there is a need to change farmers' attitudes towards investing in these efforts by increasing public awareness and the availability of soil conservation techniques. There is also a need to implement an effective incentive system to make it worthwhile for farmers to adopt soil conservation measures. Extension services and follow-up visits related to planting of seed cane, the avoidance of cane burning, and weedicide and fertilizer use are required so that an integrated model of farm practice and management for varying topography and soils can be effectively established.

APPENDIX 5.1. TYPES OF SOIL CONSERVATION MEASURES

1. Planting of vetivar grass is inexpensive and easy. It is often grown along contour lines on sloping lands. This grass is known to quickly form narrow and very dense hedge. Its stiff foliage blocks the passage of soil and debris, slows down any runoff and gives rainfall a better chance of soaking into the soil.
2. Contour planting (which is designed to carry run-off water at low velocity across the slope to grassed waterways) with trash conservation is the most cost effective water and soil conservation practice for cane farms on hilly land.
3. Trash conservation is a low-cost method where farmers leave the trash (sugarcane crop residue after harvest) on the ground to conserve soil moisture, reduce run-off rates and sediment concentration in run-off water. As well, it suppresses weed growth and reduces the likelihood of soil compaction. Without trash conservation, especially during the early growth period before close-in, the soil surface is exposed directly to the impact of rain and, hence, suffers from a high rate of erosion. This is especially so in the case of plant crop because the surface soil is soft and loose.
4. Traditional/conventional conservation is not very effective because, traditionally, farmers do not treat the whole farm but only selected spots. It consists of the erection of bunds made of stones or pieces of wood to minimise or prevent soil being washed off. This also means that the bare soil surface remains mostly unprotected until after harvest.

Chapter 6

REFORMING THE CANE AND SUGAR INDUSTRY

INTRODUCTION

The withdrawal of sugar subsidies by the EU became imminent from 1986 when agriculture was brought within the ambit of the GATT, and particularly since December 1994 following the EU's commitment to limit the value of export subsidies at the conclusion of the Uruguay Round. Thus Fiji, to some extent, was quite prepared to face the music. This is reflected in the many but futile attempts to consider sugar reform based on various inquiries and consultancies. The objective of this chapter is to review key features of these reports and other relevant studies to highlight the multi-faceted problems facing Fiji's cane and sugar industry and the possible options for strengthening its competitiveness.

THE REFORM PROPOSALS

In 1981, the Fiji government commissioned the consultancy firm Brooker Agriculture International Limited to conduct one of the earliest reform studies. But the UK-based consulting firm, Landell Mills Commodities Studies, undertook the first comprehensive *Review of the Sugar Industry in Fiji* in 1991. This was then followed by the *Sugar Industry Strategic Plan* by an Australian consultant sponsored by AusAID in 1997. In 2004, there was the report from the Indian Sugar Technology Mission, entitled, *Revival of the Sugar Industry in Fiji* (Indian Technology Mission, 2004). There were others reports: one by the consultancy firm TechEcon in 1993; the *McWhinney Report* in 1996; and the ADB Report in 2005.

Not surprisingly, there has been much criticism that these reports have cost a lot of money without resulting in any reform. In fact, the reports are seen by many to merely gather dust and an office bearer of one of the unions was quoted by *The Review* as having said, 'debating these issues endlessly will not produce an extra ounce, or an increase in the quality of sugar.' The general consensus on the reform front is that there is agreement on what needs to be done to revive the industry: but a dire lack of political will and financial resources to implement them.

Snell and Prasad (2001) voiced a similar concern. They were suspicious that the choice of experts for the consultancies depended largely upon the consensus reached with the Sugar

Commission of Fiji. This was seen to ensure that policy advice was generally in line with expectations of the FSC and sugar industry institutions as well as the ruling government. The authors were particularly critical of the benchmarking methodology, premised on international best practice, used by the *1997 Sugar Industry Strategic Plan.* They argued that this concept, while accepted and often used in the Western business schools of thought, meant little to the stakeholders in the industry. This approach to restructuring was not seen as locally sensitive to development practices, and advocated the change of power over the production process from the farmers and mill workers to the mill managers.

Now that reality has hit hard with the impending EU sugar preference erosion at the end of 2007, Fiji is forced to seriously consider restructuring its cane and sugar industry. The problems facing the industry can be broadly defined as: low productivity in cane farming; inefficiency in the sugar mills; poor weather conditions; the nature of the cane payment system; and harvesting problems. Each of these issues is discussed below with the options available for diversifying sugar production to make the industry viable.

Poor Weather Conditions

Apart from rice and tree crops, sugarcane is one of the heaviest users of water. Entirely rain-fed cane areas require a consistent and reliable rainfall pattern that meets or provides a good percentage of the crop's water demand for at least nine months of the year (James ed. 2004). In Fiji, sugarcane is planted early in the year and is harvested once every year between July and December. While December to April is the wettest season, unfortunately, cane farming conditions in Fiji are less than ideal given its total reliance on rain. Erratic weather conditions with cyclones and drought (within the same year) raise the risk of a low cane and sugar yield. Table 6.1 shows the frequency of unfavourable weather in Fiji. While dry conditions are not conducive for crop growth for obvious reasons,[1] excessive rain brings with it difficulties in harvesting, loading, transportation to the mills, and in maintaining cane yield and quality.

Table 6.1. Weather Conditions

Drought	Excessive Rain
Near dry conditions in 1979	Two cyclones each in 1979 and 1984
Two spells of dry conditions in 1980	One cyclone in 1983, 1990, 1993, 2003
1982, 1983, 1985, 1988, 1997, 2002, 2003	Floods in 1998, 1999, 2000, 2004

Rainfall causes leaching of nutrients from the soil, and adversely affects cane quality on flat lands with improper drainage.[2] Cyclones cause lodging of cane where it gets stunted, falls and gets twisted, making harvesting difficult – hence much of the stem must be cut off, thereby losing cane and, therefore, sugar. Also, heavy rains disrupt cane supply to the mills

[1] Droughts can have severe effects as seen in the 2003 season where cane crop suffered 60% damage in the hilly areas, leveling out to between 25-30% devastation in other areas (National Farmers Union 2003).

[2] Inadequate drainage was a complaint of 47% of the farmers surveyed who did not see the point of paying drainage fee. Drainage lowers the free water table to increase the root zone to enable a greater absorption of nutrients and water by the plant roots.

and the mills suspend crushing to economise on the under-utilisation of mill capacity and lower production costs.[3] Cane is a low-density, low-value, perishable product that must be moved without causing serious damage to the soil structure and cane stools – then transported quickly to prevent deterioration in cane quality (James ed. 2004).

Unfavourable weather conditions also make it (politically) necessary for farmers to be compensated, thereby reducing the funds available for improving production. For instance, as of June 2004, the government owed F$27 million to the Cane Growers Fund that was used to help farmers in times of bad weather.[4] Although the recent (2004) sugar proposal by the Indian team has recommended that irrigation (such as rainwater harvesting techniques, lift irrigation scheme and bore holes) be provided for drought years, little notice of this is being taken as seen in the 2006 *National Adaptation Strategy for the Fiji Sugar Industry*. This is possibly due to different priorities given the limited funds and the existing constraints to irrigation.

For instance, it is explained in FSC (1987) that although most cane planted along the shores can be easily irrigated due to the land being flat, these areas contain brackish to salty water at least 3 km upstream, and this does not make it viable for irrigation. Although fresh water is available upstream where the land is undulating to hilly, such terrain limits the use of travelling irrigators, as the uphill movement would damage the operators. The terrain is also likely to put additional pressure on the pumps and, as a consequence, nozzle pressure is reduced. Low nozzle pressure does not permit the water to "break", and so the cane stools can be uprooted or lodged.

FARMING PRACTICES

While sugarcane has often been described by the Fijians as a lazy man's crop requiring relatively less care than other crops, there are some farming practices involving input use, soil erosion and cane burning that could adversely affect production. While chapter four (see table 4.9) quantified the efficiency of inputs such as land, labour, bullock, tractor and fertilizer use, chapter five quantified the impact of soil erosion on output and efficiency and the resulting loss in farm and industry revenue. This section provides a qualitative discussion on some farming practices drawing on the survey interviews.

SOIL EROSION AND INPUT USE

Although most of the farmers surveyed agreed that soil erosion should be avoided, only 54% believed that, in the long term, the benefits of undertaking soil conservation outweighed the costs. This is compounded by the low profits earned by farmers, which average about F$30-F$40 per ton of cane with an average total cost[5] per ton of cane ranging from F$20-

---

[3] FSC officials in June 2004 said that their policy was to stop mill operations if they anticipate less than 65% of the crushing requirement of the mill or if they expect the fall in cane supply to continue for more than four days.

[4] Interview with Mr. Jagannath Sami, the Chief Executive Officer of the Sugarcane Growers Council, in July 2005.

[5] This includes input costs (such as planting, land preparation, purchase of fertilizer and weedicide), harvest, transport, roads and drainage fee, and land rental.

F$26 (Government of Fiji 2006a). This does not leave much to be spent on soil conservation measures. But Gawander (1998) argues that the vetivar grass – which is cheap, easy to grow and maintain, and extremely effective in controlling soil erosion – is not being used these days due to the use of lorries for transport which require more space to get into the cane land. Walter *et al.* (2003) also highly recommend hedgerows on hill slopes in Europe – but like Fiji, intensive farming in Europe has increasingly reduced the use of a hedgerow network.

Perhaps less surprising is the finding that only 30% of the farmers felt that soil erosion was a problem that needed the same attention as the other primary concerns (production costs, land tenure and poor returns on cane). In particular, when farmers were asked why did not attend soil conservation programs, they explained that although extension education assisted in heightening awareness of the soil erosion problem, there had not been follow-up farm visits by extension officers. These were necessary to observe the fields at various stages to identify problems and provide advice and assistance in the adoption of soil conservation. This failure is due to a lack of funding to employ enough extension officers – the FSC has been in financial strife since the late 1990s.

Although informal extension advice can be accessed through the media or by seeking the help of leading or best practice farmers to share their expertise, this too requires funding and incentives. Furthermore, there needs to be individualised programs rather than a one-size-fits-all approach for extension education. For instance, less educated farmers need more technical education to understand the consequences of erosion and the benefits of unfamiliar conservation practices.

On the other hand, it has been argued that neither education alone nor extension services alone are likely to be effective at the margin and that to induce adoption practices, cash payments, incentives, subsidies or some form of cost sharing must be put in place (e.g., see Sheriff 2005). For instance, expenditure on soil conservation could be made tax deductible, but this might be difficult or costly to monitor.

In the face of stretched budgetary resources, soil conservation does not appear to be at the top of the Fiji government's spending priorities. This can be seen in the *National Adaptation Strategy for the Fiji Sugar Industry* tabled on 31st August 2006 by the Fijian government. An earlier report (Leslie and Ratukalou 2002) documents serious under-resourcing of the ministries with responsibilities for agriculture and forestry, and the lack of expertise in the areas of agricultural extension in general, and soil conservation in particular. Given that a reduction in soil erosion could generate significant public and private benefits, there is the need for the government to explore avenues, perhaps with donor assistance, to devote more resources to address the problem.

There has, at least on paper, been some effort towards this end as witnessed by the endorsement of the *Rural Land Use Policy* in June 2005, which will become part of the *Land Conservation Act*. But even if a soil conservation policy is implemented, it can be expected to take a voluntary rather than a regulatory approach at this stage. The voluntary approach would be ineffective since it is difficult to discriminate between farmers who adopt the soil conservation measures and those who do not find a given practice profitable (Sheriff 2005). At the same time, the potential for changing programs to incorporate both carrots and sticks – requiring compliance with erosion reduction goals to be eligible for other price subsidies or a regulatory approach – is unlikely to enjoy high public favour among farmers. It is, therefore, not surprising that no action was taken, even though, as part of the Environment Protection Policy, an Environmental Code of Practice for Cane Farming was approved in August 2002.

This was then given to the Sugar Cane Growers Council Sector Councilors and to FSC Field Staff for implementation (Sugar Commission of Fiji Annual Report 2002).

Also, while fertilizers and weedicides (pre-emergent and post-emergent herbicides) can improve soil quality, they are not considered cheap in Fiji. The cost of fertilizer can take up, on average, about 30–40% of input costs, and weedicide can account for about 20–25% (ADB 2005). But weedicides, if properly applied, are more effective than mechanical and manual methods since weeds are killed outright and not broken off or left to desiccate.[6] Perhaps a greater concern is that, in general, knowledge on the use of the appropriate type of fertilizer and weedicide – the amount to be used, timing of application in relation to the requirements of soil nutrients in different soil types, and whether a plant or ratoon crop is grown – is lacking among farmers.

About 58% of farmers admitted they sought advice from experienced farmers and followed what the majority were using rather than finding out the necessary details from the Fiji Sugar Research Centre or the FSC. But according to Vallis *et al.* (1996), the scope for efficient use of weedicides and fertilizers may be limited by natural conditions like soil type and climate. For instance, LMC's (1991) analysis for Fiji was that the minimum rate of fertilizer application was 50 kg/acre. The survey revealed that growers are divided into those who will take the risk of a low application rate for cost considerations, and those who regard fertilizers and weedicides partly as an insurance against nutrient shortage and weed problems.

CANE TYPES

Another farming practice that may increase soil erosion is soil compaction – it slows infiltration and increases the volume of surface run-off in cane lands (Prove *et al.* 1986). The degree of soil compaction is said to be significantly less in green cane harvest than in ratoon cane (APO 2001). This is a major concern in Fiji, as currently only 4% of cane is plant cane (Sugar Technology Mission 2004). In view of this, the Government of Fiji (2006a) has adopted a Cane Development Plan that envisages a program of planting up to 70% of the existing crop area with plant cane within five years. For this to be successful, a subsidy will need to be provided as seed cane is expensive.

Due to the cost, about 72% of the surveyed farmers said they often did not purchase seed cane from the nurseries at the Cane Research Centre, but bought them at a cheaper rate from other farmers who propagated them. But seed cane, if poorly germinated (for instance if cane knives are not sterilized), can encourage disease within the plant tissue. The use of sub-standard quality seed cane causes an estimated 15%–20% yield reduction in the sugar industry (FSC 2006).

The incentive to plant ratoon cane instead of seed cane is high given: that (some varieties of) plant cane crop takes longer to grow; the higher cost of crop establishment for seed cane; and the extra time and labour required for replanting. In fact, plant cane production costs 2.12 times more than the ratoon plants (Government of Fiji 2006a) and the increase in yield was not considered sufficiently significant in the opinion of 68% of the farmers surveyed. Although the average number of ratoons was around seven in the 2003 season, it was found to

[6] Cane yield reduction as affected by weed infestation was estimated to be 40-50% (Sugarcane Research Annual Report 1992).

be above 12 in many cases (Sugar Technology Mission 2004). Table 6.2 shows crop production and yield by plant cane and ratoon age.

Table 6.2. Crop Production and Yield in 2003

	Area Harvested in hectares	Yield given by tons/hectare
Plant Crop	4026 (6.6%)	55.9
First Ratoon	4349 (7.1%)	54.1
Second Ratoon	3442 (5.7%)	46.1
Other Ratoons	49095 (80.6%)	40.5

Note: Plant crop is of ratoon age zero.
Figure in parenthesis shows proportion of total area harvested.
Source: Sugar Technology Mission (2004).

It can be seen that yield is higher for the younger cane harvested, but only 13.7% of area harvested was made up of plant cane and first ratoon. This is far cry from the 26% of total area harvested of plant cane over 1976–80 and the 26% both plant cane and first ratoon over 1995–99. The target recommended by the Sugar Technology Mission (2004) was for plant cane to make up 25% of harvested cane and that of ratoons 75% within the next three years.[7] Poor ratoon crop management – such as not cutting cane close to the ground,[8] lack of stubble shaving, off barring and root pruning – can easily hasten the decline in cane yield. While some farmers applied organic manure such as filter cake to plant cane, there was a lack of the application to ratoon crops. In addition, ratooning over many years can allow gaps to appear between the cane stalks leading to a systemic build-up of disease and infection. Also, soil erosion involving ratoon crops can be four times higher than plant cane farming (FSC 1996).

Another way cane can attract diseases that easily spread is when a disproportionately large area is planted with one variety of cane. Although there are 16 cane varieties, the survey revealed that less than 5% of farmers used more than one cane variety, while at least 90% of them used the Mana variety, which has more weight but less sugar content. This variety, which has been predominantly used since the late 1980s, is also cheaper than other varieties and can be ratooned for longer periods. In fact, the cane weevil borer has been noted to be a serious problem particularly manifested in the Mana variety (Sugar Technology Mission 2004). In general, the farmers surveyed were not aware of newer and improved varieties such as Naidiri (recommended in 2001) and the early maturing Aiwa variety (with good milling qualities) released in 1991. These may be more suitable for certain soil types and can provide up to 0.5% improvement in POCS relative to the Mana variety. A mix of cane varieties – comprising one early maturing, one mid-maturing and one late maturing[9] – will also improve allocative efficiency. This would achieve optimal cane output and help lessen queues at the mill and enable the transportation of cane to run more smoothly over the season.

[7] Interestingly, this same target was the industry policy before 1990 (see Cane Research Centre Annual Report 1987/1988) but no attention or effort was put into enforcing it. In addition, with more plant cane, the incidence of burning can be expected to be lower because harvesting plant crop and one-year old ratoon weigh more than older rations and hence earn more if burning is avoided.

[8] Harvesting in this way leads to nearly 10% loss in cane yield (Sugar Technology Mission 2004).

[9] This is recommended by the Sugarcane Research Centre in its 2001/02 annual report where growers are encouraged to grow about 30% of each cane variety.

Lastly, some inter-row crops that have been grown with sugarcane are black beans in Colombia, cucumbers and tomatillos in Mexico, sugar beet in Pakistan, Irish potatoes in Louisiana and radish in Java. While this provides a quick cash crop, tests have frequently shown that plating between rows reduces the yield of the sugarcane crop – but economic circumstances may favour an early income over a small sacrifice later (James ed. 2004). But in Fiji, intercropping is hardly practiced as the incentive to farm sugarcane was driven by the high EU sugar subsidy – but this may well change in the future. Intercropping has other advantages as leguminous intercrops: fix atmospheric nitrogen and enrich soil with nitrogen and organic matter; use nutrients available in different soil layers; and control insects and pests if crops such as garlic and onions are grown.

To Burn or not to Burn Cane

Yet another farming practice that also worsens soil quality is cane burning. Burning is environmentally harmful as it releases carbon dioxide and causes soil degradation; it brings out nutrients in the topsoil and these can be easily washed or blown away. In the long run, burning cane results in the loss of crop residue and trash retention, which affect soil quality in terms of organic matter improvement and erosion (Spain and Hodgen 1994). In fact, the transition from burnt to green cane harvesting in Australia has been shown to reduce soil loss. The green cane trash blanket provided a 95%–100% ground cover (which protects the soil surface from water erosion) compared to a 50% ground cover from the burnt cane trash blanket (Wood 1991).

In addition, the heat and smoke released from burning cane leads to environmental pollution that can destroy surrounding vegetation and pose a danger to animals grazing near or around the area. It could also cause forest fires in the pine plantations found in the dry sugar-growing areas of Fiji.[10] But cane burning itself is not a bad practice as it removes weeds, creepers and dead leaves and destroys hornets in particular (which nest in cane fields towards the end of the crushing season), thereby making harvesting easier.[11] Also, for effective milling, it has been recommended that not more than 2% extraneous matter on cane – such as tops, leaves and soil – is allowed as they interfere with sugar extraction. But it is the excessive burning of cane that poses a problem. Table 6.3 shows the sustained sharp escalation in burning after 1990,[12] while burning rates were at half of those levels in the 1970s.

---

[10] Fiji Pine Limited (1998) reports that between 1991 and 1995 cane burning triggered 146 separate forest fires, covering 1700 hectares of pine plantation. In 2000, 53 fires burnt 106 hectares. As in most years, 80% of the fires between August and October coincide with the cane harvesting season (Fiji Pine Limited 2003).

[11] Otherwise, farmers need to employ men (and they demand quite high wages given the back breaking nature of the work) to rake away the trash and dead leaves before cutting cane, and to avoid any leftover crop on farm when crushing season ends. More often than not, many cane cutters demand farmers burn cane before they start harvesting. The farmers however were not mindful of that as they felt that it was in their interest to get the cane harvested in time rather than let it stand and face the danger of not being able to sell lest the mills stop crushing.

[12] This was because up until 1989, there was a provision of delaying the payments for burnt cane for three months beyond the date of payments made to green cane suppliers. In drawing up the Master Award, this provision was strongly resisted and successfully sustained by the cane growers. And as expected, more burning has been taken place since 1990.

Table 6.3. Proportion of Burnt Cane Harvested (%)

Time Period	Burnt Cane
1971–75	16.7
1976–80	18.7
1981–95	19.2
1986–90	25.4
1991–95	40.2
1996–2000	50.0
2001	43.4
2002	36.4
2003	33.4
2004	34.8
2005	36.2

Note: Annual averages computed before 2001.
Source: Fiji Sugar Corporation Annual Reports.

Cane burning has disastrous effects on cane quality and results in revenue loss in more ways than are illustrated in figure 6.1. For instance, burning consumes much of the fibre in the leaves and tops of the cane stalks. The fibrous pulp left after all cane juice is extracted from the crushed stalks constitutes bagasse, which is a valuable fuel. It is used to generate both heat and electricity to power the energy-intensive milling operations, with the substantial excess electricity often being sold to national grids.

Burning cane in the field diminishes the fossil fuel replacement potential of bagasse fibre, something that can obligate mills to purchase extraneous boiler fuel and electricity. Deterioration in cane quality (in the form of dextran, a gum produced by bacteria during deterioration that reduces fibre content) starts from the time of burning – whereas for green cane, it starts from the time of cutting. Thus, burnt cane has high dextran levels compared to green cane making it more difficult to mill[13] and screen out the fibre particles that form an undesirable rim around non-crystallised sugar. Also, burnt cane must be cut immediately and transported. If left to stand, burnt cane absorbs a considerable amount of water diluting the sucrose content.

More than 50% of the surveyed farmers said that they burn cane about three days at a time to save the effort and time in doing it just before harvesting and transporting. In addition, cane is often burnt loose (that is, burnt and left lying on the ground) rather than tightly bundled after burning. The former method results in faster deterioration in cane quality due to its greater exposure to bacteria (*Cane Research Centre Annual Report* 1998/99). Deterioration rates also increase with humidity, thus, harvesting when the weather is too hot is not desirable.

But not all burning is illegal. In some years, there is an on-program of cane burning that has to be approved by the Sugar Tribunal in consultation with FSC, Sugar Cane Growers Council and the Sugar Commission of Fiji. This is for harvesting cane that may be left over and an announcement is usually made giving 10 days before the mills close. Stand-over cane

[13] This is because high dextran levels cause high viscosity in the liquid extracted from cane and this reduces the processing rate. The mills will then have to use chemicals to clean the evaporating surfaces, which get scaled by the high viscous liquid in the cane (Davies 1998a).

may not always be harvested the following year as it often falls over or rots away depending on the weather – so it often has to be burnt.[14]

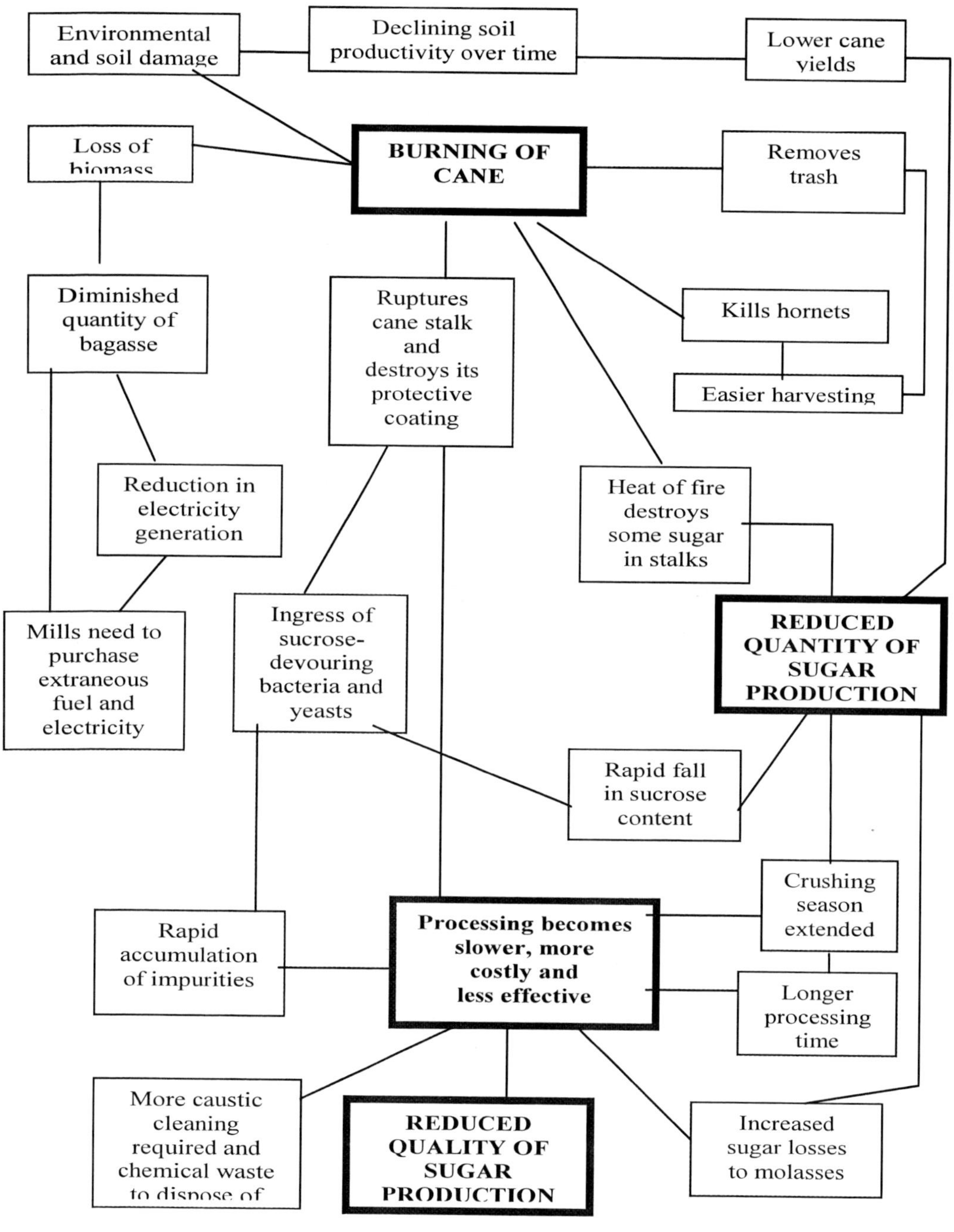

Figure 6.1. The Complex Effects of Cane Burning.

[14] Due to the May 2000 coup, when there was a large volume of cane remaining unharvested for that season, it was agreed that $5 per ton for stand-over cane be paid.

Sometimes, when the incidence of burning is high or when the crushing season starts late (which results in panic burning), the Tribunal has little choice but to allow growers to burn on-program. Some farmers in the survey said that in some years, burning was unofficially allowed and in other years it was officially allowed – thus, they were often confused as to whether or not it would be allowed. Unfortunately, cane burning is, in a sense, encouraged by the current cane payment system as set out in the Master Award.

THE MASTER AWARD

The Master Award[15] is a detailed legal document stipulating the rights, responsibilities and duties of all those associated with the growing, harvesting, transportation and crushing of sugarcane. But even with this regulatory artifice, coordination has proven to be an inexact science, with inevitable difficulties. The award has seen some minor changes since 1970 when Lord Denning first drew it up.

According to the award, cane growers are paid according to the tonnage of cane they deliver – however, apart from India, all other sugar producing countries follow a payment system based on the sugar recovered from cane delivered. Thus, there exists an economic incentive to burn cane in Fiji because payment is based on tonnage delivered. Also, good variety cane does not necessarily weigh more, so farmers may not plant them.

Farmers surveyed revealed that they voluntarily burnt cane if they believed that they were unable to get their harvested cane to the mills before the end of the crushing season. Also, there is incentive to burn cane as burnt cane is given priority in being transported to the mills to prevent a quick deterioration in cane quality. This is especially worse when farmers expect or experience prolonged wet conditions, which makes harvesting difficult and causes delays in transportation – thereby leading farmers to practice queue jumping using methods like cane burning. Interestingly, farm size was found to have the some effect on cane burning too. About 60% of the small-scale farmers indicated that harvesting gangs gave priority to large-scale farmers, which meant further delays in cutting cane – thus, they resorted to cane burning to quicken harvesting efforts.

About 80% of those surveyed agreed that the penalties as set out in the Master Award were not a sufficient deterrent considering the losses they would face if they did not burn cane. Furthermore, those who could afford to bribe field officers who reported the time of burning, found it worthwhile to do so. Moreover, in computing penalties, the FSC depends on the honesty of growers and its own field officers for accurate reporting.

The penalties vary according to the delay from burning to delivery at the mills as seen above. The revenue retained from paying a lesser price for burnt cane goes into a Burnt Cane Fund, which is divided between the miller and those growers who supplied green cane. In the years 1990–96, the Burnt Cane Fund averaged around F$4.17 million per year, although in 1997 the Fund paradoxically fell to F$1.45 million, even though there was a record burning rate that year. Davies (1998a) explains that this was due to the intense pressure put on field officers to mis-report the actual time of burning when burning rates spiral out of hand. In the seven-year period 1990–96, the industry lost an average equivalent to 20,000 tons of sugar

[15] Before the Master Award, the rights and responsibilities of growers and millers were specified in concise ten-year legal contracts.

per season due to burning. This included 11,500 tons due to the effect of burning on the POCS and 8,500 tons due to processing difficulties in the mills. This represented an annual loss in revenue of over $13 million in revenue (*ibid.*).

Table 6.4 gives an idea of the burnt cane penalty system. For instance, for cane delivered 50 hours after being burnt, from the 12% deduction from the green price, $^{5}/_{12}$ goes to the grower and $^{7}/_{12}$ goes to the millers. For cane delivered 150 hours after being burnt, from the 17% deduction from the green price, growers receive $^{5}/_{17}$ of it and the millers receive the rest. This structure reflects the escalating costs of milling cane associated with the higher levels of impurities as burnt cane ages. The extra milling cost incurred in the processing of burnt cane in 1997 was estimated to be over F$6 million, while total proceeds from sugar sales fell by about F$10 million compared to the 1996 season (Sugar Cane Growers Council 1998).

Using a game theory setting as seen in table 6.5, with a playoff matrix of two farmers with the two strategies of to burn or not burn, Davies (1998a) shows that the optimum result for the industry is for neither grower to burn – this strategy carries with it the highest risk for the individual.

Table 6.4. Burnt Cane Penalties

Number of hours from burning to delivery*	Penalty
<24	Price of green cane (i.e. no penalty)
24-28	Green cane price less 9%
48-72	Green cane price less 12%
72-96	Green cane price less 13%
96-120	Green cane price less 15%
120-144	Green cane price less 16%
144-168	Green cane price less 17%
>168	Cane rejected

Note: * The actual day of burning is ignored.

Source: 'Master Award' published by the Sugar Industry Tribunal (1997).

Table 6.5. Cane Burning in a Game Theoretic Setting

Strategies		Farmer B	
		Burn	Don't Burn
Farmer A	Burn	A, B: harvest date unchanged; income of both reduced due to sugar losses.	A: early harvest, income maximised. B: harvest relegated, income minimised (if cane not harvested).
	Don't Burn	A: harvest relegated, income minimised (if cane not harvested). B: early harvest, income maximised.	A, B: harvest due unchanged, aggregate sugar revenues maximised.

Source: Davies (1998a).

Table 6.6. Distribution of Proceeds from Sugar Sales (%)

Total Sugar Produced	Grower's share	FSC's Share
Up to 325,000 tons	70.0	30.0
For every ton over 325,000 up to 350,000	72.5	27.5
For every ton over 350,000	75.0	25.0

Source: Sugar Industry Tribunal (1997).

If A burns and B does not, the possibility exists that B's crop would not be harvested until the season's end, thus inflicting maximal possible income losses. This risk, coupled with the maximum perceived income that can be earned when one burns and the other does not, induces both to burn. But this produces a suboptimal result – the same harvesting schedule as if neither burned, and easier harvesting not compensating for reduced sugar earnings. Thus, there is a classic prisoners' dilemma situation: a non-zero sum game where minimax thinking yields a suboptimal choice of strategy. The optimal strategy, not to burn, is not chosen because of the lack of trust and the desire to pursue individual interest regardless of the effect it has on others or on the common good.

CANE PAYMENT SYSTEM

The cane payment system defines one of the most important relationships within any cane industry since it determines how revenues are distributed between growers and millers. This has a central role in determining the incentives that growers and millers face and, hence, has implications for investment decisions and the sustainability of the sugar industry. Table 6.6 shows the fixed revenue sharing system in Fiji. Over time, grower proceeds have risen from 58% in 1969 to 71%.

Periodically, the contest for the division of sugar proceeds between millers and growers illustrates the nature of this political terrain. Cumulative success for growers in this contest has resulted in a share that is among the highest in the developing world's sugar industries. In fact, the World Bank (1991) recommended a 10% reduction in the grower share of the sugar proceeds, but this was not heeded. Other studies – such as LMC (1991), the Sugar Technology Mission (2004) and ADB (2005) – have highlighted weaknesses in the existing cane system that provides insufficient incentives for millers to improve performance, since the cost of doing so is borne by the miller and the benefits are shared with the growers.

There are many types of cane payment schemes practices by various countries (as seen in table 6.7) and this indicates there is no single formula for an efficient and effective system as they all have their advantages and disadvantages. Ideally, cane payment systems should provide an incentive for growers to maximise the sugar content of the cane and for millers, to maximise recovery of sucrose at the factory. The first problem is to measure the sucrose content of cane that is fair to both growers and millers – and this requires testing procedures that are often highly complex. From the growers' point of view, sampling of cane as it enters the mill yard offers the fairest means of establishing cane quality. This way, growers are not penalised for any deterioration in the cane quality that might result from it being stored for long periods in the cane yard, and/or any sucrose losses sustained as a result of cane washing.

Clearly, the introduction of sophisticated testing techniques brings with it additional costs. In Fiji, where there are many small growers delivering small quantities of cane, the administrative burden and cost may prove too great. Instead, less technically efficient cane systems may be used that are much simpler and cheaper to administer. Such systems often rely on payments based on the average quality of cane delivered by all growers – but this brings into question the extent to which this would have an impact on the incentives to individual farmers to improve cane quality. This is because the individual grower cannot influence the price received for his cane, and has no financial incentive to produce cane of higher quality.

In April 2001, the industry stakeholders agreed to the implementation of a cane payment system based on the quality of cane. It was also agreed that the Near Infra-Red Reflectance (NIR) technology be used for the determination of cane quality for the payment system at the Lautoka mill, which is the biggest of the four mills in Fiji. This technology was first trialed in November 1999 and it was agreed by stakeholders to continue using it to assess cane quality. This technology, imported from Australia, estimates various constituents in cane and enables sugar content analysis. It also generates data that can be used as a reliable source for mill-controlled raw data input for its technical information system. This has the potential to eliminate the need for the routine analysis currently being carried out and will lead to reduced manpower.

There are, however, various difficulties in implementing this system. Two problems exist on the operational side. One is that after the trial period ended in 2001, the FSC took over the NIR scanning operations from the Sugar Commission of Fiji, but have not yet used it – there were faults in the system that have yet to be repaired, partly due to a shortage of funds. Also, the stop/start nature of crushing operations at the mills has made it difficult and uneconomical to use the NIR regularly.

The second problem is that to make the system work, a minimum 10-ton consignment is required to allow for the uniform tipping of cane into the feeder. It is difficult to assess cane quality for both small farms and large farms when they are unable to deliver this minimum consignment at one go. Sometimes this is not within the control of the farmer given problems in the transport of cane and the behaviour of cane cutting gangs. These are discussed in the next section. Also, if the area is of poor quality land, then farms must be quite large to produce enough tonnage of cane for assessment to be viable.

Table 6.7. Cane Payment Systems

Fixed Cane Price	China, Pakistan, and some parts of India
Fixed Revenue Sharing	Fiji, Mexico, Thailand
Variable Revenue Sharing	Australia
Individual Cane Quality	Australia, Jamaica, Mauritius, Thailand, and South Africa
Average Cane Quality	Mexico
Relative Payment Scheme	Australia, Jamaica, Mauritius, and South Africa

Source: Adapted from James (ed. 2004).

Philip Atherton, an Australia consultant, adapted the cane payment system in Queensland and proposed the first performance payment system in Fiji in 1998/99. This was, however, criticised for over-compensating millers and growers whenever any one of them made improvements (Lal 2006a). Another proposal for a quality-based cane payment by Kroes and McFadden (2004) was also not well received by the industry stakeholders. The criticism was based on the notion that, as a key determinant, the POCS is affected by a range of factors not necessarily within the control of the grower. Thus, the search continues for a better system to be put in place.

SUPPORT SERVICES

In this section, three types of support service in the industry are reviewed: harvesting, transport and cane research, and extension services.

Harvesting

Fiji's harvesting season lasts about six months from June to December, depending on weather conditions, and is predominantly labour intensive. Harvesting is done manually, with cut cane loaded by hand onto portable carts, transported to collection points on a rail network, or loaded onto trucks for cartage by road to the mills. Neighbouring farmers pool their labour to form a gang, requiring an average of 10 to 12 harvesters and the gang leader signs a memorandum of gang agreement with the Sugar Commission of Fiji.[16] This system has worked well in the past as first, it allows the use of the grower's own labor and secondly, it enables the grower to ensure that his harvesting expenses are earned back by working in the gang. However, for a while now, more substitute workers are being hired and there are about 12,000 seasonal harvesters in any year. Most of these harvesters are landless workers, housed by farmers who contract them only for the crush period. Harvesters pay is based on per ton of cane harvested, and the rate of about F$11-F$13 is generally the lowest paid of all categories of workers in the country.

More than 60% of the surveyed farmers found it difficult to employ harvesters as there is a dire shortage of people willing to harvest given the low pay, and this affects farmers' cane supply to the mills. Increasingly, harvesters have been recruited from the outer islands where there are even fewer wage employment opportunities, but these seasonal migrants are often unreliable. The surveyed farmers explained that the lack of harvesting discipline also stems from the fact that whenever there are mill shutdowns or problems in transport arrangements, the harvesters do not get paid and they protest in informal ways such as cane burning, delaying the harvesting[17] and "high clearance cutting". The latter involves cutting cane stems

[16] The Sugar Commission of Fiji is trying to restructure gangs to downsize them, but each gang is to have more members. While some rationalisation of gangs was successful in the late 1980s to early '90s, there are currently still over 1,000 harvesting gangs operating and this makes it difficult to manage. Personal communication with Mr.Gerald Barrack, the chairman of the Sugar Commission of Fiji, in July 2005.

[17] Harvesting at the right time is important to prevent decreases in sugar content as sugar is converted to growing energy and new tillers come about and one has to wait until they mature before harvesting. Immature cane has a high proportion of tops and such extraneous matter affects cane milling processes.

a few inches above the ground resulting in significant loss of cane weight and sugar and retarding ratoon growth. Occasionally, there have been instances where native Fijians – who make up a large portion of the cane cutters – make ethnicity a salient factor, and these pressures are accentuated when they coincide with land-lease renewals and rental assessments.

Although mechanical harvesting is a good alternative to the above problems, it is cost effective only for large farms. But most farms in Fiji are small land holdings and, thus, the turn-around time of the harvester *vis-à-vis* the time for manual harvesting is very high. The row-to-row space is also inadequate for the movement of the mechanical harvester. Unless the planting technique is modified and sufficient skills imparted to operators, shifting to mechanical harvesting methods would not be efficient (Sugar Technology Mission 2004). Furthermore, 70% of the cane farms in Fiji are on hilly areas and rendering mechanical harvesters inoperable. Nevertheless, the Sugar Commission of Fiji trialed mechanical loading and harvesting from 1997 to 2000, and currently there are three to four harvesters around. Some growers were renting them, but the program had to be abandoned due to lack of funds.[18]

Perhaps the more pressing problem in cane harvesting is the lack of monitoring of a harvesting schedule. Presently, the harvesting program is divided into two phases where 50% of the crop is harvested from each farmer first and the remainder next. There is no difference between plant cane and ratoon cane harvesting. Harvesting management is left to Sardars, who are often influenced by farmers, thereby leading to *ad hoc* harvesting schedules. Such a lack of transparency in the harvesting program leads to complaints from farmers and millers (Sugar Technology Mission 2004).

Transport

Transportation of sugarcane in Fiji is done by rail and road. The efficiency of the transport system is important to ensure adequate mill performance and to shorten 'cut to crash' delays for improving cane quality. Over time, more cane farmers are using road transport as seen from the rise of 35% of cane delivered by road in 1974 to more than 60% since 2002. This is perhaps not surprising, given that 65% of lorry cane gets crushed within 24 hours of harvesting as opposed to 30% for rail cane (Sugar Technology Mission 2004). The average distance for rail haulage is 31.2 km and cane, at best, makes it to the mill 17–18 hours after cutting – lorry transport takes below 1.5 hours, on average, to transport cane from field to mill (*ibid.*).

The rail system consists of 76 locomotives and 9,800 cane trucks. The infield operations of the rail system are of two types. One is the portable line, a traditional system, whereby light railway tracks are laid from the main line to the area being harvested and the trucks are moved to and from the main line by bullocks or tractors. This method is best suited to large harvesting gangs operating on flatter terrain. The second type of rail is the tractor winch trailer system, where trucks are transported to and from the railway by means of tractor and trailer. For infield loading, the truck is lowered onto two or three lengths of portable track that on steep land is laid on a hand-leveled site. This system is used for all terrain categories and is

[18] Communication with Mr.Gerald Barrack in July 2005.

favoured by small harvesting gangs. The FSC is bound by the Master Award to accept cane free of charge by rail, which is more dependable during adverse weather conditions.

But the rail system of sugar transportation in Fiji has, however, steadily and significantly deteriorated over the years because of under-investment in rail maintenance, inefficient harvesting and loading systems, poor labour practices and incentive systems, lost and inadequate skills, and use of old locomotives (Davies 1998b). Hence, the rail system has faced frequent breakdowns, the speed has slowed to 6 km/h from a design speed of 18km/h. For similar reasons, the Sugar Technology Mission (2004) recommended that the rail system be abolished, as strengthening and improving the current system would require F$12 million per year. However, some industry stakeholders were concerned that roads would become congested if cane were only taken to the mills by lorry. The 24-ton truck suggested by the Sugar Technology Mission was not considered suitable for Fiji's terrain and weather conditions and the loss of jobs for 400 rail workers was another concern. It was argued that if the mills were to run on a 24-hour basis, there was no way that lorries could feed the mills if there were no rail.

Truck users, in general, meet the full transportation costs,[19] but if they can prove it is not possible to use rail, there is a provision in the Master Award for payment of a transport allowance as a partial compensation towards their costs of transportation. About 73% of surveyed farmers said the FSC hardly ever pays this compensation due to a lack of such proof. Nevertheless, they felt it was still worthwhile to use lorries, as there was better control over the timing of the cane pick up and timely delivery to the mills. But a large number of lorries arriving at the mills at the same time have caused queues and delays at the mills as well. Thus, there needs to be major restructuring of pre- and post-harvesting logistics to ensure that the cane supply is smooth enough to enable optimum crushing at the mills.

Cane Research and Extension Services

Investment in applied research and extension services has a high probability of producing substantial returns in the sugar industry but, since 1970s, funding has been about F$1.2 million.[20] More importantly, up until 2003, the Fiji Cane Research Centre did not operate independently from the FSC, which owns the mills and is mostly funded by the government and the proceeds of sugar sales.[21] This is unlike the cane research centres in India and Australia that are run by independent private companies.

Thus, it is not surprising that the FSC is more interested in miller and grower operations than field research and extension services. In fact, extension services (for disseminating information to farmers) have been dismantled since 2001 and this would have had a detrimental effect on crop management, protection and improvement practices related to ratoon management, soil erosion and water management measures, fertilizer and weedicide application, cane varietal selection, etc.

---

[19] This anomaly arose because the rail system was built to service the original growers. As time went by, others wanted to farm more distant land and FSC agreed to this on the basis that the transportation cost was to the account of the grower.

[20] Personal communication with Mr. Jai Gawander, the FSC Research Manager, in July 2005.

[21] It is now jointly funded by the industry and the government.

However, in accordance to the recommendation of the Sugar Technology Mission (2004), the Government of Fiji intended to establish an independent sugar research institute by late 2006 – but the attempts were futile because of the December 2006 coup.

Mill Operations

The milling and processing of cane to extract sugar comes under the management of the FSC, which prior to 1996-97 was a profitable entity (White 2003). Table 6.8 shows the trends in reported profits. The decline in the financial performance of the FSC in recent years has been widely criticised. For instance, Lal (2006b) explains that the FSC's losses have taken place despite an increase in gross revenue, suggesting an increase in the FSC's costs. According to scientific studies, Fiji's cost of production is ranked seventh highest for the 20 ACP sugar-producing countries (*Fiji Times* 30 Sept 04). The Congressional Research Services (1985) rated Fiji's average cost of production as 60 on an index value scale of 100, which is the weighted world average for sugar production. This is bettered only by Brazil at 57, and is even lower than Australia's 62 and Philippine's 75. In fact, the current cost of production in the Fiji sugar industry is almost equal to the subsidy prices obtained by the EU (Government of Fiji 2005).

Table 6.8. Net Profits of Fiji Sugar Corporation

Year	F$million
1997	- 1.2
1998	-3.0
1999	2.0
2000	-3.3
2001	-20.9
2002	-16.4
2003	-15.8
2004	2.3
2005	51.9*
2006	-3.6

Notes:

1. Net profits are defined as profit after taxation.
2. * This is due to the government writing off its loans of F$54 million to FSC to strengthen FSC's financial position.

Source: White (2003); FSC Annual Financial Reports, year ending 31st March.

It has been further argued that the near collapse of the FSC has been at the expense of improvements to mill efficiency, investment in sugarcane farming research and the transport system (Prasad and Narayan 2004). Based on various reports on industry structuring, the FSC has been said to have spent about F$300 million in mill upgrading, averaging about F$20 million a year – but there is little evidence of any marked improvements in mill capacity. In fact, it has been noted that the four sugar mills often operate below capacity in most years, processing on average 3.5 million tons of cane – about 2 million tons below capacity. Apart from bad weather conditions, this is also due to numerous mill breakdowns and delays in crushing.[22] The current average of the crushing season is above a 30-week period, yet to be replaced with an optimal 22–24 weeks. The average stoppage hours at the mills are high at about 30–60 hours per week (Sugar Technology Mission 2004). Such downtime lengthens the crushing season (into the wet weather), which has an impact on sugar recovery rate given by POCS, which is currently about 11.25% and below the recommended rate of 13% (*ibid.*).

The low POCs and even mill breakdowns, have often been blamed on the poor quality of cane supply, which raises the costs of production. In 2002, when Japan rejected a sugar shipment on the grounds of poor quality, the FSC and the government blamed farmers for burning the cane. But in Brazil, most of the cane supplied to the mills is burnt, and yet the quality of sugar is high because of the efficient transport system that allows cane to be milled within 36 hours of harvesting (Prasad and Narayan 2004).

The point remains that replacing old and inefficient machinery alone will not lead to efficient milling and processing. This is because the root cause of the problems also involves poor governance due to the lack of accountability at all levels of management – this results in widespread principal/agent problems. This situation is bound to continue if the government keeps bailing out the FSC. For instance in 2002, in a bid to keep the FSC afloat, the government wrote off a loan worth F$34 million to the FSC, and then facilitated F$75 million in loans from the ANZ Bank, provided on a government guarantee to enable the operation of the FSC (National Farmers Union 2003). Lal (2006b) further highlights discriminatory promotion and appointment within the FSC and, hence, the lack of appropriate technical expertise and experience. This resulted in incompetent people being placed in several key positions, and is a possible explanation for the poor performance of the FSC.

VIABILITY OF THE INDUSTRY

With the all the problems mentioned above plaguing the cane and sugar industry, the foremost question in one's mind is, how likely are these issues to be resolved given that attempts to find solutions have been futile so far? In the wake of the erosion of the EU's sugar subsidy, will the plight of Fiji be similar to that of Trinidad and Tobago, which had to shut their state-owned sugar firm due to huge losses in 2003? While White (2003) is pessimistic about the viability of the industry and suggests its winding down and ultimate closure, LMC and Oxford Policy Management (2003) indicate that Fiji has the potential to either sink or swim. So, to what extent is the industry important enough to be kept alive and viable?

Despite the less than "sweet" environment, sugar remains important for Fiji on a number of levels. First, in comparison to other crops, farmers have long been involved in cane farming. Also, the geographic spread of farms has ensured that a substantial portion of the revenue derived from the sale of sugar is widely distributed throughout rural Fiji. This is one factor that no other industry has been able to replicate – and this makes it important to keep the industry alive.

---

[22] In 2003, at the Lautoka mill, F$10 million was spent on a new mill, but the capacity of this mill was 15,000 tons lower than the old mill. Also, at the start of the 2003 crushing season, the Lautoka mill broke down within the first week of crushing although the FSC spent F$6 million in mill maintenance just before.

One good possibility is offered by the horizontal expansion of sugar-related activities that can enhance Fiji's industrialisation in more ways than one. One obvious option is to develop sugar refineries to derive benefits from the highest value added component of the production chain. This has long been undermined by the EU's past preferential access that created a ready market for raw sugar, but strongly discouraged the export of processed sugar by only offering the same price as for raw sugar. But sugar quality needs to be of a high standard for export, and such capacity may require time to build. Perhaps a more important question is, how worthwhile is it to produce sugar? There is the expansion of alternative sweeteners such as caloric and non-caloric sweeteners aided by the fad for diet beverages. Also, competition from saccharin and high fructose corn syrup as sugar substitutes cannot be ignored. As world sugar prices have historically been characterised by short, sharp price rises followed by long periods of low prices and with production outstripping consumption, prices have gradually declined albeit on a wildly fluctuating trend and this is expected to continue (Oxfam 2004a).

Another option is in electricity generation from bagasse[23] (crushed cane fibre), a waste from the milling process and its disposal a problem. This will reduce Fiji's dependence on imported fossil fuels (which are less environmentally friendly) and help alleviate the current electricity crisis in the long run.

The third option is to build a distillery to convert molasses, another by-product of sugar, to produce ethanol for fuel.[24] It is, however, unlikely that Fiji is able to compete in the export market given the fierce competition from Brazil, which has been in the business for over 30 years. Thus, ethanol production needs to be considered for domestic consumption and this is heavily dependent on the government establishing an ethanol fuel blending program to create the market (as has been done in Australia and Malaysia). The FSC has, nevertheless, decided to temporarily shelve implementation of an ethanol strategy for a few years to concentrate on improving mill efficiencies and maximising cogeneration opportunities (Government of Fiji 2006a).

The potential for other by-products (like liquid carbon dioxide, additional molasses for animal feed and dry yeast, filter cake for export fertilizers) has been explored and highly recommended for Fiji by Nobel Sugar (2004). These up-stream economic activities not only add value to sugarcane production, but also generate huge employment opportunities for the more than 12,000 displaced cane farmers who will exit the cane industry when their leases are not renewed (ADB 2005). However, if these sugar-related sectors can be managed well, there is little doubt that Fiji's sugar industry can be revitalised in a profitable and sustainable way.

CONCLUSION

This chapter has highlighted the complex interactions and dependencies between the stakeholders in the cane and sugar industry that make it difficult for reform to work smoothly. Although options exist to make the industry viable, success in exploiting these options still depends on the ability of the parties to work in tandem. In the past, there were industrial disputes by the mill workers (such as in 1998 and 2000, the growers' boycott of harvest in

---

[23] Bagasse can also be used to manufacture paper and other products such as liner and corrugated board and bio-fertilizer.

[24] This form of biodiesel is not only cleaner and could possibly be a cheaper alternative to petrol.

1999, and threat to boycott carting cane by the Fiji Cane Transport Operators Association in 2004), which all happened in isolation and caused huge losses to everyone in the industry.

A series of integrated measures on mill and farm operations is required, but more importantly, a radical change from the well-established way of doing things to a new level of professionalism and commitment by all stakeholders in the industry holds the key to successful reform. The 2007 budget has identified four critical areas for sugar reform: the upgrading of mill facilities to increase mill capacity and operational efficiency; the improvement of the transportation system to the mill to reduce the cost of carting cane; the modernization of farming methods; and the diversification into value-adding opportunities. The possibility of reforming the industry along these lines does exist based on funds provided by the ADB and the EU. What remains to be seen is how effectively these funds will be used to produce the results needed to fulfill Fiji's sweet dreams for its sugar industry.

Chapter 7

THE DYNAMIC COMPUTABLE GENERAL EQUILIBRIUM MODEL

INTRODUCTION

This chapter describes the structure of the computable general equilibrium (CGE) model that is used for the empirical analyses in the next two chapters. General equilibrium models are an abstraction that is complex enough to capture the essential features of the economy, yet simple enough to be tractable. In general, any policy instrument or trade shocks have direct and indirect effects in a given country. Consequently, in any given economy it is difficult to conceive a situation where the change of a policy or shock would affect only one sector. Due to forward and backward linkages and their related strengths within a particular economy, the result is always one in which the relative mix of sectoral outputs change. This, by extension, affects the relative mix of the different factors of production in the different sectors.

Thus, general equilibrium models are popular over their partial equilibrium counterparts because they stress the interactions among different sectors. A dynamic CGE model goes a step further to consider short-, medium- and long-term effects. The partial equilibrium modelling framework presents itself as a second-best option for those countries that are not captured individually in large-scale models such as the GTAP model. However, the CGE models are the first-best option as they not only measure the first-round effects of simulated changes, but also the second-round effects, which include inter-industry effects and macroeconomic adjustments.

The Fiji CGE model can be used to assist policy makers and others to evaluate the effects of a wide range of policies and external events at both the macroeconomic and sectoral level. The model belongs to the Johansen family of CGE models (Johansen 1960; Dixon et al. 1982), with modifications to the financial and labour sectors to make it dynamic. A distinct feature of the Johansen approach is that the non-linear equation system is linearised before being solved. This can be contrasted to another approach in which the system of equations is solved in the levels of its variables (see Dervis de Melo and Robinson 1982).

The main advantage of the second approach is that it produces exact solutions. However, it requires tailor-made solution algorithms that need to be redeveloped after changes to the model specification. While the Johansen approach is subject to linearisation error, the recent development of multi-step solution algorithms has enabled fairly accurate solutions to be obtained for Johansen-type simulations. Hertel et al. (1992) have shown that the linear representation can produce the same accurate solutions as models using explicit levels equations.

Within the last decade or so, there has been a boom in CGE modelling for two main reasons. First, the development of suitable computer software and the increase in computing power has allowed huge amounts of data to be processed quickly and cheaply. Second, CGE models, unlike partial equilibrium models, have facilitated the simulation of policies in ways that are easily understood or explained, and are perceived to be relevant by decision makers.

This chapter is organised as follows. Section 2 briefly describes the CGE approach, while Section 3 sets the discussion in context by briefly reviewing previous macroeconomic models of the Fijian economy. Section 4 provides a detailed description of the structure of the Fiji CGE model. This section also includes a description of the commodity and industry categories, the input/output structure, the theoretical structure and definition of the model's equations. Section 5 explains the model closure, while Section 6 concludes.

THE COMPUTABLE GENERAL EQUILIBRIUM APPROACH

An economic model has been described as "a schematic simplification that strips away the non-essential aspects to reveal the inner working, shapes, or design of a more complicated mechanisation" (Klein 1983). In other words, economic models tend to abstract from reality by simplifying parts of this complex system. Economic models may be classified in various ways. One approach is to divide them into partial equilibrium and general equilibrium models. The latter are multi-sectoral in nature and include macroeconometric models, linear programming models (LP), input-output (I-O) models and CGE models. These models have the following general characteristics (Challen and Hagger 1983):

(i) all the relationships are represented in a specific mathematical form by means of various parameters and coefficients; and
(ii) the parameters are specific numbers that have been estimated from relevant statistical data.

The development of CGE analysis can be credited to the French economist, Leon Walras, who first proposed the concept of general equilibrium analysis in his book, *Elements d'Economie Politique* (Walras 1954). Edgeworth (1881), followed by Arrow and Debreu (1954), also made early contributions to the concept. Leontief (1936) made it possible to operationalise the Walrasian general equilibrium system when he developed the LP and I-O models for the US economy. The first CGE model was constructed by Johansen (1960) in an anaylsis of growth in Norway using the Norwegian I-O table

After Johansen's path-breaking work, there was not much development of CGE modelling until the early 1970s following a breakthrough by Scarf (1973). Scarf developed an algorithm for computing solutions to numerically specified general equilibrium models. This stimulated interest in CGE modelling in the US and Canada, initially for the analysis of taxation policy (Shoven and Whalley 1972). Since then, there has been a meteoric rise in the use of CGE models for policy analysis in both developed and developing countries. Extensive surveys of CGE studies have been conducted by Shoven and Whalley (1984), Dervis *et al.* (1982) and Dixon and Parmenter (1994).

Economic models may be classified into two main types: forecasting models and simulation models. The former provide forecasts of likely outcomes for the relevant variables, while the latter address 'what if' scenarios. In simulation models, we focus on the effects of a policy change, holding constant all other factors that influence the economic outcomes. The Fiji CGE model is designed to enable the analyst to address three 'what if' or policy issues:

(i) policies that occur at the sector level: industry, commodity, occupation
(ii) policies that occur at the macroeconomic level
(iii) changes in international economic conditions.

Examples of policies of type (i) include taxes and subsidies on industry production, exports and imports. Examples of policies of type (ii) include changes in the level and composition of government spending, changes in wage rates and changes in the exchange rate. Finally, examples of policies of type (iii) include changes in world prices or changes in Fiji's terms of trade.

The Fiji model is termed *economy-wide* because it contains a sufficient level of disaggregation that enables the effects of a policy to be traced to all the different sectors of the economy. The term 'computable' in 'CGE' refers to the fact it is a quantitative model that is solved by means of a computer. The term 'general equilibrium' refers to the fact that the production and consumption relationships, prices and the interaction between supply and demand in factor and product markets are all simultaneously considered.

In this book, we employ the CGE framework to quantify the broader (i.e. direct plus indirect) contributions of agriculture to Fiji's economy. Traditionally, the contribution of the agricultural sector to an economy is measured by its shares in gross domestic (or regional) product, employment and exports. This conventional approach shows that as an economy grows, agriculture's share declines relative to other sectors. Nevertheless, this decline of agriculture's relative share during economic growth does not necessarily imply that the overall economic significance of the sector diminishes as well. As the sector itself grows, so does its absolute contribution to the economy.

Beyond the direct contributions of the sector, one also has to take into account its contributions to the growth of light manufacturing devoted to processing agricultural produce, further value-adding, and its contribution to the growth of the transport and marketing sectors. Similarly, one also has to consider agriculture's backward linkages through which it contributes to the growth of those sectors that service farm activities. For example, the fertilizer, chemical, machinery industries and various services to the agricultural sector also benefit from expansion in agriculture. Often, the indirect contributions flowing through the linkages in production, trade and consumption are complex and may not be obvious, so that the broader contributions of the sector can easily be underestimated.

Accordingly, for a comprehensive account of the sector's contributions to the economy, a proper account should be taken of the wide-ranging linkages of the agricultural sector with the rest of the economy. Often input-output multiplier analysis, which is based on some restrictive assumptions on both the demand side and the supply side, is undertaken to capture these linkages. For example, on the supply side, this approach does not recognise any constraints on the supplies of primary factors nor does it assume any balance of payments constraints. Furthermore, a major inadequacy of the input-output approach is its inability to explicitly take into account public policies such as direct and indirect taxes, and trade and exchange rate policies.

The chapter, thus, proposes to employ a computable general equilibrium model, which does not suffer from these weaknesses, to quantify the overall contribution of agriculture. Given its theoretical superiority, a CGE approach to measuring sectoral contribution would represent an improvement over input-output methodology.

An Overview of Economy-Wide Models of Fiji

Sturton (1989) constructed the earliest economy-wide model of Fiji using a semi-input-output model to analyse the impacts of the 1987 military coup on Fiji's economy. He simulated the impacts of a 35% devaluation in the Fiji dollar following the post-coup period. This resulted in a 17% contraction of the construction sector, an 8% contraction of the private services sector, and a decline of 5% in real GDP. Other macroeconomic impacts included a 20% rise in domestic prices, a 10% decline in the terms of trade, a 3% deterioration in the balance of payments and a 3% government budget deficit. Thus, one of his main conclusions was that the 1987 coup depressed economic activity and had a significant inflationary impact on the economy.

Murphy (1992) conducted a series of simulations for the period 1976 to 1986 using a macroeconomic model of Fiji. The policies considered were: (i) devaluation of the exchange rate; (ii) increase in wages under the central system of wage fixation; (iii) an increase in sugar prices; (iv) an expansion in government spending; and (v) a tightening of monetary policy. Under the devaluation policy, real output initially rose but subsequently declined. Domestic prices rose by the full amount of the devaluation, offsetting any gains in external competitiveness. The main conclusion from this simulation was that devaluation of the currency had very little benefit for the economy without complementary policies. The policy of increasing wages results in a steady decline in real output through a decline in private investment and a reduction in the capital stock. Higher wages also had an adverse impact on the tourism sector.

An increase in sugar prices has two effects. First there is a direct increase in farm income as a result of the higher prices. Second, the increase in prices induces an expansion in sugar output. There is also an increase in imports and private consumption as a result of the higher disposal income. An expansion in government spending initially results in an increase in real output, however, it also results in a rise in public debt and a fall in foreign exchange reserves. This leads to higher taxes and a deflationary tightening of monetary policy. In the long run, it is shown that real output falls as a result of a fall in the capital stock and a rise in interest rates. The tightening of monetary policy has a deflationary effect on prices and wages and thereby improves the economy's external competitiveness. It also results in a decline in imports and a rise in foreign exchange reserves.

Levantis (1999) developed the first CGE model of the Fiji economy. Using the model that had a 1997 base year, Levantis *et al.* (2005) evaluated the following alternative options for using aid from the EU sugar preferences:

Scenario 1: Subsidy transfer from the EU by considering a removal of preferential access;
Scenario 2: Using the aid monies to fund a reduction by one-third in income tax and tariff rates; and
Scenario 3: Investment in infrastructure.

The immediate impact in Scenario 1 is a decline in economic activity. But with the substitution of factors toward other forms of production, the net impact on GDP of 1.1% is significantly less than the amount of loss in transfer payments (about 2.9% of GDP) from the EU. Diverting the funds directed to the sugar subsidy into financing a reduction in Fiji's taxes and tariffs (Scenario 2), and therefore a reduction in the distortions associated with them, delivers a significant benefit to Fiji in terms of stimulating overall production. Under this scenario, there is an initial rise in real GDP of 1.0% compared to the base situation of continued sugar preferences, which moves Fiji onto a higher growth path. Scenarios 3 and 4 (investing in infrastructure) easily deliver the biggest long-term gains for Fiji in terms of real GDP growth.

Narayan (2003) used a CGE model of Fiji to analyse the IMF recommended VAT policy for Fiji. He found that the VAT of 12.5% improved government revenue and increased real GDP by 0.6%. However, the VAT policy led to a decline in investment and a reduction in real consumption and national welfare. He concludes that the policy was misdirected and that a better alternative to the VAT policy would have been to upgrade the government's tax collecting mechanism. More recently, Narayan and Prasad (2007) have analysed the long-run economy-wide impacts of the May 2000 military coup. They found that the coup reduced real GDP by 8.2%. In addition, it led to a 2.2% decline in private savings and private consumption, a 4.8% decline in government tax revenue and a 4.4% rise in the CPI. Real national welfare declined by 7.3%, while private disposable income declined by 2.2%. All sectors of the economy declined, with hotels, transport and commerce among the hardest hit.

The studies presented in this book use the most up-to-date data by upgrading the 1997 I-O table to the 2002 base year. Also, as we show later, two additional sectors – the informal primary and informal secondary sectors – have been added to the I-O table, thus broadening the scope of the model. We next present a description of the model.

STRUCTURE OF THE FIJI CGE MODEL

Sector Detail

The Fiji CGE model comprises 36 domestic industries producing 35 commodities. Table 7.1 lists the industries and gives the corresponding classification numbers from the *Fiji Standard Industrial Classification* (FSIC). There are 14 agricultural industries, including forestry, fishing, primary informal and secondary informal. There are 10 industrial industries and 12 service industries. The main commodity produced by each industry is also outlined in Table 7.1, and, in all, there are 35 commodities. Each commodity corresponds to an industry except for gold, which is considered to be produced by two industries: the Emperor Gold Mine and the Mt Kasi Gold Mine

Table 7.1. Industry/Commodity Classification

°	Industry		Commodity	FSIC code
1	Sugarcane	1	Raw sugar	1111
2	Coconuts	2	Coconuts	1112
3	Rice	3	Rice	1113
4	Ginger	4	Ginger	1114
5	Dalo	5	Dalo	1116 (part of)
6	Root crops	6	Root crops	1116 (part of)
7	Kava	7	Kava	1116 (part of)
8	Fruit and vegetables	8	Fruit and vegetables	1116 (part of)
9	Other crops	9	Other crops	1115 and 1116 (part of)
10	Dairy	10	Dairy	1118
11	Livestock	11	Livestock products	1117, 1119
12	Forestry	12	Forest products	121, 122
13	Fishing	13	Marine products	130, 140
14	Emperor Gold Mine	14	Gold	210
15	Mt Kasi Gold Mine	14	Gold	210
16	Quarrying	15	Quarrying	220
17	Sugar manufacturing	16	Sugar products	3118
18	Beverages & Tobacco	17	Beverages & Tobacco	313, 314
19	Food processing	18	Processed foods	311/312 excluding 3118
20	Clothing, footwear	19	Clothing, footwear	321, 322
21	Other manufacturing	20	Other manufactures	33, 34, 35, 36, 37, 38, 39
22	Electricity & water	21	Electricity & water	41, 42
23	Construction	22	Construction services	51 52
24	Commerce	23	Retail/wholesale services	61, 62 excluding 6292
25	Hotels, cafes, restaurants	24	Hotels, cafes, restaurants	63
26	Transport, communication	25	Transport, comm. services	71, 72
27	Finance	26	Finance services	81
28	Insurance	27	Insurance services	82
29	Property services	28	Property services	831
30	Business services	29	Business services	832, 833
31	Other private services	30	Other private services	934, 939, 941, 949, 95
32	Health	31	Health services	932
33	Education	32	Education services	931
34	Other government services	33	Other government services	91, 92, 933, 942, 96
35	Primary informal sector	34	Primary informal	6292
36	Secondary informal sector	35	Secondary Informal	6292

Note: FSIC refers to the Fiji Standard Industrial Classification.

The gold industry is split between the two mines because the cost structures differ. New additions to the database are the primary informal and secondary informal sectors. This is considered important because the informal sector provides a significant degree of employment for those unable to find formal sector jobs. The primary informal sector refers to informal agricultural activity and the secondary informal sector refers to non-farm informal activity.

Table 7.2 lists the 35 commodities. Most of these commodities have competing imports, but as is usual in CGE models, we take the *Armington assumption* which considers imported inputs to be imperfect substitutes to the domestic varieties.

Table 7.2. List of Commodities

	Commodity	Exportable?	No.
1	Raw sugar		
2	Coconuts	Exportable	1
3	Rice		
4	Ginger	Exportable	2
5	Dalo	Exportable	3
6	Root crops		
7	Kava	Exportable	4
8	Fruit and vegetables		
9	Other crops		
10	Dairy		
11	Livestock products		
12	Forest products		
13	Marine products	Exportable	5
14	Gold	Exportable	6
15	Quarrying		
16	Sugar products	Exportable	7
17	Beverages & Tobacco		
18	Processed foods	Exportable	8
19	Clothing, footwear	Exportable	9
20	Other manufactures	Exportable	10
21	Electricity & water		
22	Construction services		
23	Retail/wholesale services	Exportable	11
24	Hotels, cafes, restaurants	Exportable	12
25	Transport, & communication services	Exportable	13
26	Finance services		
27	Insurance services		
28	Property services		
29	Business services		
30	Other private services	Exportable	14
31	Health services		
32	Education services		
33	Other Govt services		
34	Primary informal services	Exportable	15
35	Secondary informal services	Exportable	16

The commodities which are considered exportable are also listed in the table. The exportable commodities do not form the complete list of commodities which are exported, but comprise only those commodities for which the domestic market is assumed to be affected by world prices and demand conditions. For example, there is a small amount of fruit and vegetables that are exported, but the bulk of the market is domestic and prices and demand for fruit and vegetables are determined according to market conditions in Fiji. For this reason, fruit and vegetables are not classified as 'exportable'.

The manufacturing industries include the following: sugar products; food processing; beverages and tobacco; textiles; clothing and footwear; and other manufacturing. The other sectors in the model are the service sectors which include: electricity and water; construction; wholesale and retail trade; hotels and restaurants; transport and communications; financial services; insurance services; property services; business services; other private services; health, education and other government services.

Input-output Structure

The links between production and consumption within the economy, as well as links to the external economy, are represented by the model's input-output structure. The database also allows various structural coefficients – sales and cost shares – to be computed. The input-output structure of the model consists of various matrices that are briefly described below (see Figure 7.1).

		Industries (current goods) n	Industries (capital goods) n	Household consumption 1	Exports 1	Government 1	Duty	
Domestic commodities	n	A	B	C	D	E		Row sums = total usage of local commodities
Imports	n	F	G	H		I	-Z	Row sums = Total imports c.i.f.
Labour Occupations	q	K						
Capital Land Labour	1 1 1	L M N						
		Column sums = outputs of local industries	Column sums = Capital expenditure by industries	Column sums = total household expenditure	Column sums = total exports	Column sums = total government demand	Column sums = total duty	

Figure 7.1. Representation of Input-Output Database for the Fijian CGE Model.

Matrix A contains the inputs of locally-produced commodities into the production processes of local industries. Matrix B shows the local inputs into the production of capital goods. Obviously, in the case of Fiji, there will be many zero entries in B since most capital inputs are imported. Matrix C shows the consumption by Fijian households of locally produced commodities. Matrices D and E are vectors showing the flow of locally produced commodities to exports and government demands, respectively.

Matrix F shows inputs of imported commodities for current production, while G shows inputs of imported commodities for the production of capital goods. Matrices H and I are also vectors that show household and government consumption of imported commodities, respectively. Matrix Z contains the negative of the duty on imported commodities. Matrix K shows the use of the different occupation types by industry. Matrix L shows the rental value of each sector's fixed capital while M shows the rental value of land. Matrix N shows aggregate inputs of labour by each industry.

The entries in the database represent estimates of the value of output of each commodity in each industry in the base period, which is taken to be 2002. Thus, the column entries indicate the commodity composition of each sector's output. By a similar token, the row entries indicate the proportions of a particular commodity produced in each sector and the row totals show the value of output of each commodity.

Theoretical Structure

The model is based on the circular flow of funds in the economy, which is described by the Walrasian general condition in Equation 7.1. This condition requires that total supply of goods (left hand side) be equal to total demand (right hand side). Imports are placed on the right hand side of the equation because they constitute supply of externally produced commodities.

$$\text{production} + \text{imports} = \text{intermediate inputs} + \text{consumption} + \text{investment} + \text{government consumption} + \text{government investment} + \text{exports} \qquad (7.1)$$

The circular flow of funds described by Equation 7.1 (below) is explained in the model by five core equations representing the production, household, government, external and finance sectors. In addition to these equations, there are others to determine variables in the equation and a group of information equations that provide information about variables that are not part of the core model. The sources and uses of funds in this circular flow model are further explained with the aid of Figure 7.2. The sources of funds for the household sector are shown by the left-hand side terms in Equation 2 of Figure 7.2. These include payments to labour and capital by the production sector; net receipts of investments from abroad; net private unrequited transfers from abroad; and net government transfers. These funds are used for private consumption, savings and income tax payments.

The sources of the government sector's funds (left-hand side of Equation 3, Figure 7.2) are tax revenue and public unrequited transfers from abroad. These funds are used for consumption and investment expenditures and transfers to firms and households. The balance goes into the budget surplus (or deficit). Government tax revenue is derived from personal income tax, company tax, and other taxes. Total government consumption is the sum across the 35 commodities that were purchased for consumption and investment. Public unrequited transfers are assumed to be endogenous. Further details of the equations in the government sector are given below. The external sector equation (Equation 4, Figure 7.2) is the balance of payments, which describes the sources and uses of Fijian currency for foreign currency traders. The outflows of the currency are used to purchase imports or to transfer investment income abroad. These funds are applied to purchase exports, capital inflows, inflows of investment income, and net private and public unrequited transfers. Net unrequited transfers are assumed to be exogenous and therefore the balancing items in Equation 4.

Total imports for a give commodity are given by the sum of import demand for that commodity across the 33 sectors, while total exports of a given commodity are given by total supply minus total domestic demand.

The sources of funds for the financial sector (Equation 5 in Figure 7.2) are private and government savings, and net capital inflows. These funds are used for private investment. The level of private investment in each industry is determined by its profitability and interest rate and obtained by aggregating investment across the 33 industries.

Description of the Model's Equations

This section describes in a little more detail the core equations of the model and the supporting equations. We first introduce the derivation of the production sector equations, followed by equations for demand for inputs. We then discuss household demand and savings, government demands, the external sector, the finance sector, information equation and determination of commodity and factor prices. It concludes with a description of the approach to model closure and solution.

1. **Production sector**
   production = intermediate inputs + factor payments + production sector tax payments.
2. **Household sector**
   factor payments + net income flows + net private unrequited transfers + government transfers = private consumption + private savings + income tax payments.
3. **Government sector**
   tax revenue + net public unrequited transfers = government consumption + government investment + government transfers+ net government savings.
4. **External sector**
   imports = exports + net capital inflows + net private unrequited transfers + net public unrequited transfers.
5. **Finance sector**
   private investment = private savings + net government savings + net capital inflows.

Figure 7.2. Sources and Uses of Funds in the Fijian CGE Model.

Production Sector Equations

It is assumed that industries choose their inputs to current production and capital formation to minimise the costs of these activities. Input-output separability is assumed for current production so that the composition of inputs is independent of the composition of outputs. The model's equations reflect the nested structure of the input side of the production functions assumed for current production and capital creation. At the top level of the nests is the Leontief assumption of no substitution between input categories, or between them and the composite inputs. The second level allows CES substitution between sources in the formation of composites, resulting in source-specific demand functions. At each stage, the degree of substitution is determined by the values assigned to the respective substitution elasticities.

Suppose a representative industry has the following CES production function:

$$Z = (\beta_1 X^{\rho}{}_1 + \beta_2 X^{\rho}{}_2 + ,\ ,\ , + \beta_n X^{\rho}{}_n)^{1/\rho} \qquad (7.2)$$

where Z is total output; X_i is production of commodity i; and β_n and ρ are parameters.

Assuming that firms are profit maximisers and that they choose output combinations to be supplied so as to maximize revenue subject to the production function. We can derive the supply mix of commodities by solving the optimisation problem using the Lagrangian method. With lower case letters representing linearised percentage change form, the supply mix of commodities by industry is given by:

$$x_{idj} = z_j + \sigma^T.(p_i - \sum_i S_{ij}^{pr} \cdot p_i) \qquad (7.3)$$

where $S^{pr}{}_{ij}$ are shares out of the value of all output of industry j attributable to output of good i, p_i is the change in the producer supply price of good i and σ^T is the elasticity of transformation between goods. Subscript 'd' represents domestically produced goods.

Total commodity output is given by:

$$x_{id} = \sum_j B_{ij} \cdot x_i \qquad (7.4)$$

Other equations in this section define intermediate input purchases by firms, labour costs of firms, net (after tax) payments to capital, and the sum of tax payments by industry. The different categories of taxes defined in the model are production taxes, tariffs on imported intermediate inputs, and company taxes.

Demand for Inputs

The inputs into production include intermediate inputs and primary factors. We assume that substitution is not possible between intermediate inputs and primary factors. Therefore industries are assumed to have a Leontief production function of the form

$$Z = \text{minimum}\ [f_p(F_n, F_f, F_k), f_1(X_{1d}^{int}, X_{1m}^{int}), \ldots, f_r(X_{rd}^{int}, X_{rm}^{int})] \qquad (7.5)$$

where Z is output, $F_n, F_{l,} F_k$ are inputs of labour, land and capital, respectively, and $X_{id}^{int}, X_{im}^{int}$ are inputs of commodity i from domestic (d) and imported (m) sources.

The implication of the Leontief production function is that there can be substitution between labour, land and capital as inputs to production, there can be substitution between domestic and imported varieties of a commodity, but there cannot be substitution between primary factors and intermediate inputs or substitution between commodity groups. Note that the model adopts the Armington assumption referred to earlier so that the imported varieties of a commodity are imperfect substitutes for the domestically produced varieties. The functions $f(\cdot)$ are assumed to be constant elasticity of substitution (CES) functions.

Demand for Primary Factors (Land, Labour and Capital)

From the assumptions of a Leontief production function and of CES functions for $f(\cdot)$, are derived the demand for labour, land and capital equations. The equations for primary factors are expressed as follows:

$$f_{kj} = \theta_j .z_j - \sigma_j^f .[w_{kj} - (S_{kj}^f .w_{kj} + S_{kj}^f .\varepsilon_j^i + S_{lj}^f .w_{lj})] \ - \theta_j .(\lambda_{kj} + \lambda_j) \tag{7.6}$$

where k = land, labour, capital; w_{kj} = percentage change in gross rate of payment for primary factor k by industry j; S^f_{kj} = cost share of primary factor k out of all primary factor costs of industry j; ε^i_j = elasticity of substitution between i and j; θ_j = return to scale parameter for industry j; λ_{kj} = percentage change term to account for any exogenous change in productivity of primary factor k in industry j; and λ_j = percentage change term to account for any exogenous change in total primary factor productivity in industry j.

It can be seen from the above equations that substitution is only allowed between labour, land and capital, and between the imported and domestic varieties of each commodity. The second term on the right-hand side of Equation 7.6 allows demand for a given factor to respond according to changes in its relative price compared to the average price of other primary factors. For example, an increase in the relative price of labour will cause a decrease in demand for labour with the magnitude of the decrease dictated by the elasticity of substitution, σ_j^f.

Demand for Intermediate Inputs

The level of output and relative prices determines demand for inputs in each industry. The first term on the right-hand side of Equation 7.7 links output with demand for intermediate inputs – so a 1% increase in output causes a 1% increase in demand for each intermediate input. The second term allows substitution between the imported and domestically produced varieties of each commodity. For example, a rise in price of the domestic variety relative to the imported variety will cause a fall in demand for the domestic variety, and the magnitude of the fall will depend upon the size of σ_{ij}^{int}, the substitution elasticity between imported and domestic varieties of commodity group i for intermediate input usage in industry j.

$$x_{isj}^{\text{int}} = z_j - \sigma_{ij}^{\text{int}} .(p_{is}^{tf} - \sum_s S_{isj}^{\text{int}} .p_{is}^{tf}) - \lambda_{ij} \tag{7.7}$$

Demand for Labour Inputs

There are two categories of labour in the Fiji CGE model - skilled and unskilled. Equations 7.8 and 7.9 determine the level of demand for unskilled and skilled labour for a given level of labour requirement by industry *j* as follows:

$$f_{naj} = f_{nj} \tag{7.8}$$

$$f_{nbj} = f_{nj} \tag{7.9}$$

where f_{naj} = percentage change in usage of skilled labour by industry *j*; f_{nbj} = percentage change in usage of unskilled labour by industry *j*; and f_{nj} = percentage change in labour supply.

It is assumed that an industry splits its labour between the unskilled and skilled categories in fixed proportion so that an increase in labour requirement will translate to proportional increases of unskilled and skilled labour. The secondary informal sector is assumed not to use skilled labour, so Equation 7.7 for determining skilled labour does not extend to that sector.

Labour Market

A Harris-Todaro structure is used to model the labour market (Harris and Todaro 1970). Here, the labour market is dichotomized between rural and urban areas. The model distinguishes between rural and urban-based industries and it is assumed that employment in a rural or urban industry is contingent on being correspondingly located in a rural or urban area. In other words, to work in a rural industry, one must be part of the rural labour force – alternatively, one must be part of the urban labour force to work in an urban industry. In turn, urban industries are distinguished between formal employers and informal employers and all industries are considered formal employers except for the secondary informal industry (see Table 7.1), which employs informal labour only. The equations determining employment are as follows.

$$dF^{r}_{nq} = \sum_{j \in r} F_{nqj} \cdot f_{nqj} \tag{7.10}$$

$$dF^{u}_{nq} = \sum_{j \in u} F_{nqj} \cdot f_{nqj} \tag{7.11}$$

$$dF^{h}_{na} = F_{naj} \cdot f_{naj} \tag{7.12}$$

where dF^{r}_{nq} = change in aggregate demand for rural labour of skill type *q*; dF^{u}_{nq} change in aggregate demand for urban labour of skill type *q* ; dF^{h}_{nq}= change in aggregate demand for informal sector labour (unskilled); and F_{naj} = usage of labour of unskilled labour by industry *j* (coefficient).

Equation 7.10 defines aggregate skilled and unskilled employment in the rural sector as the sum of employment across rural industries, and Equation 7.11 is the corresponding equation for the urban formal sector. Since there is assumed to be no skilled informal labour, Equation 7.12 defines only total unskilled informal employment.

Labour is assumed to be mobile so that wage rates equate across industries in each sector, resulting in a single wage rate for each sector and skill level. There is no open unemployment defined in the model, but informal labour can otherwise be interpreted as labour surplus to formal employment opportunities in the urban sector. This surplus labour is to be interpreted as the combination of those earning an income from informal activities and those that are strictly unemployed. The wage for informal labour is, then, to be interpreted as the average wage across the unemployed and those engaged in informal activities.

On the basis of the Harris-Todaro structure for the model, it is assumed that there is a less than certain probability of finding formal employment in the case of unskilled labour in the urban labour market. Therefore, if one cannot find formal employment, then that person becomes surplus labour, and so part of informal employment in our model. Further details of the labour market structure are provided in Levantis (2006).

Household Demand and Savings

As indicated earlier, the household sector obtains its income from returns to factors owned by the household sector (i.e. labour and capital) and from transfers. The sources of household income include: investment income receipts from abroad; net private unrequited transfers from abroad; and transfers from the government. The determination of government transfers is discussed in the next section and the determination of investment income receipts and private unrequited transfers is explained later in the overview of the external sector equations. Household sector income is then applied to consumption, savings and income taxes. Equation 7.13 defines household savings in percentage change form as:

$$dS^{pri} = \mu.dY^{pri} + d\mu.Y^{pri} \tag{7.13}$$

where S^{pri} is total private sector savings, Y^{pr} is the aggregate disposable income of the household sector, and μ is the marginal propensity to consume out of disposable income.

Disposable income is defined in Equation 7.14 as the gross income of households (as discussed above), less income tax payments.

$$dY^{pri} = \sum_j dY_j^n + \sum_j dY_j^{kneth} + dQ^{yinf} + dQ^t + dG^{tra} - dR^w \tag{7.14}$$

where dY^n_j = change in total labour costs in industry j; dQ^{yinf} = change in gross private receipts of investment income from abroad; dQ^t = change in net private unrequited transfers from abroad; dG^{tra} = change in government transfers to households; and dR^w = change in income tax revenue.

Consumption expenditure is determined as the residual of disposable income, less savings. The marginal propensity to save is determined by Equation 7.15 and adjusts according to interest rates, so a rise in interest rates increases the marginal propensity to save.

$$d\mu = \omega.r + dh^{\mu} \tag{7.15}$$

where r = interest rate; dh^{μ} = an exogenous shift term for marginal propensity to save; and ω = parameter to measure the impact of interest rates on the marginal propensity to save.

Household purchases of commodities for consumption are assumed to be determined by the budget constraint and relative prices between commodities. On the basis of the assumption of utility maximisation, the aggregate Marshallian demand function for commodities of group i can be expressed as:

$$X_i^{pc} = X_i^{pc}(P_i^c, C) \tag{7.16}$$

where $X^{pc}{}_i$ is consumption purchases from commodity group i; $P^c{}_i$ is the weighted average price (between the domestic and imported variety) of commodity i at the consumers' purchase price; and C is aggregate consumption expenditure.

Differentiating and rearranging we get:

$$\frac{dX_i^{pc}}{X_i^{pc}} = \eta_i \frac{dC}{C} + \sum_h \varepsilon_{ih} \cdot \frac{dP_h^c}{P_h^c} \tag{7.17}$$

where η_i = income elasticity of demand for commodity i; and ε_{ih} = own and cross price elasticity of demand.

Demand for the domestic or imported varieties of commodity i are then determined according to the overall level of demand for the commodity group (as determined by Equation 7.17), and the relative prices of the domestic and imported varieties. Purchases of the composite commodity i are assumed to be determined according to the following CES function:

$$X_i^{pc} = (\beta_{id} . X_{id}^{pc\,\rho} + \beta_{im} . X_{im}^{pc\,\rho})^{1/\rho} \tag{7.18}$$

where subscripts d and m refer to the domestic and imported varieties; and the ρ and b_{is} are parameters ($s = d$ is domestic, $s = m$ is imported).

Government Sector

As indicated earlier, the change in total government tax revenue (dG^{tax}) is defined as the sum of the change in income tax revenue (dR^{w}), the change in company tax revenue (dR^{k}), the change in production tax revenue (dR^{py}), the change in tariff revenue (dR^{tf}), the change in excise tax revenue (dR^{exc}), and the change in value added tax (dR^{vat}). That is:

$$dG^{tax} = dR^{w} + dR^{k} + dR^{pr} + dR^{tf} + dR^{exc} + dR^{vat} \tag{7.19}$$

Additional equations are added to determine each of these revenue components. Government consumption expenditure (G^{con}) is defined below as simply the sum of the value of purchases of each commodity i from source s. That is:

$$G^{con} = \sum_i \sum_s P^{gfd}_{is} .X^{gc}_{is} \tag{7.20}$$

where the value of purchases is defined at final demand after VAT purchase prices ($P^{gfd}{}_{is}$) and $X^{gc}{}_{is}$ is government consumption purchases of commodity i from source s.

Government investment expenditure (G^{inv}) is similarly defined as follows:

$$G^{inv} = \sum_i \sum_s P^{gfd}_{is} .X^{gi}_{is} \tag{7.21}$$

Government transfers to the household sector (G^{tra}) are assumed to be indexed to consumer prices so that we have:

$$\frac{dG^{tra}}{G^{tra}} = \frac{d\varepsilon^c}{\varepsilon^c} \tag{7.22}$$

where ε^c is the consumer price index. The remaining government sector equations determine the company tax rate and tariff rates.

External Sector

The external sector of the model comprises equations to define aggregate imports and exports, gross private receipts from investment income earned abroad, investment income transferred abroad by each industry, foreign aid, and net private unrequited transfers abroad. Aggregate imports (M) are defined as the sum of the value of imports of each commodity at border prices. That is:

$$M = \sum_i P_{im} .X_{im} \tag{7.23}$$

where P_{im} is the import price of commodity i (subscript m indicates imports) at the border and X_{im} is the quantity of imports of i.

The value of aggregate exports (E) is similarly defined as:

$$E = \sum_i P^{efd}_{id} .X^{e}_{i} \tag{7.24}$$

where P^{efd}_{id} is the border price of exports (subscript d denotes domestically produced) and X^{e}_{i} denotes exports.

Imports of commodity i (X_{im}) are determined in Equation 7.25 as the sum of demand for imported intermediate inputs (X^{int}_{imj}), private consumption (X^{pc}_{im}), private investment (X^{pi}_{im}), government consumption (X_{im}^{gc}), and government investment (X_{im}^{gi}). In change form, this can be expressed as:

$$x_{im} = \sum_j B_{ij}^{intm}.x_{imj}^{int} + B_i^{pcm}.x_{im}^{pc} + B_i^{pim}.x_{im}^{pi} + B_i^{gcm}.x_{im}^{gc} + B_i^{gim}.x_{im}^{gi} \tag{7.25}$$

where the B's are shares.

Exports of commodity i (X_i^e) are defined as total domestic production of commodity i (X_{id}), less domestic sales, which will be the sum of that sold as intermediate inputs (X_{idj}^{int}), private consumption (X_{id}^{pc}), private investment (X_{id}^{pi}), government consumption (X_{id}^{gc}), and government investment (X_{id}^{gi}). This is also expressed in change form as:

$$B_i^e.x_i^e = x_{id} - \sum_j B_{ij}^{int}.x_{idj}^{int} - B_i^{pc}.x_{id}^{pc} - B_i^{pi}.x_{id}^{pi} - B_i^{gc}.x_{id}^{gc} - B_i^{gi}.x_{id}^{gi} \tag{7.26}$$

It is assumed that gross private receipts from investment income earned abroad (Q^{yinf}) is received in foreign currency and transferred into domestic currency, giving:

$$\frac{dQ^{yinf}}{Q^{yinf}} = e^{xch} + q^{yinf*} \tag{7.27}$$

where e^{xch} = exchange rate (Fiji dollars per unit of foreign currency) and Q^{yinf*} = gross private receipts from investment income in foreign currency, which is assumed to be exogenous; and q^{yinf*} is the change form of Q^{yinf*}.

Equation 7.28 determines, in change form, net private unrequited transfers abroad. In foreign currency, net private unrequited transfers are assumed exogenous, so in domestic currency net private unrequited transfers are simply defined as:

$$\frac{dQ^t}{Q^t} = e^{xch} + q^{t*} \tag{7.28}$$

where Q^t and q^{t*} are net private unrequited transfers in domestic currency and in foreign currency, respectively.

Foreign aid is defined similarly and is taken to be exogenous in foreign currency. In change form, the foreign aid equation is given by:

$$\frac{dQ^a}{Q^a} = e^{xch} + q^{a*} \tag{7.29}$$

where Q^a is the foreign aid term and q^{a*} is its equivalent change term.

Finance Sector

The core equation for the finance sector defines the change in nominal private investment expenditure (*dI*) as the sum of private savings (S^{pri}), government savings (S^{gov}), and net capital inflows (Q^k). That is:

$$dS^{pri} + dS^{gov} + dQ^k = dI \tag{7.30}$$

It is assumed that the net change in foreign reserves (Q^r) is endogenous. Therefore, Q^k is determined as the residual in Equation 7.30. Nominal private investment expenditure is then determined by Equation 7.31 as follows:

$$\frac{dI}{I} = \varepsilon^i + i^{real} \tag{7.31}$$

where ε^i = investment price index and i^{real} is the change in real private investment expenditure.

It is important to note that government investment expenditure is not part of *I*, as it is itemised separately. The surplus of funds from government activities is assumed to be available as part of the pool of funds that private investors can draw upon. Nominal investment expenditure and real investment expenditure are linked in change form in Equation 7.31.

Treatment of Capital

In general, most CGE models impose the restriction that either capital is fixed in each industry or that capital is completely mobile. In static models, capital is assumed to be exogenous (i.e. fixed) in the short-run, but is endogenous (i.e. mobile) in the long-run. In this model, industries are allowed to invest to target an optimal level of capacity utilisation, which they can within a period according to changes in market conditions. For example, if there is an increase in demand leading to increased profit opportunities, and increased rates of return (or price of capital), then the industry will respond by increasing its factor usage – including its capital usage (hence, utilisation), thereby increasing its supply. Further details are provided in Levantis (2006).

To determine investment, we first establish the identity below linking the capital stock level in the next period to investment and depreciation in the current period:

$$dK_j^{t1} = F_j^i - D_j \tag{7.32}$$

where, F_j^i is investment in the current period and D_j is depreciation.

This identity simply says the change in capital stock next period will equal investment minus depreciation this period. We can define depreciation simply as the actual usage of capital stock so that $D_j = F_{kj}$ and, in percentage change form, $d_j = f_{kj}$. Equation 7.31 can be expressed in change form as:

$$dK_j^{t1} = (F_j^i - F_{kj}) + (F_j^i.x_j^{pi} - F_{kj}.f_{kj}) \tag{7.33}$$

where x_j^{pi} is the percentage change in investment in industry *j*.

Equation 7.34 determines the demand for purchases of each commodity *is* for investment purchases in industry *j*. Demand for each commodity moves in accordance with changes in overall investment in industry *j*.

$$x_{isj}^{pi} = x_j^{pi} \tag{7.34}$$

Equation 7.35 aggregates investment purchases of each commodity *is* across industries, while Equation 7.36 aggregates across investment by industry to determine economy wide real investment.

$$x_{is}^{pi} = \sum_j S_{isj}^{invis} x_{isj}^{pi} \tag{7.35}$$

$$i^{real} = \sum_j S_j^{inv}.x_j^{pi} + h^{ireal} \tag{7.36}$$

where the *S*'s are investment shares and h^{ireal} is an exogenous shock term for real investment.

Finally, an equation is included to determine land supply. It is assumed that there is a fixed availability of supply of land for agriculture in Fiji. Land prices are allowed to vary from industry to industry, while reallocation of land between industries is possible. Land allocation to an industry responds to the price of land for that industry relative to the weighted average price level of land within the region. An increase in the supply of land to an industry will require an increase in the price of land relative to the weighted average price. This process is captured by Equation 7.37:

$$f_{lj} = f_l^{total} + \sigma^{land}.(w_{lj} - w_l^{total}) \tag{7.37}$$

where f_{lj} = percentage change in usage of land by industry *j*; $f^{total}{}_l$ = percentage change in total supply of land across the economy; σ^{land} = substitution elasticity in allocation of land across industries; w_{lj} = percentage change in gross rate of payment for land by industry *j*; and $w^{total}{}_l$ = percentage change in weighted average price of land across the economy.

Information Equations

Information equations refer to equations that enter into the model for informational purposes only. These include equations to determine nominal GDP, real GDP, nominal consumption, real consumption, national welfare, and other relationships. Nominal GDP in change form is defined as the sum of consumption, investment, government spending, and the trade surplus. This is expressed in change form as:

$$dGDP = dC + dI + dG^{con} + dG^{inv} + dE - dM \tag{7.38}$$

Equation 7.39, then, determines the percentage change in real GDP as the change in nominal GDP less the GDP deflator (ρ).

$$gdp^{real} = \frac{dGDP}{GDP} - \rho \tag{7.39}$$

The percentage change in real consumption expenditure is similarly derived in equation 7.40 as the change in nominal consumption expenditure less inflation as determined by the consumer price index.

$$c^{real} = \frac{dC}{C} - \varepsilon^{c} \tag{7.40}$$

National welfare is defined here as the change in the value of output of the economy that accrues to Fijians. In this sense, if the objective of a simulation is to test to what extent Fiji will be better or worse off, it is the national welfare equations that should be looked at. National welfare (V) is simply measured by adding to GDP net inflows of investment income, net private unrequited transfers from abroad, and net foreign aid receipts from abroad.

$$dV = dC + dS^{pri} + dG^{con} + dG^{inv} + dS^{gov} + dQ^{r} \tag{7.41}$$

Change in real national welfare (dV^{real}) is given by:

$$dV^{real} = dV - (C + S^{pri}).\varepsilon^{c} - (G^{con} + G^{inv} + S^{gov}).\varepsilon^{gc} \tag{7.42}$$

The remaining equations determine the percentage change in aggregate exports and aggregate imports, change in the government budget surplus as a percentage of GDP, the current account surplus as a percentage of GDP, and some useful employment aggregates in percentage change terms.

Determination of Commodity Prices

A number of equations are included in the model to define commodity prices and prices of primary factors. Commodity prices are first defined at *basic values*, from which prices under various definitions of *purchaser's prices* are derived. The price of a commodity at basic values is defined as the price received by the suppliers after all taxes have been deducted. This can be interpreted as the price level net of all tax distortions. The taxes imposed on commodities include tariffs, excises, and value added tax (VAT). It is assumed that these taxes are applied to the basic value price level in that order. Therefore, from the price level at basic values, P_{is}, where i is the commodity and s the source of supply (i.e. domestic or imported), we have the following definitions of prices:

- Prices after tariffs – $P_{is}^{tf} = (1 + T_{is}^{tf}).P_{is}$, where P_{is}^{tf} is the price level of commodity i from source s after tariffs, and T_{is}^{tf} is the tariff rate. Naturally, the tariff rate on domestically sourced commodities will be zero.
- Prices after excises – $P_{is}^{exc} = (1 + T_{i}^{exc}).P_{is}^{tf}$, where P_{is}^{exc} is the price level of commodity is after excises, and T_{i}^{exc}, is the excise tax rate of commodity i.
- Private final demand prices after VAT – $P_{is}^{pfd} = (1 + T_{i}^{pfd}).P_{is}^{exc}$, where P_{is}^{pfd} is the price level of commodity is after VAT on private purchases, and T_{i}^{pfd} is the VAT rate for private purchasers.
- Government final demand prices after VAT – $P_{is}^{gfd} = (1 + T_{is}^{gfd}).P_{is}^{exc}$, where P_{is}^{gfd} is the price level of commodity is after VAT on government purchases, and T_{is}^{gfd} is the VAT rate for government.
- Export prices after VAT – $P_{id}^{efd} = (1 + T_{i}^{efd}).P_{id}$, where P_{id}^{efd} is the price level of commodity i after VAT on export purchases (s = d denotes that the commodity is produced domestically), and T_{i}^{efd} is the VAT rate for exports of commodity i. Commodity exports are not generally subject to VAT, but VAT is normally charged on exports of tourist and other services.

The commodity price equations include import prices and the domestic price of exports. Import prices are defined in percentage change form as:

$$p_{im} = p_{im}^{*} + e^{xch} \tag{7.43}$$

where e^{xch} is the change in the foreign exchange rate and p^{*}_{im} is the price of imports in foreign currency.

The domestic price of exported commodities is defined as:

$$p_{id}^{efd} = p_{id}^{*} + B_{i}^{e}.e^{xch} \tag{7.44}$$

where p^{*}_{id} is the change in prices in foreign currency (the subscript d refers to domestically produced commodities) and B^{e}_{i} is the share of output of commodity i sold as exports.

The consumer price index (ε^{c}) is defined as the weighted sum of changes in consumer prices. That is:

$$\varepsilon^{c} = \sum_{i \in a} \sum_{s} S_{is}^{cn} . p_{is}^{pfd} \tag{7.45}$$

where S^{cn}_{is} is the share out of the value of all consumption attributable to consumption of commodity i, variety s.

Similar indices are defined for investment prices, as well as prices for government consumption, government investment, exports and imports.

Determination of Factor Prices

Price of Labour

The change in *expected* net (after tax) wage for urban (dW^{unet}_{nq}) and rural labour (dW^{rnet}_{nq}) is defined, respectively, in change form as:

$$dW_{nq}^{unet} = (1 - T_{nq}^{u}).dW_{nq}^{u} - W_{nq}^{u}.dT_{nq}^{u} \tag{7.46}$$

$$dW_{nq}^{rnet} = (1 - T_{nq}^{r}).dW_{nq}^{r} - W_{nq}^{r}.dT_{nq}^{r} \tag{7.47}$$

where T^{u}_{nq} and are T^{r}_{nq} are the *ad valorem* income tax rates for urban and rural labour, respectively, of skill type q; W^{u}_{nq} and W^{r}_{nq} are the annual gross urban and rural wage rates, respectively, for labour of skill type q.

Price of Capital

The change in the net price of capital (w^{net}_{kj}) is defined as:

$$w_{kj}^{net} = w_{kj} - \frac{1}{1 - T_{j}^{k}}.dT_{j}^{k} \tag{7.48}$$

where T^{k}_{j} is the *ad valorem* tax rate on capital returns of industry j.

Price of Land

Finally, the percentage change in the weighted average price of land across the economy (w^{total}_{l}) is defined as:

$$w_{l}^{total} = \sum_{j} S_{lj}^{f}.w_{lj} \tag{7.49}$$

where w_{lj} is the percentage change in the gross rate of payment for land by industry j, and S^{f}_{lj} is the cost share of land out of all primary factor costs of industry j, gross prices.

MODEL CLOSURE AND SOLUTION

The model's I-O database represents an initial map of the economy in a state of equilibrium, as implied by the Walrasian condition in Equation 7.1. We then impose the scenario we wish to simulate on this initial map, throwing the system out of equilibrium. The system iterates towards a new equilibrium until a final equilibrium is reached. By comparing the new map of the economy with the old one, we are able to measure the impact of a particular policy on a range of economic variables. For each year, the model can be represented as:

$$F(X) = 0 \tag{7.50}$$

where F is an n x m matrix for which the number of variables, n, exceeds the number of equations, m.

To carry out the simulations, we compute changes in the endogenous variables from their values in the initial solution caused by changes in the exogenous variables. The model is recursive dynamic, in the sense that each period is solved as a static equilibrium problem given the stock of capital and investment. The results for a particular period are used to update the database to form the basis for the next simulation, and so on. Model closure refers to the designation of the exogenous/endogenous split. Since the equation system 7.50 contains more variables than equation, we assign exogenously given values to the $(n\text{-}m)$ variables and solve for the remaining m endogenous variables.

Three types of closures are employed in the simulations: a basic closure, a forecasting closure, and a deviation closure. The basic closure is the type that is commonly used in comparative-static simulations of CGE models. The exogenous variables in the basic closure include various tax rates, export and import prices, the exchange rate (the *numeraire*), technology, various exogenous shock terms, and exports of non-exportable goods. Real government purchases are also set exogenous because we make no attempt to model government behaviour.

In the forecasting closure, we make assumptions about the growth rates of key socio-economic variables, such as population growth, output of sugar, changes in real interest rates, tourism, real government expenditure, agricultural productivity, changes in capital stocks, import prices, and exchange rates. These forecasts are summarised in Table 7.3.

The forecasts are taken from specialist agencies such as the Reserve Bank of Fiji, the IMF, the World Bank, the ADB, and the Australian Bureau of Agricultural and Resource Economics.

In the forecasting closure, these variables are set exogenously according to their forecast values. The forecasting closure produces projections for the economy through time. This can be considered as a dynamic path along which the economy is expected to move. In the deviation closure, we then test to see how the path will be affected by the introduction of a policy change. This allows us to compare the new growth path after the policy change with the path the economy would have taken in the absence of any changes (i.e. the base case or *business as usual* case). In the deviation closure, the following changes are made to the model:

Table 7.3. Forecasts of Key Macroeconomic Variables

Variable	Forecast growth rate (%)		
	2006	2007	2008–11
Domestic inflation	2.0	2.0	2.0
World inflation[e]	2.3	2.3	2.1
Population growth[a]	1.0	1.0	1.0
Tourism[b]	5.0	5.0	5.0
Commodity prices[c]			
– Sugar	16.2	5.0	2.0
– Gold	30.3	10.0	2.0
Import prices[d]	2.3	2.3	2.1
Sugarcane exports	0.0	0.0	0.0
Nominal government consumption expenditure	0.0	0.0	0.0
Real government consumption expenditure	2.0	2.0	2.0
Nominal government investment expenditure	0.0	0.0	0.0
Nominal government transfers to households	3.0	3.0	3.0

Sources:
a. Reserve Bank of Fiji; b. International Monetary Fund; c. Asian Development Bank.
d. Australian Bureau of Agricultural and Resource Economics.
e. World Bank forecasts.

- for those variables that are *exogenous* in both the basic and forecasting closures, the same shock is given as in the forecasting closure; and
- for those variables that are *exogenous* in the basic closure but *endogenous* in the forecasting closure, the shock is made identical to the corresponding endogenous (i.e. solution) values from the forecast simulations.

Additional shocks are added to the deviation closure to simulate the effects of trade liberalisation policies. The model is solved using Version 9 of *GEMPACK* (Harrison and Pearson 1996).

CONCLUSION

In recent years, computable general equilibrium models have found increasing use in policy analysis and research due to their ability to analyse complex interactions within sectors of an economy following a policy shock. In contrast to older analytical approaches, such as econometric modeling (which belong the class of partial equilibrium models), CGE models are able to measure both the first-round and second-round effects of a given policy. Furthermore, inter-industry effects and macroeconomic adjustments, including effects on households can also be evaluated.

Thus, CGE models are able to assess the effects of a broader range of policies and 'what if' scenarios, compared to other modelling approaches. In the early stages of CGE modelling, analysis using this particular approach required the help of software programmers and other technicians. However, within the last few years, the development of user-friendly Windows-based software packages has brought CGE modelling within the reach of analysts who may not necessarily be technical experts. The falling costs of computer memory and ever-increasing processing speeds have also vastly increased the size and complexity of CGE models.

Chapter 8

IMPACT OF TRADE LIBERALISATION POLICIES

INTRODUCTION

Before the Doha Development Round was launched in November 2001, there were eight multilateral trade negotiating rounds. Although developing countries greatly increased their preparation, organisation and active participation after the Uruguay Round and the creation of the WTO in 1995, they still did not perform well in 2001. Following the Cancun ministerial meeting in 2003, one criticism of developing country participation was that they opposed but did not propose in a constructive manner. This criticism has some merit since developing countries are resource constrained and, hence, are limited in their capacity to intervene in the policy process with well-considered proposals. In recent years, there has been considerable emphasis on providing financial and technical assistance to developing countries for capacity-building measures.

Despite all the high-sounding rhetoric about the democratic credentials of the WTO, the decision-making processes are opaque. Moreover, the practice of a few countries meeting behind closed doors (the so-called 'green room'), to make decisions remains an entrenched feature of WTO decision making. For instance, when ministers convened in Cancun, the main outstanding issues were agriculture, market access (tariffs) and whether to include Singaporean issues. Following a green-room meeting, the Singaporean issues (investment, competition policy, transparency in government procurement and trade facilitation) were placed at the top of the agenda. This appeared to be a strategy to shift the focus away from agricultural liberalisation.

The current WTO negotiations on trade policy reforms have important implications for Fiji. As a member of the ACP countries, Fiji has enjoyed preferential terms of access for her sugar exports to the EU market under the 1975 Lomé Convention. As a member of the PICs, Fiji also benefits from SPARTECA for exports of garments into the Australian and New Zealand markets. Under the WTO policy reforms, these preferential arrangements are to be abolished.

In preparation for eventual global trade liberalisation, the PICs have adopted a regional trade agreement (RTA), referred to as the PICTA, which took effect from January 1st 2006. PICTA aims to further integrate trade among the PICs, and requires them to gradually lower tariffs on their goods over a ten-year period. Given that a typical problem for the PICs is their smallness, PICTA aims to create an expanded market of some seven million consumers. PICTA excludes Australia and New Zealand, which have, however, been included in another recently signed agreement, the PACER. This agreement requires the PICs to begin PACER negotiations at the most eight years after PICTA comes into effect.

Although the agricultural export share of developing countries fell from 42% to 11% between 1970 and 2003, for many of these countries, agriculture remains a significant contributor to total output and employment. Therefore, it is necessary for the developing countries to exploit their comparative advantage in the wake of trade liberalisation measures. In 2001, developing countries faced an average tariff (after accounting for preferences) of 16% for agriculture and food exports and 9% for textiles and clothing – compared to only 2.5% for other manufactured goods (see Table 3.1). At the same time, the average tariff in developing countries is also relatively high, thus highlighting the need for policy reforms in both the developed and developing countries.

The purpose of this chapter is to analyse the impacts of these trade-related developments on the Fijian economy by employing the dynamic CGE model, which was described in the previous chapter.[1] The remainder of the chapter is organised in the following way. The second section briefly reviews the theoretical and empirical literature on the implications of trade liberalisation and RTAs. The next section justifies the policy scenarios employed in the simulations, followed by a presentation and discussion of the empirical results. The final section summarises the main findings and policy implications.

Table 8.1. Average Applied Import Tariffs by Sector and Region in 2001

Exporting economies	Importing economies		
	High income	Developing	World
Agriculture and food			
High-income	18	18	17.8
Developing	14	18	15.6
Textiles and wearing apparel			
High-income	8	15	12.0
Developing	7	20	9.3
Other manufactures			
High-income	2	9	4.1
Developing	1	7	2.5
All merchandise			
High-income	3	10	5.4
Developing	3	10	4.9

Source: Anderson and Martin (2006).

[1] This chapter draws on Asafu-Adjaye (2007), Asafu-Adjaye and Mahadevan (2008), and Mahadevan and Asafu-Adjaye (2008).

Implications of Trade Liberalisation and Regional Trade Agreements

'Trade liberalisation' is a rather broad term, which is used to describe a country's trade becoming more 'outward-oriented'. This is associated with a situation where trade reforms are seen as moving towards 'neutrality', 'liberality' or 'openness'. Neutrality is associated with approximately equal incentives between the export and import-competing sectors. Liberality is associated with reduced government intervention in trade; while openness is associated with an increasing importance of trade (imports and exports) in the economy (Edwards 1993). Therefore, trade reform policies – such as the simplification of import procedures, the reduction/elimination of quotas, and the removal/reduction of tariffs – can all be subsumed under the heading of trade liberalisation.

Since the establishment of the General Agreement on Tariffs and Trade (GATT) in 1947, and the WTO in 1995, the dominant view in the economics literature is that free (or freer) trade fosters economic growth. This view is bolstered by studies that show that during the last three decades, open economies grew much faster than economies with high protection levels. In addition, it has been shown that some economies that implemented import substitution policies either suffered economic crises or collapsed during the eighties and nineties (Sachs and Warner 1995; Krueger 1998).

Two main channels have been identified as the means by which trade promotes economic growth. The first is through technology and the second through investment. According to the first view, also referred to as the New Trade or Endogenous Growth Theory, countries open to trade benefit for a number of reasons including technological spillover effects from exposure to a large international market, economies of scale in R&D, higher profits for innovators, and avoidance of the replication of R&D efforts across countries (Romer 1990; Grossman and Helpman 1991; Krueger 1998).

However, others have argued that investment is the key link between trade and economic growth. For example, Baldwin and Segheza (1996) and Lee (1994) have developed theoretical models that show trade liberalisation promotes growth through the increased use of imported capital and intermediate inputs. This effect occurs because often the traded sector happens to be more capital-intensive than the non-traded sector. Baldwin and Seghezza (1996) and Wacziag (1998) have provided empirical support for the positive impact of investment on growth. Other studies, such as Coe and Helpman (1995), have also shown that trade liberalisation enhances economic growth through its positive effects on total factor productivity growth.

Not all economists agree that trade liberalisation is a major driving force for economic growth. For example, Sachs (1987, 1989) has argued that the spectacular success of the East Asian tigers was influenced more by active government promotion of exports and restriction of imports. Imbs and Wacziarg (2003) found that developing countries tend to diversify rather than specialise, thus casting doubt on comparative advantage as a key factor in economic development. Taylor (1991) has argued that there are some losses attributable to open trade and capital market policies, while Greenaway *et al.* (1997) did not find any conclusive results on the positive effects of trade liberalisation in their empirical modeling.

Regional trade agreements may be viewed as a step towards global trade liberalisation. In fact, this is the view embodied in the GATT *Article XXIV* which maintains that, provided new

RTAs do not raise trade barriers to the 'rest of the world', they contribute to the lowering of trade barriers worldwide (WTO 1995). To date, there is no consensus on the effects of an RTA. Viner (1950) suggested that trade induced by an RTA is of two types: trade creation and trade diversion.[2] According to him, where the trade-diverting effect is dominant, welfare will be reduced in the member countries as well as the rest of the world (ROW).

Bhagwati and Panagariya (1996) and Panagariya (2000) support this view. They argue that because an RTA gives preferential treatment to its members, trade will be diverted from non-members who could be least-cost suppliers. This trade diversion is likely to dominate trade creation and, therefore, reduce welfare of the members and the ROW. In their example, they show that the liberalising member loses tariff revenue and yet does not receive a lower domestic price for the imported good. However, Wonnacott (1996) argued that trade diversion is not necessarily welfare-decreasing, as firms in a trade-diverting country could exploit economies of scale by having a larger market and could become least-cost suppliers, thus increasing welfare for the diverting country and the ROW. De Melo *et al.* (1993) have shown that there can be large gains from an RTA between developed and developing countries due to different factor endowments.

The net impact of an RTA on a member country depends on a number of factors including initial tariffs, export capacity, and the world price of RTA members vis-à-vis non-members. Also, for a given country, an RTA could be trade creating in some sectors and trade diverting in others. Thus, the issue of the net impact from an RTA is strictly an empirical one. CGE models, with their high degree of sectoral disaggregation and ability to capture economy-wide interactions, are well suited for analysing trade liberalisation issues in general, and RTAs in particular. A number of studies (Brown *et al.*, 1992; Brown, 1993; Francois and Shiells, 1994) have analysed the North-American Free Trade Agreement (NAFTA) using CGE models and concluded that the trade creation effect offsets the trade diversion effects. Also, it was found that welfare increased for members of NAFTA (Canada, Mexico and the US), but decreased for excluded countries.

Haaland and Norman (1992) investigated the effects of the EU's single market and found that it increased the welfare of its members. In a study of the effects of a bilateral RTA, Hertel *et al.* (2001) simulated a Japan-Singapore RTA that considered tariff liberalisation for trade in goods only versus other elements, including trade services and e-commerce. They found that Japan would lose in a tariff-only liberalisation and gain when all elements of an RTA were included. Singapore would gain in both cases, but with larger gains for a full RTA. Non-members would lose in the tariff-only scenario, but gain in a full RTA. Finally, Scollay and Gilbert (2000) conducted a set of trade liberalisation simulations for Asia-Pacific Economic Cooperation (APEC) countries. The simulations considered a number of possible RTAs including bilateral, plurilateral, APEC liberalisation on an MFN basis, APEC liberalisation on a preferential basis, and global trade liberalisation. Welfare gains from a bilateral RTA were minimal and, under a plurilateral RTA, some APEC members lose. Gains were much larger for APEC liberalisation – both most-favoured nation (MFN) and preferential – while non-members lose in all the scenarios, except under APEC MFN liberalisation. However, the

[2] Trade creation occurs when the importing country substitutes a lower cost supply source within the area for a more costly source. On the other hand, trade diversion occurs when a more costly supply source within the area is substituted for a less costly source outside the area.

largest welfare gains for APEC members and the ROW was in the case of global trade liberalisation.

Although trade liberalisation and RTAs have been found to be welfare enhancing for a number of developed and developing countries, this issue has not been subjected to sufficient empirical investigation for the PICs in general, or Fiji in particular. Before 1989, Fiji followed an inward-looking import substitution strategy in which industries such as rice, dairy, poultry, beef, pork and tobacco were protected by a complex array of quotas, tariffs and subsidies. In the period 1989 to 1995, the agricultural sector became the focus of a national policy of deregulation, with a switch from licensing and import controls to tariff protection and a gradual reduction in tariff levels. Initial evaluation of the policy change indicated that there were benefits from increased exports (ADB 1991; Lightfoot 1994). However, in a subsequent study, Kumar and Prasad (2002) argued that the policy switch failed to deliver a high average annual growth rate. In a recent study using time series analysis, Narayan and Smyth (2005) also concluded that trade liberalisation has not contributed to economic growth in Fiji.

Many of the past studies on trade liberalisation suffer a number of shortcomings, from an empirical point of view. Firstly, many of these studies have used time-series, cross-sectional and panel estimations.[3] The problem with such approaches is that they are based on gravity or partial equilibrium models. These are unreliable for assessing policies like trade liberalisation as they have 'second round' and feedback effects on the economy effects (including inter-industry effects, demand for factors of production and other macroeconomic adjustments on output, employment, and welfare gains). Secondly, many of these studies are unable to analyse the combined effects of more than one type of trade liberalisation measure. Thirdly, the majority of these studies use aggregate data rather than country-specific data. More recent studies of trade liberalisation (Santos-Paulino 2005; Karingi *et al.* 2006a) have used the multi-regional GTAP model (Hertel 1996), which apart from using highly aggregated data, is a static model.

POLICY SIMULATIONS

We investigate the effects on the Fiji economy of five trade policies given by the following scenarios:

Scenario 1: Unilateral tariff reduction by Fiji.
Scenario 2: the impact of PICTA.
Scenario 3: the impact of an RTA comprising PICTA and PACER.
Scenario 4: the impact of partial trade liberalisation (tariff removal only).
Scenario 5: the impact of full trade liberalisation (removal of both tariff and non-tariff barriers).

These scenarios are briefly discussed below.

Table 8.2. Values of the Shocks in Scenario 1

Scenario 1 Unilateral Tariff Reduction	Shock in Tariff Rate in Period i
Rice	-5.6%, Year 1
Ginger, dalo, root crops	-5%, Year 1
Fruit and vegetables	-4%, Year 1
Dairy	-3% p.a., Years 1-3
Livestock	-3%, Year 1
Forestry	-3%, Year 1
Fishing	-5% p.a., Years 1-3
Beverages and tobacco	-6%, Year 1
Sugar products	-8% p.a., Years 1-3; -3% Year 4

Scenario 1: Unilateral Tariff Reduction by Fiji

Compared to other developing countries, the average tariff rate in Fiji is relatively high. The current average applied rate is about 18% for agriculture and food (Anderson *et al.*, 2006). Fiji could push ahead to unilaterally liberalise its trade in readiness for eventual global trade liberalisation. To simulate the effects of such a policy, we imposed phased reductions in tariff rates for a range of agricultural commodities. Goods with tariff rates that were 8% or less had the full tariff cut in Year 1, while goods with higher tariff rates had phased reductions down to zero. Details of are provided in Table 8.2.

Scenario 2: The Impact of PICTA

The signatories to PICTA have, in effect, committed themselves to a policy of trade liberalisation by agreeing to completely eliminate tariff and non-tariff barriers to trade by 2010. *Article 7* of the agreement, signed in 2001, requires all tariffs on 'originating goods' to be reduced and eliminated in accordance with the timetables set out in *Annex II* of PICTA for trade among themselves – essentially falling to zero, ten to twelve years after ratification. Those PICs classified as LDCs and Small Island States (SIS) have been given a parallel but higher schedule of reducing import duties compared to the larger PICs such as Papua New Guinea and Fiji. For the protection of 'sensitive industries' from full competition and to give them a longer timeframe to adjust, PICTA allows each country to provide an 'Excepted Imports List' that has a slower timetable of tariff reduction. The timetable for tariff reductions for all countries except LDCs and SIS are shown in Table 8.3.

[3] See an extensive survey of these studies by Santos-Paulino (2005).

Table 8.3. PICTA Timetable for Reduction and Elimination of Tariffs

	Maximum tariff on goods from				
Base tariff on goods at January 1, 2001	1/1/ 2001	1/1/2004	1/1/2006	1/1/2008	1/1/2010
More than 20%	20%	15%	10%	5%	0%
20% - 15%	15%	10%	5%	0%	
15% - 10%	10%	5%	0%		
Not more than 10%	0%				

Source: PICTA Annex II, accessed on 3rd November 2006 from http://www.forumsec.org.fj/division/TID/PACER-PICTA/PICTA%20-%20%20as%20endorsed%20and%20signed%20by%20Forum%20Leaders%2018-8-01.pdf

Currently, there is very little trade among the PICs. For example, the percentage of total import duty revenues collected by Kiribati, Samoa, and Vanuatu for imports from Fiji were, respectively, 13%, 9%, and 9% in 2003/04 (Narsey 2004). Fiji, too, imports very little from the other PICs.[4] Given this situation, and the fact that Fiji is among the most 'industrialised' countries in the Pacific region, it is assumed in this simulation that PICTA will not lead to an increase in Fijian imports from the PICs. On the other hand, we would likely to see an increase in the exports of commodities (such as sugar products and garments) for which Fiji already had a comparative advantage when the other PICs also removed their tariffs. In this simulation, a conservative assumption of 0.5% per annum growth in the above mentioned commodities is assumed.

Scenario 3: The Impact of an RTA Comprising PICTA and PACER

The PACER, which was signed and ratified by all PICs in 2001, is essentially an expanded RTA that includes Australia and New Zealand and requires the elimination of trade tariffs between the member countries. Given Fiji's comparative advantage in some areas, it is reasonable to presume that improved market access would increase exports of commodities such as kava, fruit and vegetables, forest products, and marine products.

In this simulation, we combine a complete removal of import tariffs with an increase in agricultural exports. The import tariffs are phased out over the simulation period in accordance with the PICTA timetable (Table 8.3). With agricultural exports, we impose shocks of 3% per annum on sugar exports and 1.5% per annum on the other agricultural exports. The cumulative magnitude of the shocks for sugar exports over the simulation period is fairly conservative and much lower than the increases projected by Yu and Jensen (2005) for SSA countries following global trade liberalisation.

Scenario 4: The Impact of Partial Trade Liberalisation – Removal of Tariff Barriers

This simulation considers the case of global trade liberalisation in which tariff barriers are removed worldwide. Removal of trade barriers by developed countries would result in an increase in the world export price of some commodities. This would be offset, to some degree, by an increase in the world price of goods imported by developing countries. For most developing countries, however, improved access to rich countries' markets for agricultural and other products will see an increase in their exports.

To represent tariff removal, we implemented across-the-board tariff cuts for all traded commodities, with the exception of service sectors. We then combined the tariff cuts with export price increases as projected in recent surveys of the world price effects of tariff removals. For the main agricultural commodities, we use mid-point estimates from Beghin and Aksoy's (2003) survey and, for industrial sectors, we use GTAP –simulated world prices by Cororaton *et al.* (2005).[4] We assume here that the tariff reduction is revenue neutral to the economy, as the reduction in tariff revenue is offset by the reduced price of imports.

Scenario 5: The Impact of Full Trade Liberalisation – Removal of Tariff and Non-Tariff Barriers

Non-tariff barriers include measures like export subsidies as well as domestic support subsidies, which include output subsidies, intermediate input subsidies and factor-based payments to producers. Fiji has export taxes on sugar (currently about 3%), which are removed in this simulation. Non-tariff barriers are generally difficult to model, particularly in a single-country model such as this one, which lacks information on bilateral flows from trading partners. One of the benefits of removing non-tariff trade barriers is a reduction in intra-regional trade costs (Baldwin and Venables 1995). Also, as Hummels *et al.* (1998) have shown, additional gains from full trade liberalisation include the elimination of multiple taxation on intermediate inputs in trade. A reduction in input costs while holding output constant can be viewed as an improvement in the productivity of inputs.

Therefore, to model the removal of non-tariff barriers (i.e. reduction of trade costs), we imposed a positive shock of 0.2% on the productivity of inputs used in the tradeable sectors. We then combined this shock with Scenario 4. In a sensitivity analysis, we investigated how robust our findings are to changes in the magnitude of the 0.2% shock.

EMPIRICAL RESULTS

Results are provided for each of the above scenarios for the following four key endogenous variables: real output effects; effects on non-sugar agricultural exports; employment effects; and welfare effects. The first set of results pertains to Scenario 1 (Unilateral Tariff Reduction). We then present a comparative treatment of Scenarios 2 to 5.

---

[4] These are: mining (0.9%); coconut processing (0.5%); food processing (1.1%); and other manufacturing (0.6%).

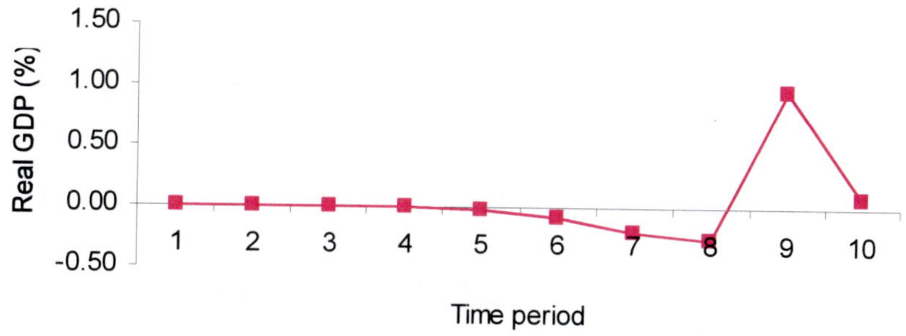

Figure 8.1. Effects of Unilateral Tariff Reduction on Real GDP.

Scenario 1: The Impacts of Unilateral Tariff Reduction by Fiji

Real Output Effects

Unilateral trade liberalisation initially has minimal effects on real output. However, starting from Year 4, we observe a gradual decline in real output (Figure 8.1). This result can be explained as follows. The extent of response to a tariff cut depends on the substitution elasticity between domestic and imported goods, the import intensity of the sector, and the baseline tariff. Some commodities in the agricultural sector (e.g. dairy and livestock) have high tariff bases and import elasticities. Therefore, the tariff cut in these sectors induces an increase in imports and a reduction in domestic production due to lower domestic demand. Sectors like food processing, which use a lot of imported inputs, are able to expand production and exports. However, other sectors lose their comparative advantage and there is an overall decline in real output. There is a reallocation of factors of production that leads to higher real output. Figure 8.1 shows an increase in real output in Year 9. However, this effect is transitory, as real output declines again in the following year.

Effects on Non-Sugar Agricultural Exports

The tariff cut under unilateral trade liberalisation (Scenario 2) has an initial terms-of-trade effect, leading to a real exchange rate depreciation and a reduction in exports. However, as can be seen from Figure 8.2, there is a recovery after Year 8 as non-sugar agricultural exporters take advantage of the cheaper imports to increase output. However, this growth is not sustained in the long-run. Trade barriers and market protection in other countries result in a decline in non-agricultural exports.

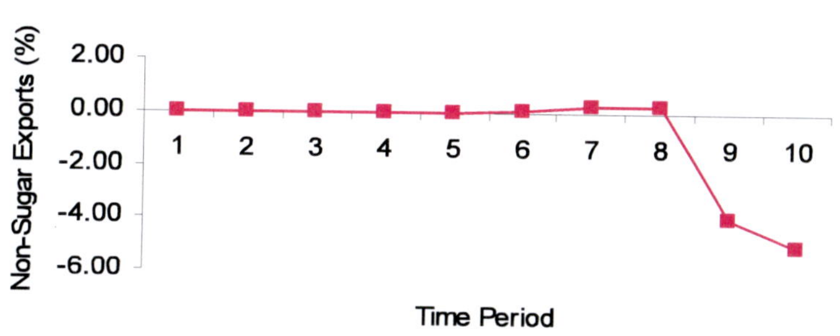

Figure 8.2. Effects of Unilateral Tariff Reduction on Non-Sugar Agricultural Exports.

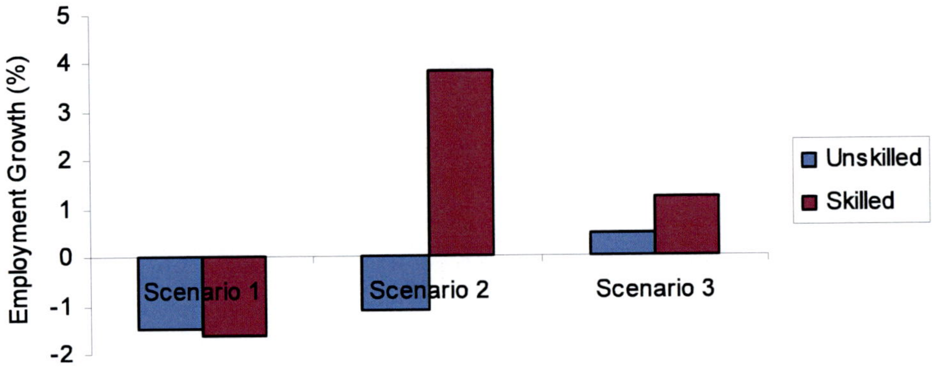

Figure 8.3. Effects of Unilateral Tariff Reduction on Employment.

Employment Effects

Unilateral trade liberalisation increases skilled employment, but appears to have an adverse impact on unskilled employment (Figure 8.3). The explanation for this result is that unilateral trade liberalisation is more beneficial to the manufacturing sector, which is urban based and employs more skilled workers.

Real National Welfare Effects

The final set of results pertains to a comparison of real national welfare effects of the policy simulations. 'National welfare' is defined here as the change in the value of output of the economy that accrues to Fijians. This is measured by the sum of changes in private consumption, private savings, government consumption, government investment, net private unrequited transfers from abroad, and net foreign aid receipts from abroad. By considering net inflows of income from abroad accruing to locals, this variable is a better measure of welfare than real GDP. Unilateral trade liberalisation has negative effects on real national welfare in the short-term.

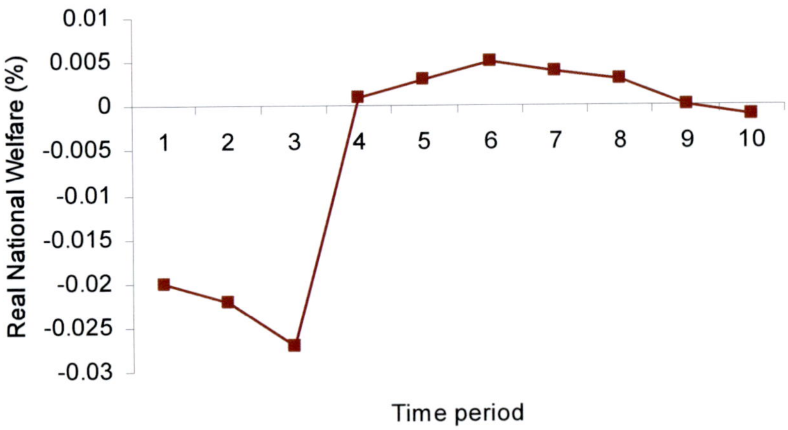

Figure 8.4. Effects of Unilateral Tariff Reduction on Real National Welfare.

Although the tariff reduction results in a fall in the consumer price index, which determines real household consumption, there is an overall welfare loss (Figure 8.4). This is due to a decline in household disposable income from reduced factor remuneration and reduced government transfers, coupled with a decline in tariff revenues for the government.

A Comparison of Scenarios 2 to 5

It is important to note that Scenarios 2 to 5 all involve tariff cuts. Scenario 2 assumes tariff cuts for PICs, which amounts to a unilateral tariff cut for Fiji in this model. On the other hand, the tariff cuts in Scenarios 3, 4 and 5 include the Australia, New Zealand, the EU markets and the rest of the world (although this is not modelled explicitly because we are using a single country model). In general, given a tariff reduction, we expect the price of imported goods to fall, triggering a substitution away from domestically-sourced inputs to imported inputs, which results in an increase in imports. However, the degree of response to the tariff cut depends on the substitution elasticity between domestic and imported goods, the import intensity of the sector (i.e. the share of imports relative to domestic consumption), and the baseline tariff.

Commodities such as dairy and livestock, which have high tariff bases and/or import elasticities, will experience an increase in imports because of the tariff reduction, leading to a decline in domestic production. However others, such as food processing that use a lot of imported inputs, will be able to expand production and exports. Overall, industries in the traded sectors are expected to enhance their external competitiveness and increase their output, while those producing for the domestic market will experience a fall in output. In the analysis below, we compare the outcomes for the four policy scenarios, beginning with the macroeconomic impacts.

Figure 8.5 shows that of the four policy scenarios, PICTA has the lowest impact on real output, with real output reaching a level of just 0.4% by the end of the 12-year simulation period. PICTA and PACER are the next best policies, followed by partial trade liberalisation and full trade liberalisation with removal of both tariff and non-tariff barriers, in that order. The results for changes in trade volumes (Figure 8.6) are fairly consistent with those in Figure 8.5.

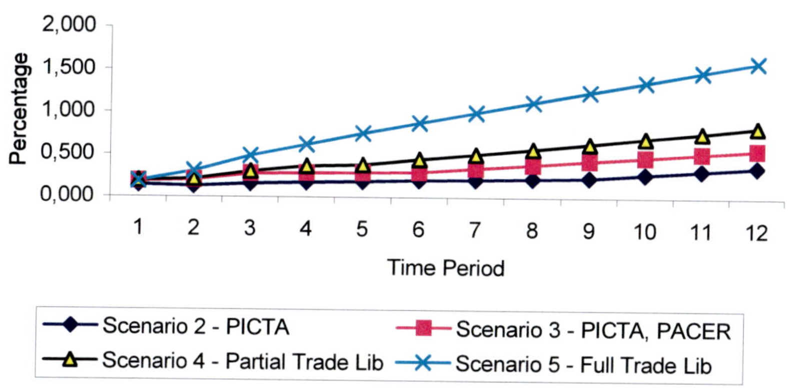

Figure 8.5. A Comparison of Real Output Effects.

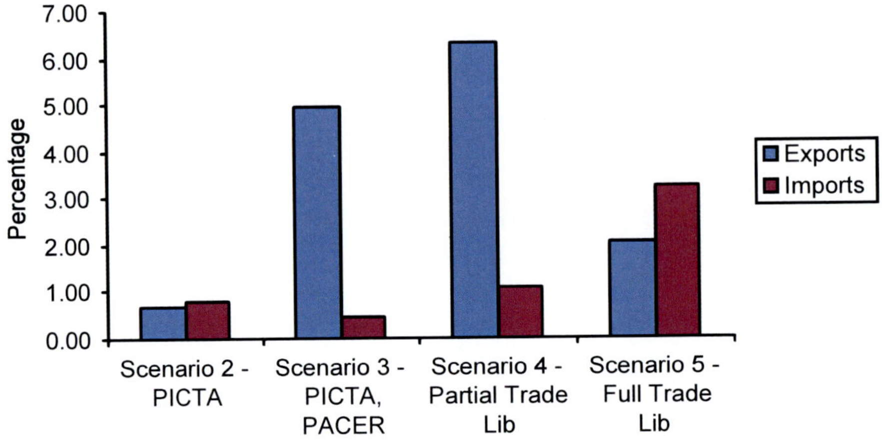

Figure 8.6. A Comparison of Trade Effects.

It can be seen here that the implementation of PICTA has the smallest impacts on trade. On the other hand, PICTA and PACER and partial trade liberalisation are seen to be more trade enhancing, in particular, in the area of export promotion. By and large, the results generally provide some empirical support for the view that regional economic integration among developing countries will pose few benefits for the participants.

In the case of the PICs, using Fiji as an example, merely removing tariffs has minimal impacts on growth and welfare on account of various constraints such as relatively small populations, low incomes per capita, poorly developed communications and trading links (especially for the transport of goods), poor infrastructure, lack of investment and poor resource endowments.

Figure 8.7 shows the real national welfare effects of the Scenarios 2 to 5. Once again, it can be seen that PICTA delivers the lowest benefits over the simulation period. However, contrary to the trends observed in Figure 8.5, tariff only trade liberalisation (Scenario 4) delivers the highest long-term benefits, while trade liberalisation involving removal of tariff and non-tariff barriers (Scenario 5) and PICTA and PACER (Scenario 3) provides identical long-term benefits. The superiority of Scenario 4 over Scenario 5 in terms of welfare effects can be explained by changes in the terms of trade. The terms of trade (not reported here) improves in Scenario 4 (by 2.31 % on average) while it deteriorates in Scenario 5 (by 0.34% on average). Therefore, under the former simulation, there is an increase in purchasing power from export revenue which therefore enhances welfare. Another interesting observation in Figure 8.5 is that in Scenario 2, it takes about nine years to see an improvement in welfare. This is because, in the PICTA scenario, there is a very small increase in real income (Figure 8.5) and, as a result, people take a longer time to change their consumption and savings patterns and, therefore, take more time to generate wealth.

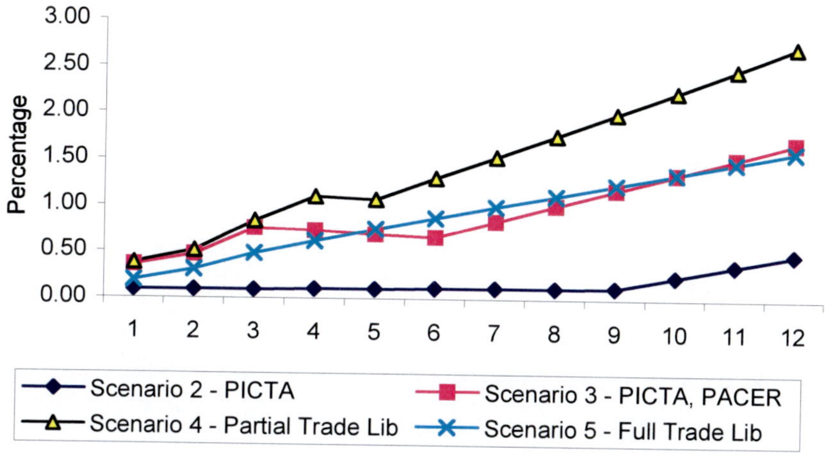

Figure 8.7. A Comparison of Real National Welfare Effects.

The next set of results pertains to employment effects (Figure 8.8). It can be seen that unskilled employment declines progressively as we move from Scenario 3 to 5, while skilled employment increases. This trend can be explained as follows. As real GDP increases from Scenario 3 to 5, the economy becomes more industrialised and there is a decline in demand for unskilled workers. However, with the increase in incomes, workers can afford more education and better training to meet the demand for skilled workers.

The results obtained so far for the four scenarios can be summarised as follows. Whereas full trade liberalisation involving tariff and non-tariff barrier reduction provides the greatest benefits in terms of real output effects, it is outperformed by partial trade liberalisation in welfare, trade creation, and employment effects. For example, full trade liberalisation involving removal of tariff and non-tariff barriers increases imports more than exports compared to tariff only trade liberalisation. A possible explanation for this is that domestic firms are unable to take advantage of the reduced resource costs and efficiency gains arising from the removal of non-tariff barriers to increase their exports.

In the final set of results, we attempt to look at the implications of the four policies at the sectoral level. Given the large number of sectors and the long simulation period, we display results for three sectors: sugarcane, root crops, and the informal sectors. The results for root crops are typical of the results for the non-sugar agricultural sector. Sugarcane output increases by substantial amounts in all of the scenarios except PICTA due to improvement in market access (Figure 8.9). The increase is higher for the trade liberalisation scenarios due to the additional benefit of an increase in world commodity prices for sugar following the removal of tariff and non-tariff barriers.

On the other hand, Figure 8.9 shows that the root crop sector experiences no change under PICTA, and actually declines in the PICTA and PACER and the partial trade liberalisation scenarios. However, full trade liberalisation, in which both tariff and non-tariff barriers are removed, sees an average increase of about 0.2% per annum in root crop production. This possibly reflects a move to diversify away from sugar production to capitalise on increased market access for other crops as well.

Figure 8.8. A Comparison of Employment Effects.

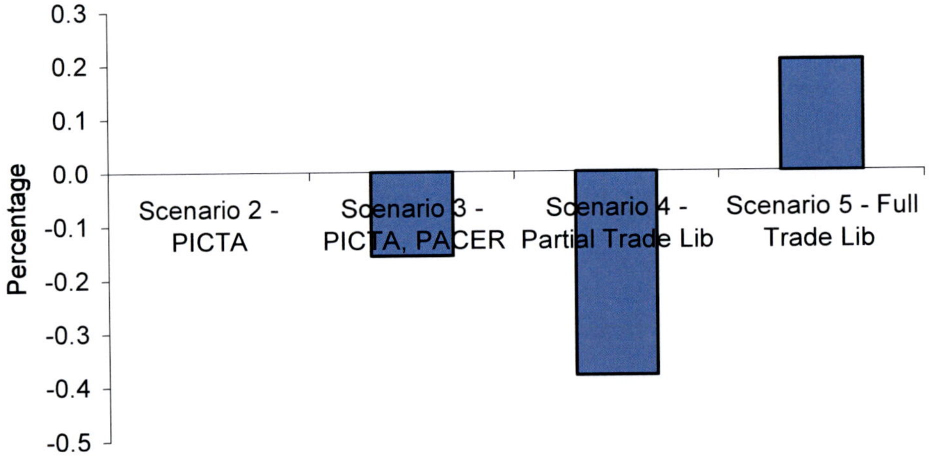

Figure 8.9. A Comparison of Effects on Sugarcane Production.

Impacts in the informal primary sector (Figure 8.10) closely mirror those in the root crop sector. That is, PICTA and PACER and partial trade liberalisation hurt informal sector activities, while removal of tariff and non-tariff barriers results in an increase in both informal primary and secondary production. The trends observed in Figures 8.9 and 8.10 are because the removal of non-tariff barriers allows competition in various other parts of the economy that tend to nurture competition. This view is supported by the observation that other sectors which decline in Scenario 4 – such as hotels, transport and communication services, and the tourism sector (not reported here) – show increases in Scenario 5.

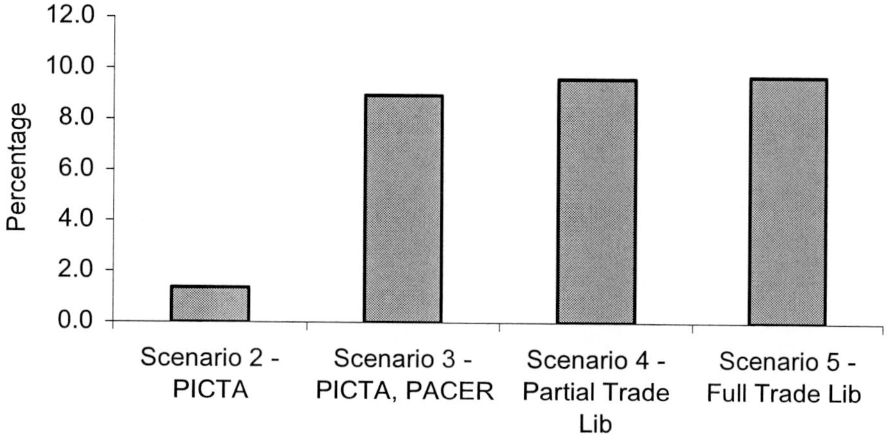

Figure 8.10. A Comparison of Effects on Root Crop Production.

CONCLUSION

The objective of this chapter was to analyse the impacts of trade-related policies, using Fiji as a case study. To capture the feed-back effects of such a complex set of policies, we employed a dynamic CGE model of the Fijian economy. The policies simulated were unilateral tariff reduction by Fiji, the impact of PICTA, the impact of an RTA comprising PICTA and PACER, the impact of partial trade liberalisation (tariff removal only) and the impact of full trade liberalisation, with removal of both tariff and non-tariff barriers.

Unilateral trade liberalisation, in the form of across-the-board tariff reduction, increases real output and non-agricultural exports in the medium term. However, this growth is not sustained in the long-term. This finding suggests a number of implications for trade policy reform in Fiji in particular, and developing countries in general. First, in the face of high protectionism in the advanced countries, there is little benefit for developing countries to unilaterally liberalise their agricultural sectors. Our results show that any such benefits would be gradually attenuated.

Tariff protection in developing countries can be used to shelter farmers from import surges in periods when world prices drop significantly (Valdes and Foster 2002). For example, in India, it has been shown that unilateral liberalisation of agricultural trade has proved to be politically unsustainable, as farmers are subjected to large world price swings and import surges of subsidised commodities (Gulati and Narayanan 2002). Therefore, as shown by the results in Scenario 5, the best outcome for developing countries is full trade liberalisation. Even though both developed and developing countries use tariffs to protect domestic production, the barriers are higher in the former –especially in the OECD countries. There is, therefore, a need for a substantial reduction in OECD agricultural support policies for developing countries to reap significant gains from the current WTO negotiations on agriculture.

In the comparison of PICTA versus a regional RTA (PICTA and PACER) and full trade liberalisation (removal of tariff and non-tariff barriers), it was found that PICTA consistently provided the least benefits across macroeconomic indicators, including real output, welfare, trade volumes, and employment. Full trade liberalisation, involving the removal of tariff and non-tariff barriers, provided the greatest benefits in real output compared to the other scenarios. However, it was outperformed by PICTA and PACER and partial trade liberalisation in welfare effects, trade volumes and employment. In relation to sectoral impacts, it was found that full trade liberalisation and PICTA and PACER had significant impacts on traditional exports like sugarcane. With the exception of full trade liberalisation (removal of tariff and non-tariff barriers), all the other policies tended to have adverse impacts on non-traded food crops such as root crops rice, and dalo.

Our results contradict a number of popularly held views about trade liberalisation. First, it is widely believed that the unilateral removal of tariffs by a developing country would lead to a flood of cheaper imports resulting in the demise of domestic industries. This view is not supported in any of the scenarios simulated here. On the contrary, it was found that tariff reduction gives a boost to the output of traded industries and industries that use imported inputs and investments through a lowering of their resource costs. Second, the World Bank (2002) has expressed the view that an economic union involving a developing country and a developed country may result in a welfare loss to the former due to the encouragement of trade diversion from the latter. Our results do not concur with this view.

In fact, the evidence suggests that the eventual granting of market access to the EU and the rest of the world through a successful conclusion of the Doha Round is likely to result in trade creation rather than trade diversion. Following the abrogation of the Lomé Convention and the withdrawal of preferential treatment, it is inevitable that an ACP country such as Fiji will suffer welfare losses in the short-run. However, our results indicate that the country will, in the long run, benefit from multilateral trade liberalisations such as the EU's Economic Partnership Agreements and the Doha Round.

Given the muted impacts of the PICTA scenario in this chapter, our results give some credence to the view that south-south trade, in the PIC sense, may not be as rewarding as north-south trade for a host of reasons. These include the lack of opportunities to benefit from technology transfers and the general smallness of markets in the south. However, the benefits of the PICTA may be seen more in the form of preparing the PICs for eventual full integration into a globalised world economy. For this transition to be successful, a number of policy measures are required.

First, our results show that trade liberalisation is likely to adversely affect non-traded food crops and, hence, there is a need for a suitable assistance package to boost production and thereby the incomes of farmers in this sub-sector. Second, for the PICs to reap the full benefits of trade liberalisation, technical assistance is needed from the developed nations such as the EU and Australia to help address the numerous supply constraints that dampen a response to improved market access. Such constraints include lack of transport and telecommunication services, inefficient ports and handling facilities, and cumbersome customs procedures.

Chapter 9

THE LOSS OF EU SUGAR PREFERENCES, IMPACT OF EU DEVELOPMENT AID, THE EPA, AND FIJI'S STRUCTURAL REFORM

INTRODUCTION

The primary objective of this chapter is to assess the effects of expected (likely) changes to the ACP-EU sugar protocol on the Fijian economy. In 2004, with preferential prices and market access to the EU, the value of exports to the EU (above world market prices) was about €63 million,[1] amounting to a significant 3.3% of Fiji's GDP. The sugar protocol expired at the end of 2007 and was to be replaced by the prospective signing of the EPA, which was to come into force by 1st January 2008. In addition, it is said that the EPA also intended to go beyond a trade agreement with implications for development in a wider context – in the words of European Commissioner for trade, Peter Mandelson, "the word 'partnership' in Economic Partnership Agreement is not there by accident."

The Pacific, in particular, has the following key objectives:[2] improved market access for goods in relation to rules of origin with duty free and quota free access; market access for service suppliers; an agreement on investment as well as reforms to existing financial mechanisms to help the development of small and medium enterprises; a multilateral fisheries agreement that includes access; and an EPA adjustment facility.

While the EU will not be directly or fully compensating countries for the loss of sugar preferences, it nevertheless has committed to help the ACP countries with grants for development. For instance, Fiji has been allocated F$40 million for 2007,[3] and a total of F$350 million (€167 million) over an eight-year period. However, these funds cannot be used for commercial activities except when there is a particular social need (as in microfinance and housing construction programs), or when confined to technical assistance for feasibility studies or to promote diversification in cane belts (Government of Fiji 2006b). The latter is in

[1] This was computed using EU preferential prices for the 156,000 tons and the Special Preferential Sugar agreement for about 20,000 tons from Fiji's sugar imports to the EU in 2004.

[2] Speech by Dr Roman Grynberg, the Director of Economic Governance at the Pacific Islands Forum Secretariat's Regional Workshop on Trade in Services in the EPA and PICTA, 26th March 2007, Fiji.

[3] This has been stalled due to the economic and political uncertainty brought about by the November 2006 coup, but the EU has agreed to disburse the funds when the new government is legally elected.

the provision of support for sustainable activities in agriculture, forestry and off-farm activities though development of post-harvest and marketing infrastructure, research and extension, and farmer training. The EU grants will also focus on supporting cane farming related to cane replanting, research and extension for cane farming systems, and rural infrastructure support (such as drainage systems and farm access roads).

In light of these developments, it is timely to analyse the impact of the EPAs, the loss of EU sugar preference and development aid on the ACP economies. It should also analyse structural reform options, such as industrial policies, for Fiji to best manage the situation from the loss of the sugar subsidy. Previous studies – such as Alexandraki and Lankes (2004), Milner *et al.* (2004), LMC International and Oxford Policy Management (2003), and Herrmann and Weiss (1995) – used partial equilibrium models to study the impact of the loss of EU sugar preferences on ACP countries. More recently, Perez (2006), Karingi *et al.* (2006b), Keck and Permartini (2005), and Levantis *et al.* (2005) have used the more extensive general equilibrium model for analysis. All but the last of these studies used the GTAP model to look at the effect of EPA arrangements on the ACP region, and Eastern and the South African countries (but not Egypt and South Africa), and South African Development Community, respectively. The study by Levantis *et al.* focused on the loss of EU sugar preferences and development aid on Fiji in particular.

The contribution of this chapter to the existing literature is threefold. First, Fiji makes a good test case for the study of sugar preference erosion, as it is the recipient of the second largest EU sugar quota allocation. Given the high level of heterogeneity within the ACP region, a single country analysis has more to offer by unmasking impacts on a wide range of macroeconomic variables as well as the effect on key sectors of the economy. More generally, Panagariya (2000) warns that the impacts of liberalisation vary for developing and developed countries within a particular region.

Even within the Pacific group itself, the heterogeneity of the economies (due to geographic, economic, ethnic and cultural differences) does not allow for generalisation of results. For instance, Tisdell (1996) explains that for PNG and Fiji, international trade is important, but for Tuvalu and Kiribati, it is of little or no importance – for Western Samoa, it is of moderate importance. He further argues that within the PICs, various social groups and communities (due to cultural and ethnic diversity) have widely varying degrees of dependence on such trade. Furthermore, other natural barriers to trade (such as size, availability and diversity of resources, and their physical cost of accessing international markets) are substantial and are likely to remain even when man-made barriers to trade are reduced.

The second contribution is that, unlike previous studies, concrete information on the EU price cuts and development aid to the ACP are considered to allow more precise and realistic policy environments to be analysed. The third contribution is in the analysis of scenarios combining development aid with the loss of sugar preferences and the EPA. While this could not be done in the single-region CGE analysis of ACP undertaken by previous studies, Levantis *et al.* (2005), on the other hand, considered the EU's development aid under some assumptions, with no attempt to combine the aid scenario and the loss of sugar preferences. Lastly, it is hoped that the analysis in this chapter motivates and paves the way for more single-country analyses for comparison, and to facilitate a better understanding of the different adjustments and costs faced by both developed and developing countries within the ACP region.

The rest of the chapter is organised as follows. The next section details ways in which the loss of EU sugar preferences, the EPA, and development aid can be analysed for simulating shocks to the economy. The impacts of these scenarios are then discussed in section three to devise possible policy options for Fiji and the challenges it faces. Section four concludes.

MODELLING THE SCENARIOS

While it was clear that the sugar protocol was to be replaced or modified at some stage, the reality of the withdrawal of sugar preferences was accelerated by the August 2004 win in the World Trade Organization (WTO). This case against the EU's high sugar subsidies was led by disputes registered by Australia, Brazil and Thailand. Thus, the EU was forced to consider major sugar reforms for its domestic economy and this meant that changes to the ACP-EU sugar protocol also had to fall in line. Hence, there has been speculation since 2004 that price cuts could be as high as 40% for the ACP economies, and the threat of it taking place immediately was a concern then.

Here, we consider the European Commission's (2006) recent announcements about the sugar price cut for the ACP countries in two different ways (partial and full price liberalisation) and compare them with and without development aid. On the assumption that there are no more *coup d'états*, Fiji will receive a grant of about F$40 per annum from 2008 for eight years. To simulate this environment as realistically as possible, we draw on Fiji's 2006 *National Adaptation Strategy for the Sugar Industry* (see Government of Fiji 2006a). It was indicated that 35% of the aid money would be devoted to restructuring the sugar industry to enable productivity increases in sugar production to reach a target level of 3.55 million tons in 2008, 3.85 in 2009, 4.10 in 2010 and 4.22 from 2011 onwards. This represents a production increase of 7.44% in 2008, 16.52% in 2009, 24.18% in 2010 and 27.72% from 2011 onwards, using 2002 sugar production levels, in line with our 2002 database.

It must be noted that the EU sugar prices, even after the gradual price cuts (partial price liberalisation), will still be higher than world prices (European Commission 2006). To consider full price liberalisation by the EU (where sugar preferences are completely eroded), we consider the impact on sugar prices when the EU abandons all regulations of its sugar market. According to LMC International and Oxford Policy Management (2003), this will result in a sugar price of €350 per ton.

Lastly, we consider alternative EPA arrangements. First, the Generalised System of Preferences (GSP) and the Everything But Arms (EBA)[4] are ruled out as possible alternatives as they fail to adhere to the legally-binding requirements of the Cotonou *Article 37.6* calling for a framework for trade that is equivalent to the existing situation and in conformity with WTO rules (Oxfam 2006c, Bilal and Rampa 2006).[5] In addition, Bilal and Rampa (2006) consider three other alternatives: the explicitly recognised special and differential treatment;

[4] The GSP option is open to developing countries and covers a large but not complete list of products, while the EBA is only open to least developed countries (LDCs) and covers all products (except arms) under which tariffs will be gradually reduced to zero (in 2006 for bananas and in 2009 for rice and sugar).

[5] While Perez (2006) argues that the GSP and EBA options would allow welfare and output losses to be less important than the partial price liberalisation scenario we consider, Curran (2007) maps out the problems and inaccuracy in Perez's modeling of the GSP option that warns readers to exercise caution in the conclusions of Perez's study.

an EPA with binding provisions for development-related liberalisation; an EPA for ACP non-LDCs only; and the EBA for the ACP LDCs. By carefully considering their arguments based on key features – WTO compatibility, regional integration prospects, scope for development and policy space and political feasibility for each of the three alternatives for Fiji and the Pacific in general – it appears that none of these options are as feasible as the two EPA options considered below.

The first is the proposition by the European Commission for a reciprocal WTO-compatible free trade agreement. This is where the ACP countries eliminate their tariffs on 80% of their imports from the EU, while the EU grants duty-free access to all ACP products to its market over a period of around 12 years. The agreement uses the standard interpretation by the EU of 'substantially all trade' and 'reasonable length of time' as per the General Agreement on Tariffs and Trade *Article XXIV* (Perez 2006). To simulate this scenario, we consider the fact that Fiji currently sources less than 2% of its total imports from the EU. Given that the price elasticity of imports for Fiji is about 1.0 (Narayan and Narayan 2005), an 80% tariff cut is simulated as a 2% fall in Fiji's import tariff rate, because the model does not incorporate bilateral trade flows between the EU and Fiji. This is the standard EPA scenario.

The second EPA scenario considered is that of Bilal and Rampa's (2006) 'EPA light' approach. This is a minimalist approach that focuses, in the first stage, on the opening of ACP markets to the minimum level necessary for securing WTO compliance; and, in the second stage, at a speed and extent to be defined by the ACP countries themselves. Negotiations with the EU could centre on a long-term approach, addressing supply-side constraints such that further liberalisation takes place from the ACP side. We draw on Bilal and Rampa's study and liberalise 30% of imports tariffs into Fiji.

SIMULATIONS

All the scenarios below are considered with and without development aid.

1) Partial price liberalisation of the EU sugar price:
   Cumulative reduction in €/ton of 21% in 2007, 9.7% in 2008, 25% in 2009 and no more reduction from 2010 onwards.
2) Full price liberalisation in the EU sugar price:
   Total abandonment of all regulations of the EU sugar market will result in 38% fall in sugar prices given in €/ton. This is followed by a one off reduction of 27.7% to match partial price cuts as above.
3) Standard EPA:
   An 80% one off cut in import tariffs is implemented as a 2% across the board cut in import tariffs.
4) EPA Light (gradual cut over time):
   An import tariff cut of 1.25% in 2008, 1.5% in 2009, 1.75% in 2010 and 2% in 2011.

Empirical Results and Discussion

With partial liberalisation, Figure 9.1a shows that real output immediately contracts by 1.0% and declines further to 1.5% in 2009, with similar annual declines for the remainder of the simulation period. The full price liberalisation policy, on the other hand, results in smaller reductions in real output. After 2010, sugar export revenue falls by 26% on average with partial (full) liberalisation policy.

The declines in real output and exports are smaller under full price liberalisation compared to partial price liberalisation because even though the price reductions are more immediate for the former, there is a higher gain in competitiveness as unproductive farmers are likely to move out leaving the more efficient ones. With aid, the situation is reversed with the partial price liberalisation providing more gains, and this reverse situation is also found between the two EPA scenarios (Figure 9.1b).

Without aid, unlike the sugar price cuts, both types of EPAs get Fiji onto a positive growth path, with the standard EPA outperforming the EPA Light policy by increasing real output by 1.7% per annum. The tariff cut in the EPAs reduces import prices, resulting in an increase in consumption that makes consumers better off. Also, sectors producing import-competing goods switch from domestic to cheaper foreign sources of inputs and are now able to increase domestic output.

For real output effects, aid works well with partial price liberalisation to smooth adjustment costs more effectively than the big-bang approach of full price liberalisation. The fact that the outcomes are considerably different with aid in the price cuts and EPA options highlights the importance of careful negotiations with the EU. For instance, without aid in the long run, the partial price liberalisation leads to large decreases in sugar exports over time in the magnitude of 30% relative to full price liberalisation, which leads to a decline of 24% per annum (Figure 9.2). This indicates that the full price cut forces the economy to adjust more quickly than gradual price cuts. This is because resources get diverted into other sectors, as seen by the smaller reduction in both skilled and unskilled rural employment (Figure 9.3) and greater increases in non-sugar exports (Figure 9.4a) and total exports too (Figure 9.5a).

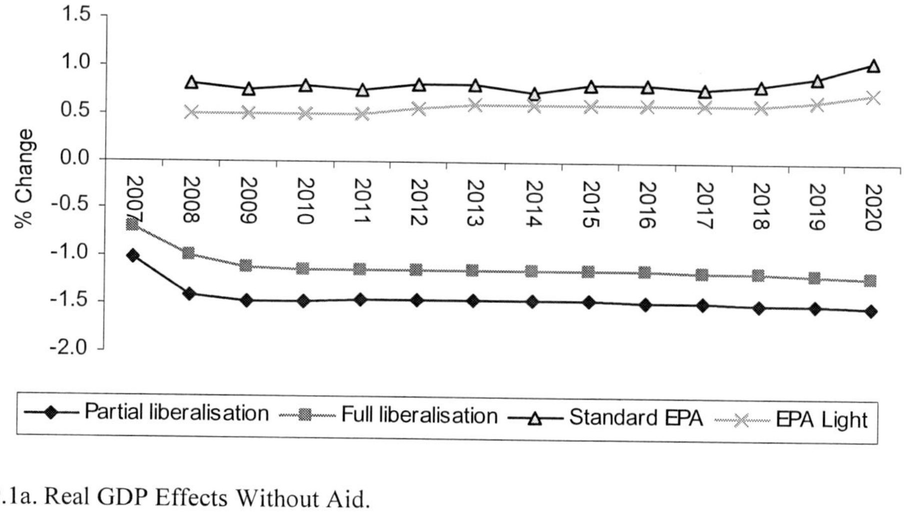

Figure 9.1a. Real GDP Effects Without Aid.

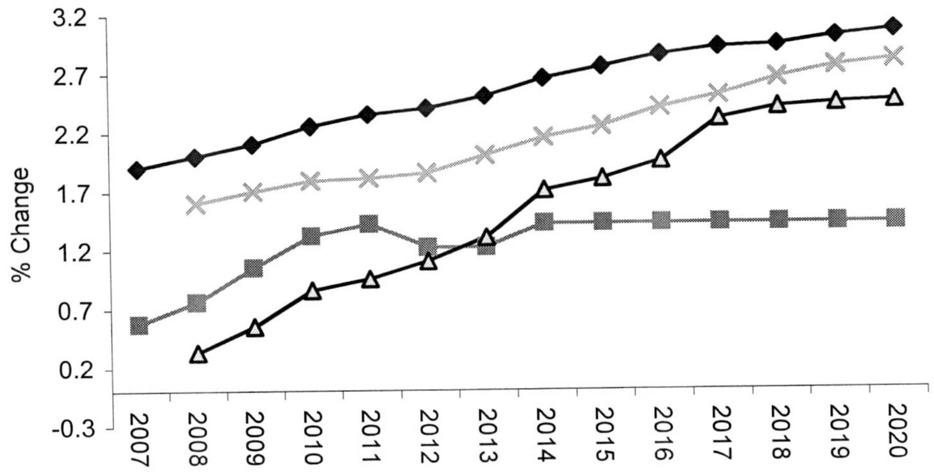

Figure 9.1b. Real GDP Effects With Aid.

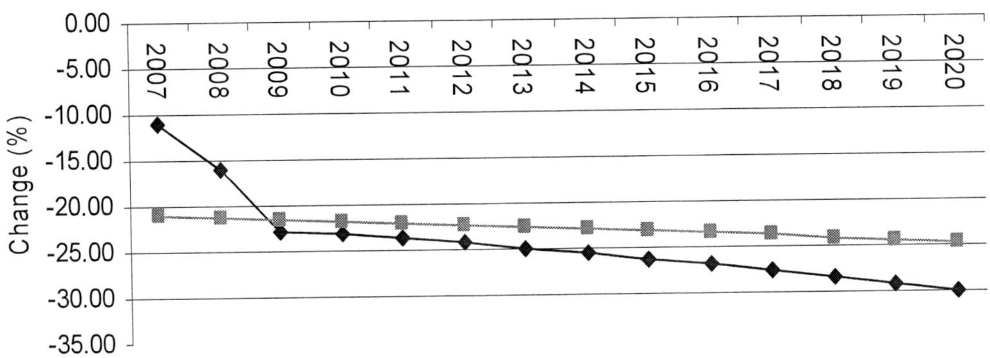

Figure 9.2. Sugar Exports Without Aid.

However, allocative efficiency may not be sufficiently optimal. Supply side constraints hinder the economy (Government of Fiji 2006b) from broadening its production and export base sufficiently to allow non-sugar exports to negate declines in the sugar industry as real output still falls as seen in Figure 9.1a. On the other hand, with aid, sugar export levels increase by about 75% under both prices cuts by 2011 (result not shown). With aid, EPA Light shows a higher growth in real output compared to the Standard EPA, as the trade balance is healthier in the former (as seen in Figure 9.5b).

Figure 9.3 reports results for rural employment effects, an important focus because the overwhelming majority of agricultural workers reside in rural areas. All four policies have a negative effect on rural employment, and in particular, the employment of unskilled labour. As expected, the situation is reversed when the policies are complemented by the aid package, which is aimed at increasing sugar production. It therefore sees rural unskilled employment increase by about 17%, with the majority of the employment gains in the sugar sector.

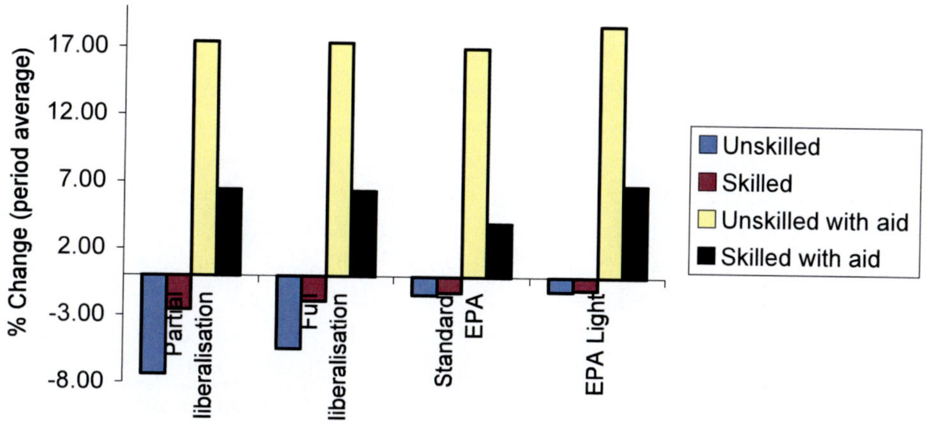

Figure 9.3. Rural Employment Effects.

Figure 9.4a shows that, without aid, the standard EPA option has larger effects than the EPA Light, be it an increase or decrease in the various non-sugar exports. This is because the former is a one-off cut and, thus, the period average is expected to be higher than the EPA Light option – but, with aid, the impacts are similar (Figure 9.4b). Although not large in magnitude, under the EPA options without aid (Figure 9.4a), there is a fall in fish exports and larger increases in the export of textile, clothing and footwear products relative to the price cuts.

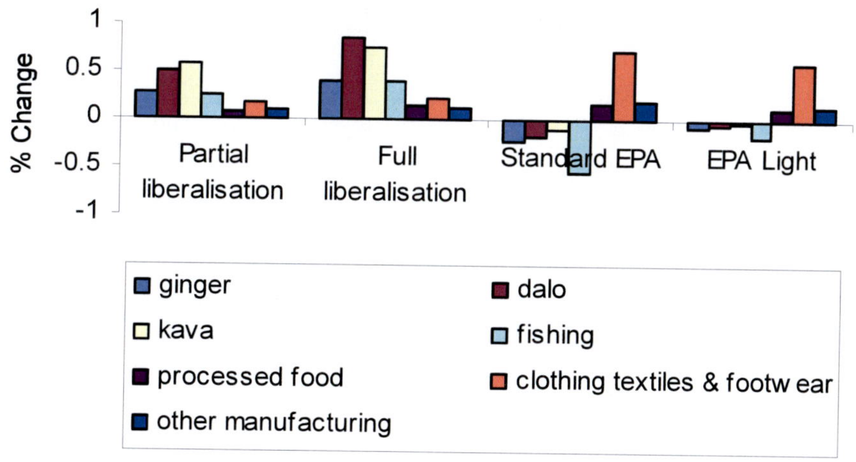

Figure 9.4a. Effects on Non-Sugar Exports Without Aid.

One explanation is that, since fishing is an activity dominated by foreigners, lower import prices do not provide sufficient protection – discouraging production and, hence, exports.

With the textile clothing and footwear industry, the fall in import prices encourages more cloth to be imported into Fiji. However with aid, all four scenarios see the largest export increase in the textile, clothing and footwear products (Figure 9.4b). This is because the tax revenue from the rise in sugar exports, in conjunction with the aid package, might enable the government to continue subsidising this sector which, according to Fiji's *Strategic*

Development Plan 2007-2011, has been earmarked to continue providing employment for women. In view of this, and because of the expiry of the multi-fibre agreement with the US at the end of 2004, the Fijian government, in late 2004, managed to convince the Australian government to extend Fiji's export agreement under the SPARTECA for an additional seven years.

With the current account balance, when no aid is provided, full price liberalisation results in a smaller deficit than partial price liberalisation because of larger increases in non-sugar exports in the former than the latter. Following the gradual loss of sugar preferences, there is a reduction in the terms of trade, leading to a depreciation in the value of the Fijian dollar, which stimulates non-sugar exports (Figure 9.4a) – but this is insufficient to dampen the fall in sugar exports. The Standard EPA scenario, on the other hand, gives the largest current account deficit since the fall in non-sugar agricultural exports is not compensated by the boost in industrial exports because they are smaller.

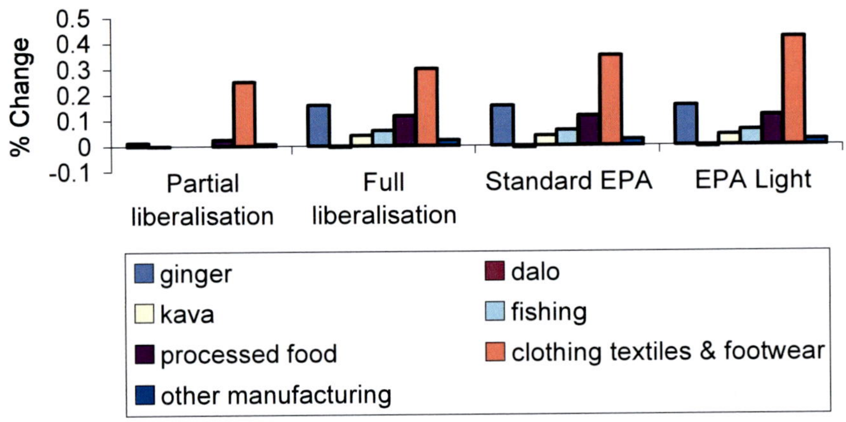

Figure 9.4b. Effects on Non-Sugar Exports With Aid.

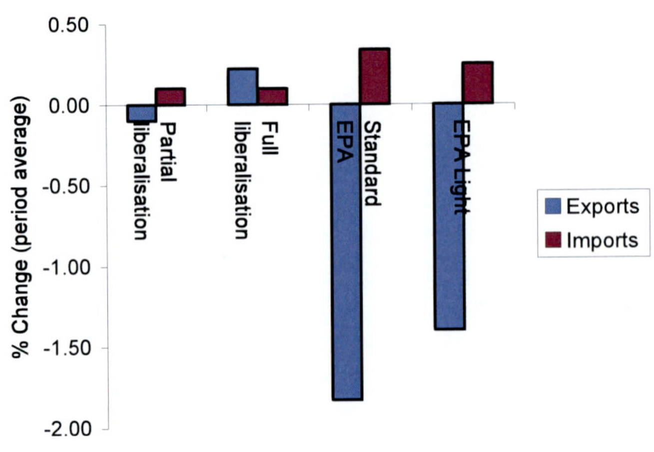

Figure 9.5a. Trade Effects Without Aid.

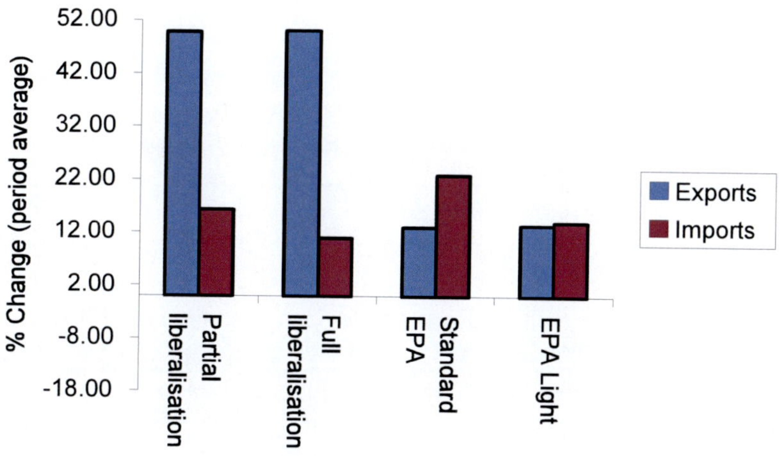

Figure 9.5b. Trade Effects With Aid.

This indicates that any complementary or adjustment program should be directed at strengthening the agricultural sector, as this is where Fiji's comparative advantage lies. With aid, the EPA scenarios still result in a trade deficit, while the price cuts allow a current account surplus. The rise in import growth with the aid package is not necessarily unhealthy, as the sugar export earnings allow the purchase of imported consumer goods and intermediate inputs (more so under the EPA scenarios due to lower import prices).

In terms of tariff revenue, the rise in imports seen in all four scenarios with or without aid (Figures 9.5a and 9.5b) does not matter much for Fiji because of the unitary import price elasticity from Narayan and Narayan (2005).

What Now for Fiji?

From the above analysis, and with regards to both types of price cuts not accompanied by aid, the results show that the non-sugar agricultural sector rather than the industrial sector still holds promise for Fiji. This is seen in the absorption of displaced workers from the sugar industry into the non-sugar agricultural sector. Thus, the 2006 implementation of the Alternative Livelihood Program by the Asian Development Bank in Fiji is a move in the right direction to diversify agricultural production. This is, however, not enough for Fiji to get onto a higher growth path in the absence of aid (Figure 9.1a) because agricultural productivity is still very low. This is because of supply side constraints such as: the lack of micro-finance programs for agricultural investment; the poor functioning of the market for leasehold land; the absence of an integrated system of formal property rights system; and there being no well-established markets and procedures for buying, selling, and improving the quality of non-sugar agricultural produce. This leaves farmers in a vulnerable position. The lack of commercialisation of agricultural production is another hindrance to economic growth (Seavoy 2000) as most farmers in Fiji are small-scale producers, including sugarcane farmers.

With the aid package, it is unclear whether directing it at raising sugar production levels is an optimal strategy given the finding in Chapter 4 that sugarcane farmers in Fiji are only

75% technically efficient. In fact, following the EU's withdrawal of preference for bananas, its aid in the form of the Special System of Assistance in 1994 and Special Framework of Assistance in 1999 was found to have limited power in raising the banana industry's competitiveness. Evaluations have called for diversification in the use of aid instead of the focus on the banana industry (LMC International and Oxford Policy Management 2003).

Political instability in Fiji also does not help, but creates uncertainty for investment in both agricultural and non-agricultural production. It disrupts any reform process as it results in a loss of human and financial capital. For instance, skilled labour migration from Fiji[6] has led to deficiencies in the work force that have adversely affected productivity in the non-agricultural sectors such as manufacturing and services (Reddy *et al.* 2004a). Apart from that, the Government of Fiji (2006b) has identified various institutional factors and poor infrastructure that increase the risks and costs of doing business, sometimes to the point where transactions no longer take place.

Thus, the concern of the impact of the type of sugar price cuts and EPAs on the ACP countries may be overstated. Panagariya (2005) explains that the more serious barriers to development for the developing countries in light of trade liberalisation are the internal policies and supply side constraints that are of their own making. One option is to use EU development aid to address the binding constraints directly with proper technical or administrative support and advice. This is more easily said than done, as it requires political will to seek help and work with another country in dealing with its internal affairs. So far, negotiations and agreement on how development aid will be used have progressed very slowly. It also remains to be seen how effectively aid will be disbursed, as Oxfam (2006b) highlights the poor track record of the EU in its five-year financing cycle of the European Development Fund assistance package. The study shows that since 1975, the percentage of total allocation disbursed from 1975 to 2007 has declined from 43% to about 25% in the last five-year period.

CONCLUSION

The results obtained here contradict two common beliefs. One finding is that EPAs are not necessarily contractionary, although imports rise because consumers are made better off and production increases using cheaper inputs. The other is the finding that gradual sugar price cuts, compared to the one-off cut, does not smooth out adjustment costs more effectively, at least for Fiji. One reason why the big-bang approach of 'pain now: gain later' works better for Fiji, is because farming is still a labour-intensive activity with little heavy investment in capital or land – thus, displaced workers are able to move quickly to other non-sugar agricultural production.

However, with aid directed at raising sugar production levels while the EPA Light is a preferred choice over the Standard EPA, the gradual rather than the immediate price cut is more satisfactory. This result is the reverse of the situation without aid, thereby indicating the crucial role that aid plays. An important extension of this work would be to compare and contrast the different uses of aid – for instance, in infrastructural development, education and

[6] McKenzie (2006) reports that 13.5% of Fiji's population is living abroad and most of them are skilled workers.

health rather than helping the affected sector (sugar in this case). This will shed light on the form in which aid could be provided for sustainable growth in Fiji.

Another extension would be to study the price cuts in combination with the various EPA scenarios because of the overlap in the occurrence of these two events. Although this was attempted, the results of such a combination were dominated by the price cuts, partly because the alternatives to the EPA scenarios are relatively less well defined in import price cut simulations. In addition, the implications for regional trade within the ACP due to the EPAs cannot be captured in the single country analysis done here.

STRUCTURAL REFORM RESPONSE

In this section, we consider a different response for Fiji in relation to the loss of EU sugar preferences and its development aid. One constraint of the EU development aid is that it cannot be used for commercial activities except when there is a particular social need, as in microfinance and housing construction programs, or when confined to technical assistance for feasibility studies, or to promote diversification in cane belts (Government of Fiji 2006b). This is in the form of provision of support for sustainable activities in agriculture, forestry and off-farm activities through development of post-harvest and marketing infrastructure, research and extension, and farmer training.

The EU grants will, however, focus on those parts of Fiji's *National Adaptation Strategy for the Sugar Industry* outlined in August 2006, which directly support cane farming. Thus, it is necessary for Fiji to not just rely on reforming the sugarcane sector, but also to undertake other forms of structural reform to manage the transition from the loss of sugar preferences and ensure that the economy as a whole is able to cope with the situation. This can be done by promoting industrial policies to boost the performance of Fiji's leading sectors.

It can be seen in Figure 9.6 that the share of sugar exports in total exports has declined to 13% in 2005 after reaching a high of 16% in 1995. From 1997 to 2001, garments replaced sugar as the country's leading export sector.

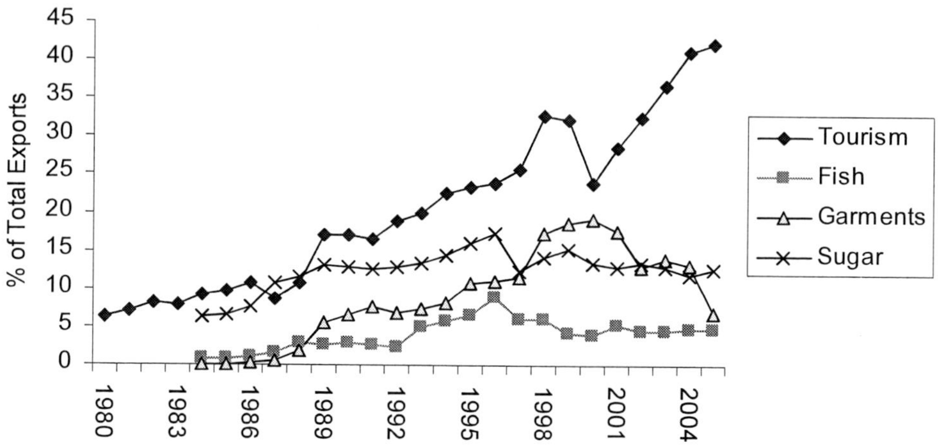

Figure 9.6. Export Trends of Fiji's Key Industries

Before the coup in 2000, the garment industry employed between 12,000 and 15,000 workers, mostly women (Hannan 2005). Garment exports reached a high of 19% of total exports in 2000 and have been declining since. This is due to a combination of factors, including: increased competition from China and Southeast Asia; the end of the tax-free factor and import credit schemes in 2000; the erosion of the preferential trading agreements under SPARTECA; and the expiry of the multi-fibre agreement at the end of 2004 (Storey 2005).

MODELLING THE SCENARIOS

In conjunction with the loss of sugar preferences in Scenario 1 representing partial price liberalisation, the following are considered. Scenario 5a models sugarcane reform in achieving half the targets set for cane production, unlike the earlier scenarios. This is to allow for the possibility that sugar industry reform may not be as successful as planned.

In Scenario 5b, we compare the above scenario with one that includes structural reform related to diversifying the agricultural sector to minimise risk and address resource misallocation due to the EU sugar subsidy, which provided the incentive to concentrate on the production of sugar. These are the aims of the Asian Development Bank's Alternative Livelihood Project in operation in Fiji since 2006. To simulate this, a 10% increase in the production of major crops is allowed in Scenario 2b in line with the government's recent strategic development plan (Government of Fiji 2006b) to double non-sugar agricultural exports from 2007 to 2011 and reduce the annual food import bill (which stood at F$350 million in 2005).

In Scenario 5c, in addition to diversifying the agricultural export base, we consider the strategy to address the United Nations' Third Millennium Development Goal of promoting gender equality and empowering women. One identified strategy towards this goal is to increase the share of women in wage employment in the non-agricultural sector, which was 36% in 2004 (Government of Fiji 2006b). The avenue for that lies in revitalising the garment sector, which predominantly employs women. More importantly, to raise the productivity of the garment sector for sustainable growth, a 5% increase in this variable is simulated.

The sixth scenario models efforts to boost the tourism sector by 20% in tourism exports. This is plausible given that the average tourism export earnings after the 2000 coup was 12% of GDP up until 2005, and the government is committed to improving infrastructure development, up-market accommodation, and construction of a Tourism and Hospitality Training School commenced in 2005. The last scenario captures the effects of a 20% increase in fisheries sector exports. The Fijian government is aware of the need to review outdated legislation governing this sector by including provisions for aquaculture, management of artisanal fisheries and the post-harvest handling and processing of fish to increase value adding in the sector (Government of Fiji 2006b). In addition, the indigenous community of native Fijians is heavily involved in this sector, thereby making it politically necessary for the government to be active in this scene.

SIMULATIONS

All the structural reform scenarios are considered simultaneously with the erosion of trade preferences as set out in Scenario 1 of the partial price liberalisation in sugar cuts.

Scenario 5a: Reforming the sugar industry with half of the cane production targets from 2008 to 2011.

Scenario 5b: Scenario 5a plus diversification of agricultural sector with a total of 10% increase in agricultural production of rice, ginger and dalo, simulated as a 2.5% increase from 2008 to 2011.

Scenario 5c: Scenario 5b plus a total of 5% increase in the productivity growth of the garment sector, simulated as a 1% increase from 2008 to 2012.

Scenario 6: Boosting tourism exports by a total of 10%, simulated as a 2.5% increase for 8 years from 2008.

Scenario 7: Expanding exports in the fisheries sector by a total of 10%, simulated as a 2.5% increase for 8 years from 2008.

EMPIRICAL RESULTS AND DISCUSSION

Real Output Effects

Figure 9.7a reports the real output effects of the first four policies. The impact of the policy change on real output growth is much less than the actual extent of the loss in EU transfer payments. This is partly due to the fact that sugar has now been outstripped by tourism as the main driver of Fiji's exports, which now accounts for over 40% of total exports.

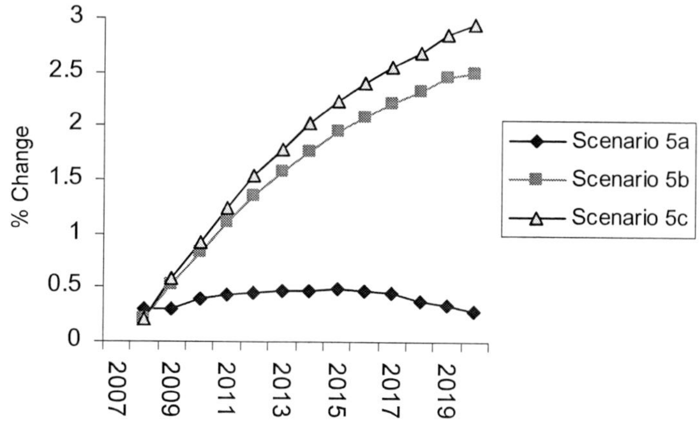

Figure 9.7a. Real Output Effects, Scenarios 5a to 5c.

The results for this scenario indicate that the economy is unable to substantially redirect the redundant labour and capital inputs into other sectors following the fall in sugar production. Although there is some improvement in the export growth of alternative crops such as coconuts, ginger and dalo (see Figure 9.10a), this is negligible. At the end of the simulation period, the growth rate of real output is below the level that would have been attained in the absence of the policy change.

When the sugar price cuts are combined with sugar industry restructuring using EU aid (Scenario 5a), there is a slight improvement in real output growth to about 0.48% by 2015, but this declines to 0.29% by 2020 (Figure 9.7b). Also, the targeted aid to the sugar sector results in a stunting of growth for the non-sugar agricultural sector (see Figure 9.10b). Scenario 5b, which combines the sugar industry reform with diversification of the agricultural sector, results in rapid real output growth starting from about 0.2% in 2007 and steadily reaching a rate of 2.5% by the end of the simulation period. In Scenario 5c, we superimpose a 5% productivity growth in the garment sector (which predominantly employs women) on Scenario 5b. The results show real output growth outstripping that of the previous scenario to reach a rate of nearly 3% by 2018.

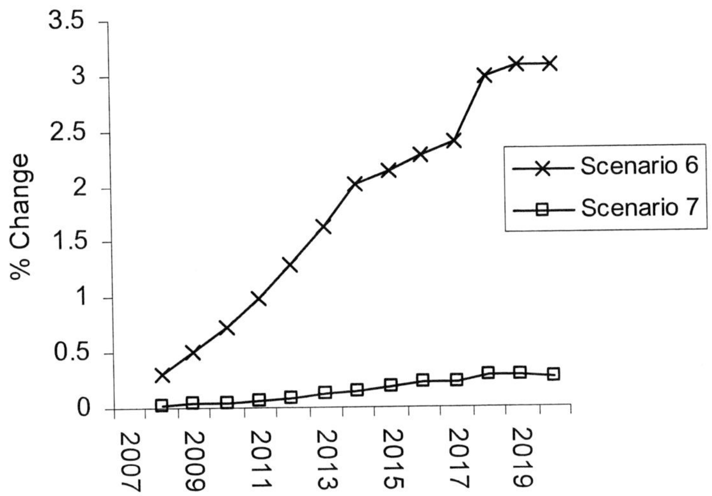

Figure 9.7b. Real Output Effects, Scenarios 6 and 7.

In Figure 9.7b, boosting tourism exports (Scenario 6) enables real output to grow by 0.3% in 2007 and reaches a growth rate of just over 3% by the end of 2020. On the other hand, increasing fisheries exports (Scenario 7) results in output growth of just 0.02% in 2007 before increasing sluggishly to a maximum of 0.29%. The failure of fisheries exports to significantly impact on real output is due to a number of factors. The sector is starting from a low base (constituting only 5% of total exports) and currently lacks adequate numbers of domestic fishing fleets and appropriate facilities for processing the fish catch onshore, thereby limiting value adding by this sector.

Effects on Real National Welfare

Given the significant numbers of Fijians who are dependent on the sugar industry, it is not a surprise that the EU sugar price cuts put the brakes on growth of real national welfare (Figure 9.8a). The price cuts lead to adverse terms of trade for the sugar sector, resulting in high-income losses for farmers in the long run. Here, we see that after hardly a change in the growth rate of real national welfare during the first six years of the policy, the growth rate of welfare declines rapidly after 2012, reaching a low of 0.24% by 2020.

As was the case for real output, restructuring the sugar industry alone does not result in sustained welfare growth. This is seen by the decline in real national welfare starting from 2012 and reaching a low 0.88% by the end of the simulation period. However, by targeting more sectors in the economy, the best outcome is achieved with Scenario 5c. The impacts on real national welfare for boosting tourism and fisheries exports (see Figure 9.8b) closely mirror those of their real output effects. Boosting tourism exports initially results in 0.3% growth in welfare, and this increases exponentially to 13.4% by 2020. On the other hand, boosting tourism exports produces marginal increases in real national welfare growth by reaching a high of about 0.7% in 2017.

Trade Effects

As expected, the removal of the EU's sugar price subsidies results in a reduction of sugar production and, consequently, causes total exports to contract. Over the simulation period, total exports decline by 0.3% on average and imports decline by twice that amount (see Figure 9.9). Both sugar industry reform and diversification of the agricultural sector reverse the decline in exports, with the latter having a bigger impact.

However, the remaining simulations indicate that the best option for significantly lifting the growth of exports is through broad-based export promotion involving the agricultural, manufacturing, and tourism sectors. Results also show that targeting a single sector for development will not bring about an even spread of benefits. For example, reforming the sugar sector, or promoting tourism and fisheries exports will depress the growth of the non-sugar agricultural sector (Figures 9.10a and 9.10b). Here we observe 'Dutch Disease' type of effects whereby a booming tourism sector, characterised by significant inflows of foreign currency and foreign direct investment, results in an appreciation of the Fijian dollar. The net effect is that the other sectors are rendered less competitive and experience a reduction in their exports.

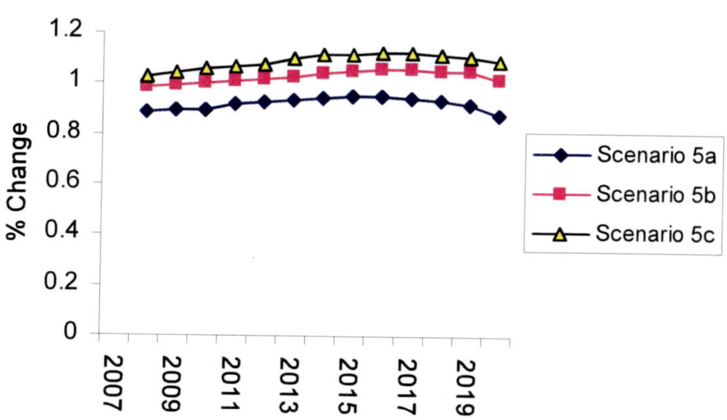

Figure 9.8a. Real National Welfare Effects, Scenarios 5a to 5c.

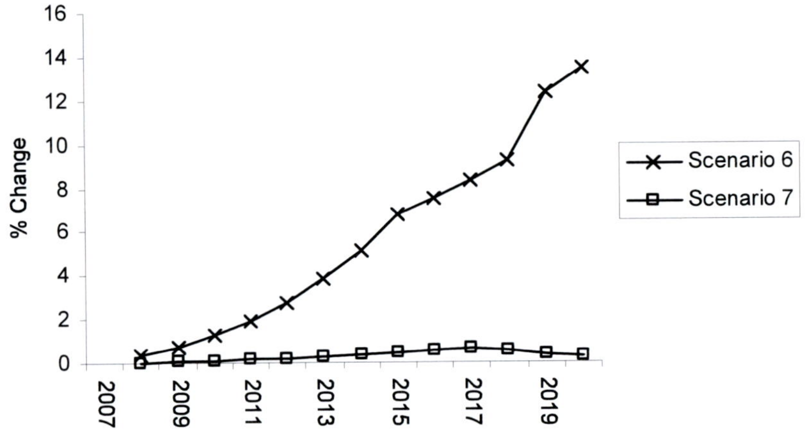

Figure 9.8b. Real National Welfare Effects, Scenarios 6 and 7.

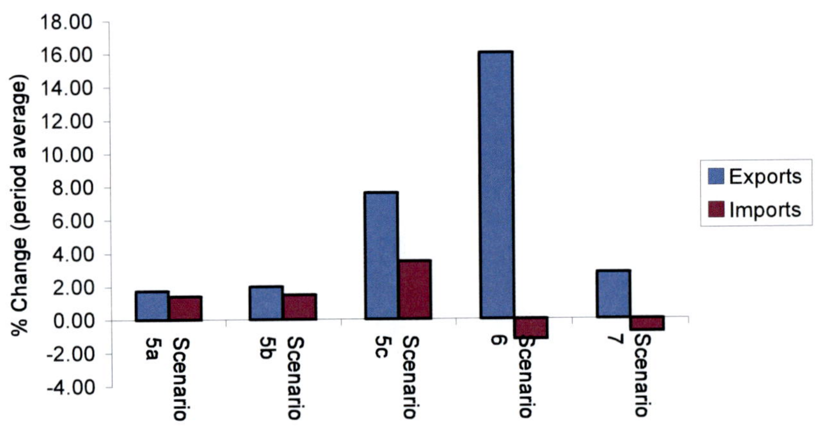

Figure 9.9. Trade Effects.

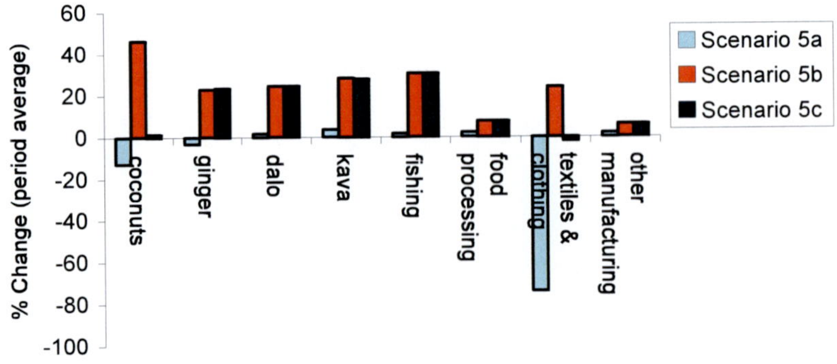

Figure 9.10a. Effects on Non-Sugar Agricultural Exports, Scenarios 5a to 5c.

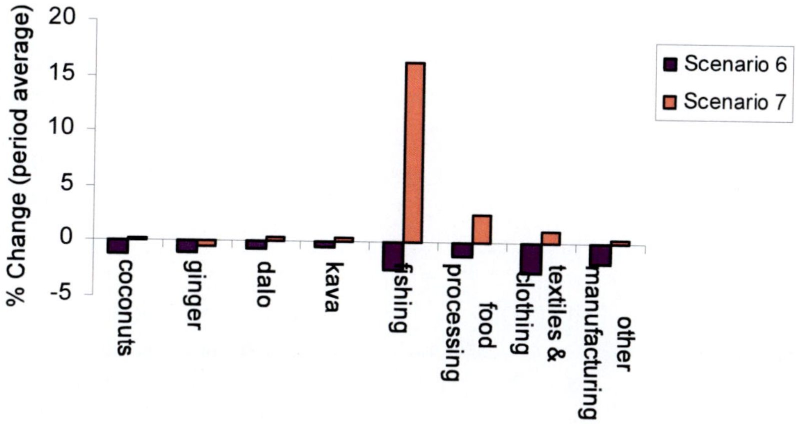

Figure 9.10b. Effects on Non-Sugar Agricultural Exports, Scenarios 6 and 7.

Rural Employment Effects

Scenario 5a shows that sugar industry reform for cane production targets need to be more than half successful to halt the decline in rural employment (Figure 9.11). However, as is the case with the other indicators, broad-based diversification involving agriculture and manufacturing achieves the best results in rural employment. Tourism expansion results in a small contraction of rural employment because this industry is mainly focused on urban centres and there are few linkages with rural industries. Finally, expanding fisheries exports increases rural employment, with skilled labour growing faster on average relative to unskilled labour. This is not surprising given the relatively specialised nature of export activities such as tuna fishing and processing.

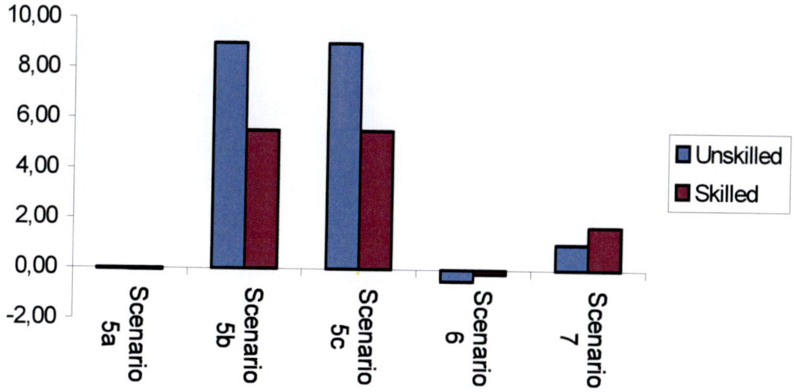

Figure 9.11. Rural Employment Effects.

Conclusion

A number of policy implications can be drawn from the results of structural reform. With partial price liberalisation, we have attempted to address the important question of whether other sectors in the economy can absorb the labour and capital inputs made redundant following the fall in sugar production. Our results indicate that diversion of these factors into other industries is minimal due to a combination of reasons, including low levels of labour skills and institutional rigidities that discourage investment in these sectors. There is, however, great potential for the informal and non-traditional export sectors to absorb the large pool of unemployed. From 2000–05, the informal sector contributed about 2.6% of total GDP. The main problems faced by informal workers in both urban and rural areas include low skill levels and access to credit. To encourage the development of alternative export crops, assistance would be required in areas such as marketing development and transport networks.

The results for Scenarios 5a and 5b highlight the impact of a narrow reform vis-à-vis broad-based agricultural reform. It is shown that targeting the sugar sector alone for assistance in response to the loss of the EU subsidies is counterproductive in the long run. In fact, the expansion of the tourism or fisheries sectors in isolation is also undesirable for welfare and employment effects. The optimal policy for Fiji is broad-based diversification of the export sector.

It is further argued that apart from the above structural reforms, it is necessary for appropriate complementary policies to be implemented for long-term sustained growth. That is, for the Fijian economy to remain competitive, there is a need to address supply side constraints such as: the lack of access to credit for agricultural investment; the poor functioning of the market for leasehold land; the absence of an integrated system of formal property rights; the poor transport and telecommunication services; inefficient ports and handling facilities; and cumbersome customs procedures.

Chapter 10

FIJI AT ITS CROSSROADS: WHERE TO NOW?

In recent times there have been few studies that have conducted a comprehensive analysis of the impacts of trade policies on agriculture. The few that have done so have focused almost exclusively on developed countries and a wide range of developing countries in Asia, South Asia, and South America. Therefore, there has been a dearth of research into small Pacific island countries. This book has analysed the impacts of trade liberalisation, the loss of the European Union's preferential access to sugar, agricultural reforms and various types of regional and global trade arrangements on a small island country, using Fiji as a case study.

A key feature of this book is the use of Fiji's sugar industry as the basis to discuss agricultural reform in general. The focus on the sugar industry not only provides important lessons for the 121 countries worldwide that produce sugar, but also offers the opportunity to consider policy making in a holistic framework. In this regard, this case study of Fiji highlights the importance of an integrated and well-coordinated approach to policy implementation, especially when an industry is tightly and vertically integrated.

Chapter 1 provided a background for the study by introducing Fiji as a country and explaining the rationale for using it as a case study to analyse the implications of structural reforms and trade liberalisation policies. Chapter 2 put the discussions in context by providing an overview of the Fijian economy. The chapter began with a brief overview of Fiji's history and macroeconomic performance, as well as past economic policies. It was seen here that after gaining independence in 1970, the promising economic growth prospects with an annual average GDP growth of just over 4% were soon dashed by the two military coups in 1987. Although, the economy rebounded somewhat in the ensuing years, the attempted coup of 2000 sent the economy into another tailspin from which it has not fully recovered.

The latest coup in December 2006 will almost certainly drive economic growth into negative territory again. One of the adverse impacts of the political uncertainty created by the coups d'état has been the decline in savings as well as domestic and foreign investment. The sectoral analysis indicated that although the share of agriculture in GDP has been declining, it still remains a significant contributor to economic growth and employment. The causality analysis also confirmed that agricultural and tourism exports are the main drivers of Fiji's economic growth. The key conclusion from this chapter, which set the stage for the analytical work in chapters 8 and 9, is that there is a need to increase productivity in the agricultural sector and to diversify the export base in order to offset possible income losses from the EU reforms.

Chapter 3 conducted an in-depth analysis of Fiji's sugar industry, which was used as the focus for the analysis of the structural reforms. It began by providing a brief insight into the world market for sugar, which is the most widely traded commodity. This included a brief discussion of protectionism in the sugar market, followed by a discussion of the EU's sugar regime, which was the subject of the analytical work in Chapter 9. The high costs of inefficiency and waste generated by the EU sugar regime was highlighted. The EU-ACP economic partnership agreement, which is the new arrangement to succeed the Cotonou agreement, was then discussed. It was noted that it is highly unlikely that the negotiations on the EPAs would be completed in time to take effect on January 1st 2008, as mandated.

Furthermore, agreement on the transition period and product coverage for reciprocal market access, as well as how to deal with development issues, is yet to be concluded. A good part of the chapter was devoted to describing the sugar industry. This included its structure and performance, and the political economy of the industry. The latter included the key players in the industry and the issue of land ownership. It was noted that the involvement of various institutions in the sugar industry, each with their own agendas, makes it extremely difficult to achieve a consensus on reform. Nevertheless, it was noted that reform was inevitable at all levels to meet the challenges in the industry.

The productivity performance of sugarcane farmers was the subject of analysis in chapter 4. Analysis at the micro level is required to assess the scope for improvement after the EU sugar subsidies are withdrawn. The analysis here improves on the only existing work by Reddy and Yanagida (1999) with the application of parametric and non-parametric approaches to estimate the efficiency measures for a sample of sugarcane farmers. The chapter began with a discussion of the key issues facing farmers, including the declining cane yield and the land tenure system, followed by an outline of the survey methodology employed in the chapter.

After introducing the theoretical models, results for overall technical efficiency, scale efficiency and input-specific technical efficiency were presented. The parametric approach indicated quite high levels of input use efficiency, but labour and tractor use were relatively less efficient. In contrast, it was found that bullocks were commonly used and it was concluded that gains in cane output could be made by farmers using about 10% less of bullock hours. Labour was found to be the least efficiently used input. The results showed that, on average, sugarcane production was about 27% below the maximum possible output due to inefficiency in the use of inputs and technology. A disaggregation of efficiency by ethnicity indicated that native Fijian farmers, on average, produced 10% less cane than their Indian counterparts.

Given the need to improve efficiency in the wake of the loss of the EU sugar subsidies, it was suggested that native Fijians could be encouraged to undertake alternative crop farming in line with the Alternative Livelihood Project in Fiji that began in 2006. Such a strategy would also serve to diversify Fiji's agricultural exports and minimise the risks associated with price variability resulting from the sugar policy reforms. The chapter also identified the need to increase farm size by amalgamating land leases to achieve economies of scale in output and enhance efficiency through better use of inputs and technology.

The previous chapters established the fact that sugarcane yield in Fiji has been declining for some time, and this was attributed to a number of factors, including the uncertainty over sugarcane leases and declining land quality. However, a major contributory factor to the decline in sugar yield is land degradation (in particular soil erosion), which according to anecdotal evidence, is on the increase. In Chapter 6, the results of an empirical analysis of soil erosion on sugarcane farms were reported. The chapter sought solutions to two problems. The first was to determine the effect of soil erosion on cane output and what it cost cane farmers and the sugar industry – the second was to determine the factors affecting the perception of the soil erosion problem and the extent of soil conservation effort on cane farms.

The chapter began with a description of the environmental impacts of sugar cultivation, followed by the hypotheses and theoretical model for the empirical investigation of the first problem above. This was then followed by the discussion of empirical results and farming practices to shed light on policy options for soil conservation. The next section provided the empirical results to address the second problem above and discussed the implications for soil conservation policy. The cost of soil erosion from forgone cane output was found to be quite significant for the individual farmer and the industry. Yet, it was noted that soil conservation is very low on the policy agenda. A number of problems were noted. At the institutional level, there is weakness in implementing and enforcing environmental legislation. At the farm level, there is lack of government support for education and extension services. Therefore, there is an urgent need for efforts to increase the public awareness of land degradation, to educate farmers on the availability of soil conservation techniques, and to implement an effective incentive system to make it worthwhile for farmers to adopt soil conservation measures.

The issue of the need to undertake reforms in Fiji's sugar industry is not new, dating back to 1981. Chapter 6 began with a review of the key features of past reports on reform for the industry, followed by a discussion of sugar-farming practices. The latter included the common practice of burning cane. Although this practice has some advantages (such as facilitating the removal of weeds and destruction of pests), it results in a deterioration of soil quality and an increase in environmental pollution. It was shown that cane burning has virtually been sanctioned by the current cane payment system as set out in the Master Award. The system provides an economic incentive to burn cane because payment is based on tonnage delivered to the mill rather than on the sugar content.

Given all the problems outlined in the chapter and the loss of the EU sugar subsidies, the question was asked as to how viable the sugar industry is. It was concluded that, of all the locally grown crops, sugar is the only one that has the widest geographic spread and, thus, has the greatest impact on poverty. Therefore, it is important to keep this industry alive. A number of options for value adding were offered: one was to develop sugar refineries, another to generate electricity from bagasse; a third was to produce ethanol. Furthermore, it was noted that there is the potential to generate by-products such as liquid carbon dioxide, molasses for animal feed, dry yeast and filter cake for fertilizers.

Chapter 7 was devoted to describing the dynamic CGE model used in the analytical work reported in Chapters 8 and 9. The discussion began with a description of the features of CGE models, which belong to the family of general equilibrium models. The particular CGE method adopted in this book, the Johansen approach, was contrasted to another approach commonly used by the World Bank and in North America. Basically, the Johansen method facilitates model solution by linearising the non-linear equation systems. While this approach could lead to some linearisation errors, the use of multi-step solution algorithms minimises these errors. The model used in the analysis is essentially a recursive dynamic model. That is, each period is solved as a static equilibrium problem given the stock of capital and investment, and the results are then used to update the database to form the basis for the simulation of the next period. In that respect, it is not an inter-temporal optimisation model.

After giving a brief overview of previous macroeconomic models of the Fijian economy, the remainder of the chapter was devoted to describing the structure of the Fijian CGE model. The discussion included descriptions of the commodity/industry classifications, the input-output structure, the theoretical structure and definition of the key model equations. Because of space limitations, the description of model equations was confined to the labour market and capital stock.

The conclusions on the impacts of trade liberalisation, the loss of the EU's sugar subsidies, agricultural reforms and various types of regional and global trade arrangements were reported in Chapters 8 and 9. Chapter 8 dealt with trade liberalisation, while Chapter 9 tackled the impacts of the loss of EU subsidies, the EPAs and structural reforms. The focus in Chapter 8 was on the impacts of a range of trading arrangements.

A number of scenarios were simulated: unilateral trade liberalisation by Fiji; the impacts of PICTA; the impacts of PICTA and PACER; and two forms of trade liberalisation (the first, partial trade liberalisation involving the removal of tariff barriers only; the second was full trade liberalisation involving the removal of both tariff and non-tariff barriers). In the medium term, unilateral trade liberalisation was found to have some positive benefits, but these dissipated in the long run. Thus, it was concluded that while there may be some benefits from a country liberalising trade on its own, the positive effects would be limited if other countries maintained their trade barriers. Regional trade agreements (in the form of PICTA, and PICTA and PACER) were then compared to the two forms of global trade liberalisation.

PICTA was found to deliver the lowest benefits based on all the macroeconomic indicators, lending some support for the view that south-south trade may not be as beneficial as north-south trade. On the other hand, there were mixed results for PICTA and PACER, partial trade liberalisation and full trade liberalisation. Full trade liberalisation delivered the highest benefits in terms of real output growth. However, it was outperformed by PICTA and PACER and partial trade liberalisation for welfare effects, trade volumes and employment.

In general, full trade liberalisation was found to not only enhance traditional exports, but also promoted the production of non-traded food crops such as root crops, rice, and dalo. Therefore, on balance, the main conclusion of this chapter was that full trade liberalisation would be more beneficial compared to the various regional trade agreements. This conclusion flies in the face of various opinions expressed in the popular press that trade liberalisation would have adverse effects on developing countries because local industries would be wiped out by cheap foreign imports. However, our results do indicate that trade liberalisation could adversely affect the production of non-traded food crops and, as such, policies are required to deal with this.

The analysis reported in Chapter 9 was conducted in two parts. The first part considered the loss of the EU sugar subsidies and the impacts of the EPAs, whereas the second part considered options for reforming the sugar sector and boosting growth in other sectors. In the first part, the following four scenarios were simulated: partial liberalisation of the EU sugar price involving phased price reductions; full liberalisation of the EU sugar price involving a one-time cut in the EU sugar subsidy; a Standard EPA involving a cut in import tariffs; and an EPA Light scenario involving a smaller cut in import tariffs. These scenarios were then repeated including the provision of aid to the sugar sector. It was shown that although the price cuts in the full price liberalisation scenario were more immediate compared to partial price liberalisation, the reductions in real output and exports were smaller for the former. This was due to a higher gain in competitiveness as unproductive farmers were likely to move out leaving the more efficient ones. With aid, the situation was seen to be reversed, with the partial price liberalisation policy providing more gains.

The two types of EPA were found to have a positive impact on economic growth, with the Standard EPA outperforming the EPA Light policy by increasing real output by 1.7% per annum. The tariff cuts in the EPAs reduce import prices, resulting in an increase in consumption that makes consumers better off. Also, sectors producing import-competing goods switch from domestic to cheaper foreign sources of inputs, and are now able to increase domestic output. Two important findings from this analysis were that firstly, the EPAs are not necessarily contractionary as has been speculated (although imports rise as could be expected); and, secondly, the one-off cut appears to smooth the adjustment costs more effectively than a gradual price cut. However, when aid to the sugar sector is included as part of the EPA package, the above results are reversed with the EPA Light scenario outperforming the Standard EPA.

In the analysis of the structural reforms in the second part of Chapter 9, we considered the following additional alternatives for reforming the sugar sector and diversifying Fiji's export base:

- partial EU sugar price liberalisation and reform of the sugar industry with half of the government's cane production targets from 2008 to 2011 (Scenario 5a)
- Scenario 5a plus diversification of agricultural sector (Scenario 5b)
- Scenario 5b plus productivity growth of the garment sector
- expansion of tourism
- expansion of fisheries.

It was shown that partial price liberalisation combined with sugar sector reforms lead to some improvement in real output that is not sustainable. This policy was also found to be injurious to the non-sugar agricultural sector. However, sugar industry reform combined with diversification of the agricultural sector resulted in rapid real output growth. When these policies were also combined with productivity growth in the tourism sector, we found even more rapid growth. However, targeting the tourism sector for growth was found to have adverse impacts on the non-sugar agricultural sector.

Finally, increasing fisheries exports had insignificant impacts on the key macroeconomic indicators. The general conclusion from this particular section of the chapter is that broad-based diversification of the economy will have more far-reaching economic effects for growth and employment than a narrow focus on a particular sector, be it tourism or agriculture. Therefore, what is required to enhance sustainable economic development for Fiji is broad-based reform directed at the agricultural, industrial and service sectors.

Fiji, like many other Pacific island countries, is faced with several hurdles in competing with larger economies in today's globalised world. These include:

- a small domestic market, which imposes diseconomies of scale in production and consequent high costs, resulting in restricted ability to compete in either domestic or (more especially) export markets for goods.

- the high cost of infrastructure services relative to the population, and the high unit costs of transport to and from major markets (due to both distance and diseconomies of scale), adding further to the cost disadvantage
- extreme openness resulting from the above factors (and consequent heavy dependence on imports), leading in turn to a high structural trade deficit – traditionally offset by protected commodity exports (sugar in Fiji's case)
- a limited tax base, with a traditionally high level of dependence on import duties
- diseconomies of scale in the public sector, which results in the latter accounting for a relatively large share of GDP, leading to significant structural budget deficits
- a proneness to natural disasters (particularly climatic), which result in periodic demands for high public expenditure on rebuilding infrastructure and housing.

In the past these handicaps were offset through the protected market provided by Britain (as a colonial power) for Fiji's single export crop (sugar). At the same time, grants from the colonial government helped maintain an adequate level of public administration and infrastructure – that is, based on standards higher than could have been afforded if the territory had been solely dependent on its own domestic economic resources. However, these privileges, including the more recent EU sugar subsidies, are now things of the past. The country would need to seriously consider a total reform of its institutions and development of policies to increase the external competitiveness of its industries. On the basis of the material presented in this book, these reforms and policies are summarised below under the following categories: reform of the cane and sugar industry, addressing structural constraints in the economy, human capital development, and export diversification. Each of these is briefly discussed.

Although reforms in the sugar industry have been talked about for a long time, now is the time for action given the immense challenges facing the industry. The three crucial areas that need to be addressed are increasing productivity, institutional reform, and increased value adding. In the area of productivity, there is an urgent need to improve farming practices. This could be achieved through providing more farmer education on aspects such as efficient input use, soil preparation, planting of seed cane, fertilizer application and farm drainage. As shown in Chapter 6, farmers prefer to plant lower yielding ratoon cane due to the costs of the higher yielding plant cane crop. However, a mix of cane varieties is required to optimise cane output.

Therefore, the FSC's plan to target an intensive replanting program of 60–75% of the existing crop area is a step in the right direction.[1] Given the high cost of seed cane, we have suggested that farmers should be subsidised in this exercise. A major adverse environmental impact of current farming practices is the burning of cane, which not only contributes to CO_2 emissions, but also leads to rapid loss of soil nutrients, soil erosion, and a decline in soil quality. As indicated above, the current payment system, which is based on tonnage rather than on sugar quality, indirectly encourages the burning of cane. Thus, reform of the cane payment system is required not only for environmental reasons, but also to improve the quality of cane produced. Although such a system had been suggested earlier, there appears to be lack of political will to carry it through.

[1] News report on *fijilive* on 24 October, 2007, accessed on:www.fijilive.com/business/show/news/2007/10/16/news3.html

Still on the subject of productivity in the sugar industry, the analysis has indicated that the industry is dominated by a large number of small-scale producers. One option we have suggested to increase productivity at the farm level is to have larger farms by amalgamating land leases. Such a move would not only result in the achievement of economies of scale, but would also make it easier for farmers to obtain credit. As indicated earlier, productivity could be improved by using mechanical harvesting, which is more suited to large farms.

A major bottleneck in sugar production is the transportation system. Over time, the rail infrastructure has deteriorated due to lack of adequate maintenance and underinvestment. Many farmers have had no alternative but to use trucks to transport their cane to the mills. However, this practice also leads to long queues and delays at the mills. Thus, there is an urgent need to critically evaluate the pre- and post-harvest logistics of cane transportation. Another issue that needs addressing is that of improving mill efficiency. Although the FSC is planning to construct a fifth sugar mill in the Seaqaqa area in the Labasa region,[2] it is essential to upgrade the efficiency of the existing ones. As noted earlier, Fiji's cost of production is amongst the highest of the ACP sugar producers. Of major concern is the fact that the mills have been producing below capacity due to a host of factors including delays in crushing and plant breakdowns.

Another key issue is the reform the FSC management to improve mill efficiency. We have noted the need to appoint competent and qualified people at all levels of management, and the wanton neglect of cane research and extension services was highlighted. In its efforts to contain costs, it is surprising that the FSC has curtailed the very activities that have the potential to substantially increase profits. In this respect, the recent decision by the government to establish an independent sugar research institute is a step in the right direction.

The issue of land degradation is of serious concern given the significant financial costs it imposes on farmers in particular, and the external costs borne by society in general. In the area of sugar production, this problem is likely to worsen because, faced with uncertain land tenure, Indo-Fijian farmers are unlikely to undertake long-term investments in soil conservation. However, sugar production is not the only area where land degradation is a problem. For example, soil erosion is also high in the cultivation of ginger. Therefore, there is a need to take a comprehensive look at the issue of land degradation and to institute policies to address the problem. We would like to suggest increased government expenditure to improve public education and awareness about land degradation. Farmers, in particular, need to be educated on affordable technologies in soil conservation. Given the externalities associated with soil conservation and the cost implications for farmers, there is some justification for the government to enter into cost-sharing soil conservation schemes. Another arrangement to consider would be the possibility of assisting farmers to gain access to credit to help them finance soil conservation.

In the long run, output and employment in the sugar sector could be significantly improved by value adding generated from initiatives such as sugar refining, electricity generation and ethanol production. Value adding could also be achieved by encouraging downstream processing of sugar by products. Examples given include the production of animal feed, liquid CO_2, and fertilizer. It would be impossible to undertake such projects through public investment alone – which is the main reason why the government should

[2] News report on *fijilive*, accessed on 25 October 2007 at: www.fijilive.com/news/show/news/2007/10/15/news7.html

create favourable conditions to attract private investment into these areas. In this respect, the areas needing urgent attention are investment policies and the general environment of registering and conducting business.

In the latest *Doing Business Report*, the World Bank has ranked Fiji fifth overall in the East Asia and Pacific region for the ease of doing business.[3] Singapore, Hong Kong, Malaysia and Thailand are ranked ahead of Fiji, and Fiji is ranked first in the Pacific island region. Although this is encouraging, to successfully compete against these countries for foreign direct investment, Fiji needs to improve in specific areas such as licensing, registration of property, taxation and trade restrictions. As noted earlier, the maintenance of political stability is a key ingredient to attracting both foreign and domestic investment.

Fiji is committed to a policy of trade liberalisation. This is evident in its acceptance of PICTA and PACER and the signing of an interim EPA with the EU. However, there is an urgent need for policies and actions to place exporters in a position that will enable them to take advantage of foreign trade opportunities. At the present time, our assessment is that they are ill-equipped to compete in the global market. In this book, we noted a number of constraints that deter an adequate supply response to price signals. These constraints pertain mainly to structural problems in the economy and include poorly developed transport and telecommunications infrastructure, inadequate ports and handling facilities, tedious customs procedures, lack of marketing networks, lack of knowledge about standards, lack of microfinance programs, and poor functioning of markets for leasehold land.

The government could use development aid from the EU to address some of these constraints. In the area of agriculture, there is a need to move from small-scale, subsistence agriculture to commercial production of non-sugar crops. It was noted in Chapter 2, for example, that the tourism sector sources most of its food inputs from overseas. We indicated that this could be due to the poor quality and unreliability of local produce. Commercial agricultural production in line with international standards would not only serve local tourism industries but could also service export markets.

A critical constraint in boosting industrial and agricultural production, especially fro absorbing workers made redundant from the loss of the EU sugar subsidies, is a lack of skills. Thus, the government needs to invest in human capital development with specific emphasis on low- and middle-level skills training. Such a strategy would improve value adding in the manufacturing and tourism industries. It could also be a precursor to linking the agricultural and manufacturing sectors through the development and processing of agricultural produce. The development of the technical skills of the large pool of unskilled workers, coupled with a program to assist them to obtain credit, would also enable some of them to establish or expand their farms to feed the agro-based industries.

Agriculture will remain the major provider of national income and employment in Fiji for some time to come. However, given the high variability in the prices of the major agricultural commodities, there is a need to diversify agricultural exports in particular, and merchandise exports in general. In this respect, one area where Fiji has a significant resource endowment is fisheries, given its extensive economic exclusive zone. It was noted that the sector is presently under-resourced due to a lack of skills and infrastructure. Much of the revenue from the fisheries sector is derived from the issuance of fishing licences to foreign fleets.

[3] *Doing Business*, accessed on 25october 2007 at: http://www.doingbusiness.org/economyrankings/?regionid=1

Despite Fiji's remoteness from the major export markets, there is a potential to target niche markets for processed fish products. However, once again, what is required is a policy package that will attract investment (both domestic and foreign) into this sector. Such a package should include tax incentives, financial assistance to local producers, and infrastructure development schemes. The results presented here indicate that the best strategy to achieve sustainable economic growth is a broad-based development approach that does not target a specific sector. Targeting one sector for development will have adverse impacts on others. Thus, we advocate a strategy that aims to strengthen the linkages between the agricultural, fisheries, tourism and manufacturing sectors.

To conclude, the pace of economic development in Fiji, like many other small island states, depends crucially on the outcomes of the current trade negotiations such as the EPAs and the Doha Round. The empirical evidence presented in this book indicates that unilateral trade liberalisation will not have lasting positive effects unless matched by global trade liberalisation. Thus, access to other markets including the EU would be a significant development. However, market access will not in itself lead to the transformation of developing countries' economies as, currently, the playing field is not level. Therefore, even with fairer WTO trading rules, developing countries such as Fiji would still need assistance from advanced countries to restructure their economies and effectively participate in global trade.

References

Akram-Lodhi, AK 1998, 'Fiji and the Sugar Protocol: A Case for Trade-based Development Corporation', *Development Policy Reform*, vol. 16, no. 1:39–60.

Alexandraki, K and Lankes, HP 2004, 'The Impact of Preference Erosion on Middle-Income Developing Countries', *IMF Working Paper*, no. 04/169, International Monetary Fund, Washington DC.

Anderson, K and Martin, W 2006, 'Agriculture, Trade Reform, and the Doha Agenda', in *Agriculture Trade Reform and the Doha Development Agenda*, K Anderson and W Martin (eds.), The World Bank, Washington, D.C.

Anderson, K, Martin, W and van der Mensbrugghe, D 2006, 'Market and Welfare Implications of Doha Reform Scenarios', in *Agricultural Trade Reform and the Doha Development Agenda,* K Anderson and W Martin (eds.), The World Bank, Washington, D.C.

Arrow, KJ, and Debreu, G 1954, 'Existence of an Equilibrium for a Competitive Economy', *Econometrica*, vol. 22:265–90.

Asafu-Adjaye, J 2007, 'Liberalising Trade in the Agriculture Sector of a Small Island State: The Case of Fiji', *World Economy*, vol. 30, no. 10: 1550–1567.

——2008, 'Factors Affecting the Adoption of Soil Conservation Measures: A Case Study of Fijian Cane Farmers', *Journal of Agricultural and Resource Economics*, vol. 33, no. 1: 99–117.

Asafu-Adjaye, J and Mahadevan, R 2008, 'Regional Trade Agreements versus Global Trade Liberalisation: Implications for a Small Island Developing State', *World Economy*, forthcoming.

Asian Development Bank (ADB) 2006, *Country Report: Key Indicators,* ADB, Manila.

——2005, *Fiji: Sugar Sector Analysis,* ADB, Manila.

——1991, *Fiji Agricultural Pricing and Marketing Study*, ADB, Manila.

Asian Productivity Organisation (APO) 2001, *Productivity Improvement in Sugar Cane Plantations in Asia,* Asian Productivity Organisation, Tokyo.

——2003, Technical Survey Report on Site-visit for Green Productivity Demonstration Project in Fiji, APO Project no. SPE | GPDP | 00.

Baldwin, RE and Segheza, E 1996, 'Trade Induced Investment-Led Growth', NBER Working Paper no. 5582, NBER, Cambridge, MA.

Baldwin, RE and Venables, AJ 1995, 'Regional Economic Integration', in G Grossman and K Rogoff (eds.), *Handbook of International Economics*, vol. III, Elevier, Amsterdam.

Barrack, GW 1996, *The Future of the Fiji Sugar Industry*, Mimeo, Sugar Commission of Fiji, Suva.

Barrows, R and Roth, M 1990, 'Land Tenure and Investment in African Agriculture: Theory and Evidence', *Journal of Modern African Studies*, vol. 28, no. 2: 265-297.

Battese, G and Coelli, T 1995, 'A Model of Technical Inefficiency Effects in a Stochastic Frontier Production for Panel Data', *Empirical Economics*, vol. 20: 325-332.

Beghin, JC and Aksoy, A 2003, 'Agricultural Trade and the Doha Round: Lessons from Commodity Studies', Briefing Paper 03–BP 42, Centre for Agricultural and Rural Development, Iowa State University, Ames.

Bhagwati, J and Panagariya, A 1996, *The Economics of Preferential Trade Agreements*, AEI Press, Washington, D.C.

Bhagwati, JN 1984, 'Splintering and Disembodiment of Services and Developing Nations', *World Economy*, vol. 7, no. 2: 133–143.

Bhalla, SS and Roy, P 1988, 'Mis-Specification in Farm Productivity Analysis: The Role of Land Quality', *Oxford Economic Papers*, vol. 40: 55–73.

Bilal, S and Van Hove, K 2002, *An Overview of ACP-EU Negotiations: Issues and Timeframe*, European Centre for Development Policy Management, Maastricht, The Netherlands.

Bilal, S and Rampa, F 2006, *Alternative to EPAs: Possible Scenarios for the Future ACP Trade relations with the EU*, European Centre for Development Policy Management, Maastricht, The Netherlands.

Bouet, A, Bureau, JC, Decreux, Y, and Jean, S 2005, 'Multilateral Agricultural Trade Liberalisation: The Contrasting Fortunes of Developing Countries in the Doha Round', *World Economy*, vol. 28, no. 9: 1329–1354.

Brenton, P 2003, 'Integrating the Least Developed Countries into the World Trading System: The Current Impact of European Union Preferences Under Everything But Arms', *Journal of World Trade*, vol. 37, no. 3: 623–646.

Breusch, T and Pagan, AR 1979, 'A Simple Test for Heteroscedasticity and Random Coefficient Variation', *Econometrica*, vol. 47: 1287–1294.

Brown, DK 1993, 'The Impact of the North American Free Trade Area: Applied General Equilibrium Models', in BP Bosworth and RZ Lawrence (eds.), *Assessing the Impact of North American Free Tra*de, N Lusting, The Brookings Institution, Washington, DC.

Brown, DK, Deardorff, AV and Stern, RM 1992, 'A North American Free Trade Agreement: Analytical Issues and Computational Assessment', *World Economy*, vol. 15: 11–29.

Byiringiro, F and Reardon, T 1996, 'Farm Productivity in Rwanda: Effects of Farm Size, Erosion, and Soil Conservation Investment', *Agricultural Economics*, vol. 15: 127–136.

Challen, DW and Hagger, AJ 1983, *Macroeconometric Systems: Construction, Validation and Applications*, Macmillan, London.

Chand, G 1998, 'The Labour Market: A Decade of Restructuring', in *Fiji: Coups, Crisis and Reconciliation 1987–1997*, G Chand and V Naidu (eds.), Fiji Institute of Applied Studies: 33–68.

Charemza, WW and Deadman, DF 1992, *New Directions in Econometric Practice*, Edward Elgar, Hants, UK.

Clarke, WC and Morrison, RJ 1987, 'Land mismanagement and the development imperative in Fiji', in HC Brookfield and PM Blaikie, *Land Degradation and Society*, London, Methun: 176–185.

Coe, DT and Helpman, E 1995, 'International R&D Spillovers', *European Economic Review*, vol. 39: 859–887.

Coelli, TJ 1996a *A Guide to DEAP Version 2.1: A Data Envelopment Analysis (Computer) Program*, Centre for Efficiency Productivity and Analysis Working Paper, no. 8/96, Department of Econometrics, University of New England.

——1996b) *A Guide to FRONTIER Version 4.1: A Computer Program for Stochastic Frontier Production and Cost Function Estimations*, Centre for Efficiency Productivity and Analysis Working Paper, no. 7/96, Department of Econometrics, University of New England.

——Rao, P and Battese, G 1998, *An Introduction to Efficiency and Productivity Analysis*, Kluwer Academic Publications, Boston.

Congressional Research Services 1985, *World Sugar Trade and US Sugar Policy*, Washington DC.

Conroy, JD 2006, *Successful Microfinance in the Pacific: Achieving Financial Inclusion*, Foundation for Development Corporation, Australia.

Cororaton, CB, Cockburn, J and Corong, E 2005, 'Doha Scenarios, Trade Reforms, and Poverty in the Phillipines: A Computable General Equilibrium Analysis', in TW Hertel and LA Winters (eds.), *Putting Development Back Into the Doha Agenda: Poverty Impacts of a WTO Agreement*, Palgrave Macmillan, New York.

Curran, L 2007, 'Response to the Article "Are the Economics Partnership Agreements a First-best Optimum for the ACP Countries?"', *Journal of World Trade*, vol. 41, no. 1: 243–244.

Davies, J 1998a, 'The Causes and Consequences of Cane Burning in Fiji's Sugar Belt', *Journal of Pacific Studies*, vol. 22, no. 1&2: 1–26.

——1998b Efficiency Problems in Fiji's Sugar Cane Rail System, Working Paper No. 98.7, Department of Economics, University of South Pacific, Suva.

de Melo, J, Panagariya, A and Rodrik, D 1993, 'The New Regionalism: A Country Perspective', in J de Melo and A Panagariya (eds.), *New Dimensions in Regional Integration*, Cambridge University Press, Cambridge.

Department of Environment, Food and Rural Affairs 2002, *Sugar Beet and the Environment in the UK*, Report by the UK in accordance with Article 47(3) of Council Regulation 1260/2001.

Dervis, K, de Melo, D and Robinson, S 1982, *General Equilibrium Models for Development Policy*, Cambridge University Press, Cambridge.

Dixon, PB, Parmenter, BR, Sutton, J and Vincent DP 1982, *ORANI: A Multisectoral Model of the Australian Economy*, North-Holland, Amsterdam.

Dixon, PB and Parmenter, BR 1994, Computable General Equilibrium Modelling *Preliminary Working Paper No. IP-16*, July, Centre of Policy Studies, Monash University: Melbourne.

Dolado, JJ and Lükepohl, H 1996, Making Wald tests work for cointegrated VAR systems, *Econometrics Reviews*, vol. 15: 369–386.

Dorfman, J.H. 1996, 'Modeling Multiple Adoption Decisions in Joint Framework', *American Journal of Agricultural Economics*, vol. 78: 547-557.

Duncan, R, Cutherbertson, S and Bosworth, M 1999, 'Pursuing Economic Reform in the Pacific', *Pacific Studies Series No.18*, ADB, Manila.

Edgeworth, FY 1881, *Mathematical Psychics*, Kegan Paul, London.

Edwards, S 1993, 'Openness, Trade Liberalisation and Growth in Developing Countries', *Journal of Economic Literature*, vol 31: 1358–93.

Ervin, CA and Ervin, DE 1982, 'Factors Affecting the Use of Soil Conservation Practices: Hypotheses, Evidence and Policy Implications', *Land Economics*, vol. 58: 277–292.

European Commission 2002, *Agriculture in the European Union – Statistical and Economic Information*, European Commission, Brussels.

——2003, *Reforming the European Union's Sugar Policy: Impact of Assessment Work.*

——2006, *The European Sugar Sector: A Long-Term Competitive Future.*

Fare, R, Grosskopf S, and Lovell, CAK 1994, *Production Frontiers*, Cambridge University Press.

Feder, G and Onchan, T 1987, 'Land Ownership Security and Farm Investment', *American Journal of Agricultural Economics*, vol. 69, no. 2: 311–320.

Fiji Islands Bureau of Statistics 2006, *Key Statistics*, Suva, Fiji.

Fiji Development Bank 2003, *Annual Report 2003*, Fiji Development Bank, Suva.

Fiji Ministry of Agriculture and Forests 1978, *Ministry of Agriculture and Forests Report,* Government of Fiji, Suva.

Fiji Sugar Corporation 2006, *Annual Report 2006*, Fiji Sugar Corporation, Suva, Fiji.

——2002, *Environmental Strategic Plan 2002–2012.*

——1987, *Sugar Cane Research Annual Report.*

——1989, *Sugar Cane Research Annual Report.*

——1996, *Soil Erosion at Drasa, Lautoka.*

——1997, *Sugar Industry Strategic Plan 1997.*

Francois, JF and Shiells, CR 1994, 'AGE Models of North American Free Trade', in JF Francois and CR Shiells (eds.), *Modeling Trade Policy, Applied General Equilibrium Assessments of North American Free Trade*, Cambridge University Press, Cambridge.

Galletly, JG and Swartz, GL 1974, *Land Conservation in Fiji*, Soil Conservation Authority of Victoria, Melbourne, Australia.

Gawander, J 1998, 'The Rise and Fall of the Vetivar Hedge in the Fijian Sugar Industry', *Advances in GeoEcology*, vol. 31: 959–964.

Ghani, A 2005, 'Fiji's Emigrant Transfers and Potential Macroeconomic Effects', *Pacific Economic Bulletin*, vol. 20, no. 2: 117–128.

Giles, JA, and Williams, C 2000, 'Export-led Growth: A Survey of the Empirical Literature and Some Non-Causality Results', *Journal of International Trade and Economic Development*, vol. 9, no. 3: 261–337.

Gong, BH and Sickles, RC 1992, 'Finite Sample Evidence on the Performance of Stochastic Frontiers and Data Envelopment Analysis Using Panel Data', *Journal of Econometrics*, vol. 51: 259–284.

Government of Fiji 1985, *Fiji's Ninth Development Plan: 1986-1990*, Suva: Government Printer.

——2005, *Fiji Country Sugar Adaptation Strategy*, Draft Report.

——2006a, *National Adaptation Strategy for the Fiji Sugar Industry.*

——2006b, *Strategic Development Plan 2007-2011.*

Grabowski, R 1994, 'The Successful Development State: Where Does It Come From?', *World Development*, vol. 22, no. 3: 413–422.

Granger, CWJ 1969, 'Investigating Causal Relations by Econometric Models and Cross-Spectral Methods', *Econometrica*, vol. 37, no. 3: 424–438.

Greenaway, D.W., Morgan, W. and Wright, P. (1997), 'Modeling Growth and (Liberalisation) Using Smooth Transitions Analysis', *Economic Inquiry*, vol.35: 798-814.

Griffiths, WE 1972, 'Estimation of Actual Response Coefficients in the Hildredth-Houck Random Coefficient Model', *Journal of The American Statistical Association*, vol. 67: 633–635.

Groombridge, M 2001, *America's Bittersweet Sugar Policy*, The Cato Institute Trade Briefing Paper No.13, Washington DC.

Grynberg, R 1993, 'Trade Liberalisation in the Post-Cold War Era and its Implications for the Fiji Sugar Industry', *Journal of Pacific Studies*, vol. 17:133–160.

Gudoshnikov, S, Jolly, L and Spence, D 2004, *The World Sugar Market*, Woodhead Publishing Limited, England.

Gulati, A and Narayanan, S 2002, 'Managing Import Competition when Developing Countries Liberalize Trade: The Indian Experience', Mimeo, IFPRI, Washington, DC.

Grossman, GM and Helpman, E 1991, *Innovation and Growth in the Global Economy*, Cambridge, MIT Press, MA.

Haaland, J and Norman, D 1992, 'Global Production Effects of European Integration', in LA Winters, (ed.), *Trade Flows and Trade Policy After '1992'*, Cambridge University Press, Cambridge.

Hannan, K 2005, 'Fiji: Sugar and Sweatshirts, Migrants and Remittances', in *Globalisation and Governance in the Pacific Islands*, S Firth (ed.), Conference Proceeding, see <http://epressanu.edu.au/ssgm/global_gov/mobile_devices>

Harris, JR and Todaro, MP 1970, 'Migration, Unemployment and Development: A Two Sector Analysis', *American Economic Review*, 60.

Harrison, JW and Pearson, KR 1996, 'Computing Solutions for Large General Equilibrium Models Using GEMPACK', *Computational Economics*, vol. 9: 83–127.

Hemraj, V 1982, 'Getting More Tonnes of Sugar from Each Tonne of Cane', *Fiji Sugar* 26th June 1982, Sugar Advisory Council.

Herrmann, R and Weiss, D 1995, 'A Welfare Analysis of the EC-ACP Sugar Protocol', *Journal of Development Studies*, vol. 31, no. 6: 918–941.

Hertel, TW (ed.) 1996, *Global Trade Analysis: Modelling and Applications*, Cambridge University Press, Cambridge.

Hertel, TW, Horridge, JM and Pearson, KR 1992, 'Mending the Family Tree: A Reconciliation of the Linearized and Levels Schools of AGE Modelling', *Economic Modelling*, 9:385–407.

Hertel, TW, Walmsley, T and Itakura, K 2001, 'Dynamic Effects of the 'New Age' Free Trade Agreement Between Japan and Singapore', GTAP Working Paper No. 15, Center for Global Trade Analysis, Purdue University.

Hildredth, C and Houck, JK 1968, 'Some Estimators for Linear Model with Random Coefficients', *Journal of The American Statistical Association*, vol. 63:764–768.

Hoestenberghe, KV, and Roelfsema, H 2006, Economic Partnership Agreements between the EU and Groups of ACP Countries: Will They Promote Development? *United Nations University – Comparative Regional Integration Studies Occasional Papers No. 2006/27.*

Hummels, D, Rapoport, D and Yi, K 1998, 'Vertical Specialization and the Changing Nature of World Trade', *Federal Reserve Bank of New York Economic Policy Review*, 79–99.

Indian Technical Mission, 2004, *Revival of the Sugar Industry in Fiji*, Report to the Government of Fiji, Suva.

Imbs, J and Wacziarg, R 2003, 'Stages of Diversification', *American Economic Review*, vol. 93, no. 1: 63–68.

James, G (ed.) 2004, *Sugarcane*, Blackwell Science Limited, Oxford, UK.

Japanese International Cooperation Agency 1998, *Study on Watershed Management and Flood Control for the Four Major Viti Velu Rivers in the Republic of Fiji Islands*, Progress Report to Suva: Ministry of Agriculture.

Johansen, L 1960, *A Multisectoral Study of Economic Growth*, North-Holland, Amsterdam.

Kaldor, N 1967, *Strategic Factors in Economic Development*, Ithaca, Cornell University of Industrial and Labor Relations.

Karingi, S, Oulmane, N, Sadni-Jallab, M, Lang, R and Perez, R 2006a, Assessment of the Impact of the Economic Partnership Agreement between the COMSEA countries and the European Union', *Africa Trade Policy Centre, Work in Progress No. 37, Economic Commission for Africa.*

——Perez, R and Hammouda, HB 2006b, 'Could Preferences Reward Sub-Saharan Africa's Participation in the Doha Round Negotiations?', *World Economy*, vol. 30, no. 3: 383–404.

Kalirajan, K and Obwona, M 1994, 'Frontier Production Function: The Stochastic Coefficients Approach', *Oxford Bulletin of Economics and Statistics*, vol. 56, no. 1: 87–96.

Keck, A and Permartini, R 2005, The Economic Impact of EPAs in SADC Countries, *WTO Staff Working Paper No. ERSD-2005-04, Geneva, World Trade Organisation.*

Klein, LR 1983, *Lectures in Econometrics*, North-Holland, Amsterdam.

Kingi, T and Kompas, T 2005, 'Communal Land Ownership and Agricultural Development: Overcoming Technical Efficiency Constraints Among Fiji's Indigenous Sugarcane Growers', Working Paper 05-11, Asia Pacific School of Economics and Government, Australian National University.

Kopp, RJ 1981, 'The Measurement of Productive Efficiency: A Reconsideration', *Quarterly Journal of Economics*, vol. 97: 477–503.

Kroes, S and McFadden, J 2004, 'A Proposed Cane Payment Formula for Fiji', *Proceedings of the Australian Society of Sugar Cane Technology*, vol. 26: 76–89.

Krueger, AO 1998, 'Why Trade Liberalisation is Good for Growth', *Economic Journal*, vol. 108, no. 450:1513–22.

Kumar, P and Prasad, BC 2002, 'Fiji's Economic Woes: A Nation in Search of Development Progress', *Pacific Economic Bulletin*, 17, 1–23.

——2004, 'Environmental Impacts of the Lome Trade Agreement and Fiji's Sugar Exports', *Fijian Studies: A Journal of Contemporary Fiji*, vol. 2, no. 1: 75–110.

Kumbhakar, SC 1988, 'Estimation of Input-Specific Technical and Allocative Inefficiency in Stochastic Frontier Models', *Oxford Economic Papers*, vol. 40: 535–549.

Kurer, O 2001, 'Productivity and Ethnicity in Fiji's Sugar Industry', University of South Pacific Economic Commentary Series No. 01/1, Suva.

Lal, P 2006a, 'An Analysis of Potential Efficiency Gains in the Fiji's Sugar Industry: The Performance Payment System', *Pacific Economic Bulletin*, vol. 21, no. 2: 117–139.

——2006b, 'Agency Costs, Corporate Governance and the Fiji Sugar Corporation', *Pacific Economic Bulletin*, vol. 21, no. 2: 70–93.

——and Rita, R 2005, *Sugar Cane Production in Fiji: Farmer Profile and Farm Profitability*, Draft Report (based on 2003 survey on sugarcane farms), Lautoka, Fiji.

Landell Mills Commodities 1991, *A Review of the Sugar Industry in Fiji*, LMC International Ltd, Oxford.

——2002, *The LMC Worldwide Survey pf Sugar and HFCS Report and On-line Service, Executive Survey.*

Larson, D and Borrell, B 2001, Sugar Policy and Reform, *Policy Research Working Paper Series 2602, World Bank, Washington DC.*

Lee, JW 1994, 'Capital Goods, Imports and Long-Run Growth', NBER Working Paper No. 4725, NBER, Cambridge, MA.

Leslie, D and Ratukalou, I 2002, *Rural Land Use Policy Statement for Fiji*, Report prepared for the Ministry of Agriculture, Sugar, and Land Resettlement and Secretariat of the South Pacific Community/German Technical Co-operation, Suva, Fiji.

Leontief, WW 1936, 'Quantitative Input and Output Relations in the Economic System of the United States', *Review of Economics and Statistics* 18:105–25.

Levantis, T 1999, *Working Manual for the CGE Model of the Fiji Economy*, Ministry of National Planning, Suva.

——2006, *Model Documentation for the Dynamic CGE Model of the Fiji Economy, FijiGEM Version 8*, ACIAR Working Paper 2006-1, School of Economics, University of Queensland, Brisbane.

—— Jotzo, F and Tulpulé, V 2005, *'Sweetening the Transition in EU Sugar Preferences'*, World Economy, vol. 28, no. 6:893–915.

Lightfoot, C 1994, *Fiji: Trade Liberalisation*, United Nations Economic and Social Commission for Asia and the Pacific, Port Vila.

Liedtke, H 1989, *'Soil Erosion and Soil Removal in Fiji'*, Applied Geography and Development, vol. 33: 68–92.

LMC International and Oxford Policy Management 2003, *Addressing the Impact of Preference Erosion in Sugar on Developing Countries*, LMC International, UK.

——2004, *Safeguarding the Benefits of the Sugar Protocol to ACP Countries*, LMC International, UK.

Lynne, GD, Shonkwiler, JS and Rola, LR 1988, 'Attitudes and Farmer Conservation Behaviour', *American Journal of Agricultural Economics*, vol. 70: 12–19.

Maerten, C 2005, *Economic Partnership Agreements: A Development Perspective,* Presented at the Workshop of the Informal European Network on Agriculture, Trade and Development, Stockholm, Sweden, 12 January 2005.

Mahadevan, R 2008a, 'The Less Than Sweet Solution to Fiji's Sugar Industry Problems', *Journal of International Development*, Forthcoming.

——2008b, 'The Viability of Fiji's Sugar Industry', *Journal of Economic Studies*, Forthcoming.

——2008c, 'The Twin Challenges of Efficiency and Soil Erosion in Fiji's Sugar Industry', *Ecological Economics*, vol. 66: 468–477.

McGregor, A 2006, 'Special Products and Special Safeguards Mechanism: The Fiji Islands Country Study', Report Prepared for Trade and Development Office, Suva, Fiji.

McDonald, JF and Moffitt, RA 1980, 'The uses of Tobit analysis', *Review of Economic Statistics,* vol. 62: 318–321.

McKenzie, D 2006, 'Remittances in the Pacific', Paper presented at the Werner-Sichel Lecture on 15th Feb, University of Western Michigan.

Milner, C, Morgan, W and Zgovu, E 2004, 'Would All Sugar Protocol Exporters Lose from Sugar Liberalisation?', *European Journal of Development Research*, vol. 16, no. 4: 790–808.

Milner, C 2006, 'An Assessment of the Overall Implementation and Adjustment Costs for the ACP Countries' in Grynberg, R and Clarke, A 2006, *The European Development Fund and Economic Partnership Agreements*, Commonwealth Secretariat Economic Affairs Division.

Morrison, RJ 1992, *An Assessment of Soil Erosion in Fiji*, The World Conservation Union (IUCN) and Environmental Services, Australia, Suva: Department of Town and Country Planning.

Murphy, C 1992, 'A Macroeconometric Model of Fiji', Economics Division Working Papers – South Pacific, Research School of Pacific Studies, Australian National University, Canberra.

Narayan, PK 2003, 'The Macroeconomic Impact of the IMF Recommended VAT Policy for the Fiji Economy: Evidence from a CGE Study', *RURDS*, vol. 15, no. 3: 226–237.

——2004, 'Do Public Investment Crowd Put Private Investment? Fresh Evidence from Fiji', *Journal of Policy Modeling*, vol. 26, no. 6: 747–753.

——and Smyth, R 2005, 'Trade Liberalisation and Economic Growth in Fiji. An Empirical Assessment using the ARDL Approach', *Journal of the Asia Pacific Economies*, vol. 10:96–115.

——and Narayan, S 2005, 'Estimating Income and Price Elasticities of Imports for Fiji in a Cointegration Framework', *Economic Modelling*, vol. 22, no. 3: 423–38.

——and Prasad, BC 2007, 'The Long-Run Impact of Coups on Fiji's Economy: Evidence from a Computable General Equilibrium Model', *Journal of International Development* 19(2):149–60.

Narsay, W 2004, 'PIC development: Remittances and Other Alternatives to Regional Integration', Paper presented at a Workshop on 'Remittances, Microfinance and Technology: Leveraging development impact for Pacific States', Brisbane 10th and 11th June 2004, organised by The Foundation for Development Cooperation, Brisbane.

National Farmers Union 2003, 'Dark Clouds on the Sugar Horizon', *Fijian Studies*, vol. 1, no. 2: 381–387.

NEI 2000, *Evaluation of the Common Organisation of the Markets in the Sugar Sector*, NEI, Rotterdam, The Netherlands.

Oxfam 2002, *The Great EU Sugar Scam: How Europe's Sugar Regime is Devastating Livelihoods in the Developing World*, Oxfam Briefing Paper No. 27, Oxfam International.

——2004a, *Dumping on the World: How EU Sugar Policies Hurt Poor Countries*, Oxfam Briefing Paper No. 61, Oxfam International, London.

——2004b, *The Fiji Garment Industry*, Oxfam New Zealand.

——2006a, *Fishing for a Future: The Advantages and Drawbacks of a Comprehensive Fisheries Agreement between the Pacific and the European Union*, Oxfam New Zealand.

——2006b, *Unequal Partners: How EU-ACP EPAs Could Harm the Development Prospects of Many of the World's Poorest Countries*, Oxfam Briefing Note.

——2006c, *Offering a Realistic Alternative: The EU's Obligation to Provide Alternatives to the Economic Partnership Agreements*, Oxfam New Zealand.

Panagariya, A 2000, 'Preferential Trade Liberalisation: The Traditional Theory and New Developments', *Journal of Economic Literature*, vol. 38: 287–331.

Perez, R 2006, 'Are the Economic Partnership Agreements a First-best Optimum for the African Caribbean Pacific Countries?', *Journal of World Trade*, vol. 40, no. 6: 999–1019.

Prasad, B 2006, 'Resolving the Agricultural Land Lease Impasse in Fiji', *Pacific Economic Bulletin*, vol. 21, no. 2: 177–193.

——and Narayan, P 2004, 'The Relationship between Fiji's Sugar Corporation's Profitability and Sugarcane Production', *Pacific Economic Bulletin*, vol. 19, no. 2:1–14.

Prasad BC and Tisdell C 2006, *Institutions, Economic Performance and Sustainable Development: A Case Study of the Fiji Islands*, Nova Science, New York.

Prove, BG, Truong, PN and Evans, DS 1986, 'Strategies for Controlling Caneland Erosion in the Wet Tropical Coast of Queensland', Proceedings of the Conference of the Australian Society of Sugar Cane Technologists, Australian Society of Sugar Cane Technologists, Brisbane.

Quarase, Hon. L 2004, *Tabling of the Report of the Sugar Select Committee of the House of Representatives*, Transcript of speech was accessed at Fiji Government Online at <http://www.fiji.gov.fj> on 20th September 2005.

Ram, AN, Gawander, JS and Soli, NS 2003, 'Effect of Intercropping o the Growth of Sugarcane in Fiji', *Journal of the South Pacific Agriculture*, vol. 10, no. 1/2: 37–39.

Raworth, K 2002, *The Great EU Sugar Scam*, Oxfam Briefing Paper No. 27, Oxfam International, Washington DC.

Reddy, M 2003, 'Farm Productivity, Efficiency and Profitability', *Fijian Studies*, vol. 1, no. 2: 225–241.

——Mohanty, M and Naidu, V 2004a, 'The Economic Cost of Human Capital Loss from Fiji: Implications for Sustainable Development', *International Migration Review*, vol. 38, no. 4: 1447–1461.

——Prasad, B, Sharma, P, Vosikata, S and Duncan, R 2004b, *Understanding Reform in Fiji*, Research Paper prepared for the Global Development Network, Accessed on 3rd Mar 2007 from <http://www.gdnet.middle.php>

——Naidu, V and Mohanty, M 2003. 'The Urban Informal Sector in Fiji: Results from a Survey', *Fijian Studies*, vol.1, no.1: 127–154.

——and Prasad, B 2002, 'Affirmative Action Policies and Poverty Alleviation in Fiji: An Examination of Post-Coup Policies and Programs', *Development Bulletin*, vol. 60: 58–61.

——and Naidu, V 2001, 'Land Tenure System in Fiji: The Poverty Implication of Expiring Leases', *Development Bulletin*, vol. 55: 33–35.

——and Yanagida, JF 1999, 'Technical Efficiency Analysis of Fiji's Sugar Industry: An Application of the Stochastic Frontier Production Function Approach', *South African Journal of Economic and Management Sciences*, vol. 2, no.1: 77–92.

Reserve Bank of Fiji (RBF), *Reserve Bank Fiji Quarterly Review*, RBF, Suva.

Romer, PM 1990, 'Endogenous Technological Change', *Journal of Political Economy*, vol. 98: 71–102.

Rutz, HJ 1978, 'Ceremonial Exchange and Economic Development in Village Fiji', *Economic Development and Cultural Change*, vol. 26, no. 4: 777–805.

Sachs, J 1987, 'Trade and Exchange Rate Policies in Growth-Oriented Adjustment Programs', in V Corbo, M Goldstein and M Khan (eds.), *Growth Oriented Adjustment Programs*, IMF, Washington, DC.

——1989, 'The Debt Overhang of Developing Countries', in G Calvo, R Findlay, P Kouri and J Braga de Macedo (eds.), *Debt, Stabilization and Development: Essays in Memory of Carlos Diaz-Alejandro,* Basil Blackwell, Oxford: 80–102.

——and Warner, A 1995, 'Economic Reform and the Process of Global Integration', *Brookings Papers on Economic Activity: 1*, 1–118, Brookings Institution.

Santos-Paulino, AU 2005, 'Trade Liberalisation and Economic Performance: Theory and Evidence for Developing Countries', *World Economy*, vol. 28, no. 6: 783–821.

Scarf HE 1973, *The Computation of Economic Equilibrium*, Yale University Press, New Haven.

Scollay, R and Gilbert, JP 2000, 'Measuring the Gains from APEC Trade Liberalisation: An Overview of CGE Assessments', *World Economy*, vol. 23, no. 2: 175–197.

Seavoy, R 2000, *Subsistence and Economic Development*, Praeger Publishers, Connecticut.

Sheriff, G 2005, 'Efficient Waste? Why Farmers Over-Apply Nutrients and the Implications for Policy Design', *Review of Agricultural Economics*, vol. 27,no. 4: 542–557.

Shoven, JB and Whalley, J 1972, 'A General Equilibrium Calculation of the Effects of Differential Taxation of Income from Capital in the U.S.', *Journal of Public Economics*, 1: 281–321.

——1984, 'Applied General Equilibrium Models of Taxation and International Trade: An Introduction and Survey', *Journal of Economic Literature* 22: 1007–51.

Siliverstovs, B and Herzer, D 2007, 'Manufacturing Exports, Mining Exports and Growth: Cointegration and Causality Analysis for Chile (1960–2001)', *Applied Economics*, vol. 37: 153–167.

Sims, CA 1972, 'Money, Income and Causality', *American Economic Review*, vol. 62, no. 4: 540–552.

Snell, D and Prasad, S 2001, 'Benchmarking and Participatory Development: The Case of Fiji's Sugar Industry Reforms', *Development and Change*, vol. 32: 255–276.

Spain, AV and Hodgen, MJ 1994, 'Changes in the Composition of Sugarcane Harvest Residues During Decomposition as a Surface Mulch', *Biological Fertility of Soils*, vol. 17: 225–231.

Stoeckel, A and Borrell, B 2001, *Preferential Trade in Developing Countries: Bad Aid After Bad Trade*, Rural Research and Development Corporation, Canberra.

Storey, D 2005, 'End of Line? Globalisation and Fiji's Garment Industry', in S Firth, (ed.), *Globalisation and Governance in the Pacific Islands*, Conference Proceeding, see <http://epressanu.edu.au/ssgm/global_gov/mobile_devices>

Studenmund, AH 2000, *Using Econometrics: A Practical Guide*, Addison Wesley Longman, New York.

Sturton, M 1989, 'Modeling the Fiji Economy', Pacific Islands Development Program, East-West Center, University of Hawaii.

Sugar Commission of Fiji 2006, *Annual Report for the Year Ended 31 December 2005*, Sugar Commission of Fiji, Suva.

Sugar Industry Tribunal 1997, *The Master Award*, Sugar Industry Tribunal, Fiji.

Sugar Technology Mission 2004, *Action Report on Improvement in Sugar Productivity in Fiji*, Technology Information Forecasting and Assessment Council, Government of India.

Swami, S 2004, 'Watershed Management in Fiji', Paper presented at a workshop on Trade Liberalisation, Agriculture and Land Degradation in Fiji: Implications for Sustainable Development Policies, Suva, 15-16 April, 2004.

Tamata, B, Kubuabola, S and Fung, C 1996, Water Quality in the Qawa River during the Sugar Cane Crushing Season of 1995, Institute of Applied Sciences Environmental Report No. 82, University of South Pacific Suva.

Taylor, L 1991, 'Economic Openness: Problems to the Century's End', in T Banuri (ed.), *Economic Liberalisation: No Panacea*, Oxford University Press, Oxford and New York: 99–147.

Tisdell, C 1996, 'Small Island Economies in a World of Economic Change', in R Gabbay, R Ghosh, and M Siddique (eds.), *Economics of Small Island States*, Delhi: New Age International.

——and Fairbairn, TI 1984, 'Subsistence Economies and Unsustainable Development and Trade: Some Simple Theory', *Journal of Development Studies*, vol. 20, no. 2: 227–241.

Toda, H and Phillips, PCB 1993, 'Vector Autoregressions and Causality', *Econometrica*, vol. 61, no. 6: 1367–1393.

Toda, HY and Yamamoto, T 1995, 'Statistical Inference in Vector Autoregressions with Possibly Integrated Processes', *Journal of Econometrics*, vol. 66: 225–250.

Topp, V 2001, *Trade Preferences: Are They Helpful in Advancing Economic Development in Poor Countries?*, Australian Bureau of Agricultural and Resource Economics Report TP01, November.

United Nations Development Program 2006, *Human Development Report 2006: Beyond Scarcity: Power, Poverty and the Global Water Crisis*, UNDP, New York.

Valdes, A and Foster, W 2002, 'On the Management of Price risk in the Context of Trade Reform in LDCs', mimeo, UNCTAD, Geneva.

Vallis, I, Parton, WJ, Keating, BA and Woord, AW 1996, 'Simulation of the Effects of Trash and N Fertilizer Management on Soil Organic Matter Levels and Yields of Sugarcane', *Soil and Tillage*, vol. 38: 115–132.

Viner, J 1950, *The Customs Union Issue*, Carnegie Endowment, New York.

Wacziag, R 1998), *Measuring the Dynamic Gains from Trade*, Policy Research Working Paper No. 2001, World Bank, Washington, DC.

Walras, L 1954, *Elements d'Economie Politique Pure*, 4th Edition, Lausanne, 1900, translated by William Jaffe, *Elements of Pure Economics*, Irwin.

Walter, C, Merot, P, Layer, B and Dutin, G 2003, 'The Effect of Hedgerows on Soil Organic Carbon Storage in Hillslopes', *Soil Use and Management*, vol. 19, no. 3: 201–207.

Ward, R 1995, 'Land, Law and Custom: Diverging Realities in Fiji', in R Ward and E Kingdon (eds.), *Land, Custom and Practice in the South Pacific*, Cambridge University Press, Cambridge: 198–249.

Watters, RF 1969, *Koro: Economic Development and Social Change in Fiji,* Oxford: Clarendon Press.

White, H 1980, 'A Heteroskedasticity-Consistent Covariance Matrix Estimator and a Direct Test for Heteroskedasticity', *Econometrica*, vol. 48: 817–838.

White, M 2003, 'The Financial Viability of Fiji Sugar Corporation: An Assessment From the Corporation's Annual Financial Reports', *Fijian Studies*, vol. 1, no. 2: 287–300.

Wonnacott, RJ 1996, 'Free Trade Agreements: For Better or Worse?', *American Economic Review,* vol. 86, no. 2: 62–66.

Wood, AW 1991, 'Management of Crop Residues following Green Harvesting of Sugarcane in North Queensland', *Soil and Tillage*, vol. 20, no. 1: 69–85.

World Bank, Washington DC 1995, *Fiji: Restoring Growth in a Changing Global Environment.*

——2002, *Pacific Islands Regional Report.*

——2006a, *World Development Report 2007: Development and the Next Generation.*

——2006b, *Home and Away: Expanding Job Opportunities for Pacific Islanders Through Labour Mobility*

World Trade Organisation (WTO) 1995, *Regional Trading Arrangements and the World Trading System.* WTO, Geneva.

Yu, W and Jensen, TV 2005, 'Tariff Preferences, WTO Negotiations and the LDCs: The Case of the 'Everything But Arms' Initiative', *World Economy*, vol. 28, no. 3: 375–405.

Zapata, HO and Rambaldi, AN 1997, 'Monte Carlo Evidence on Cointegration and Causation', *Oxford Bulletin of Economics and Statistics*, vol. 59, no. 2: 285–298.

INDEX

A

B

C

D

E

F

G

H

I

J

K

L

M

N

O

P

Q

R

S

T

U

V